The Psychology of Coaching, Mentoring and Learning

The Psychology of Coaching, Mentoring and Learning

SECOND EDITION

Ho Law

WILEY Blackwell

This edition first published 2013
© 2013 John Wiley & Sons, Ltd

First edition published 2007 John Wiley & Sons, Ltd

Wiley-Blackwell is an imprint of John Wiley & Sons, formed by the merger of Wiley's global Scientific, Technical and Medical business with Blackwell Publishing.

Registered Office
John Wiley & Sons, Ltd, The Atrium, Southern Gate, Chichester, West Sussex, PO19 8SQ, UK

Editorial Offices
350 Main Street, Malden, MA 02148-5020, USA
9600 Garsington Road, Oxford, OX4 2DQ, UK
The Atrium, Southern Gate, Chichester, West Sussex, PO19 8SQ, UK

For details of our global editorial offices, for customer services, and for information about how to apply for permission to reuse the copyright material in this book please see our website at www.wiley.com/wiley-blackwell.

The right of Ho Law to be identified as the author of this work has been asserted in accordance with the UK Copyright, Designs and Patents Act 1988.

Wiley also publishes its books in a variety of electronic formats. Some content that appears in print may not be available in electronic books.

Designations used by companies to distinguish their products are often claimed as trademarks. All brand names and product names used in this book are trade names, service marks, trademarks or registered trademarks of their respective owners. The publisher is not associated with any product or vendor mentioned in this book.

Limit of Liability/Disclaimer of Warranty: While the publisher and author have used their best efforts in preparing this book, they make no representations or warranties with respect to the accuracy or completeness of the contents of this book and specifically disclaim any implied warranties of merchantability or fitness for a particular purpose. It is sold on the understanding that the publisher is not engaged in rendering professional services and neither the publisher nor the author shall be liable for damages arising herefrom. If professional advice or other expert assistance is required, the services of a competent professional should be sought.

Library of Congress Cataloging-in-Publication Data

Law, Ho.
    The psychology of coaching, mentoring and learning / Ho Law. – Second edition.
        pages   cm
    Includes bibliographical references and index.
    ISBN 978-1-119-95466-8 (pbk.)
1. Personal coaching. 2. Executive coaching. 3. Mentoring. 4. Learning, Psychology of. I. Title.
    BF637.P36L4 2014
    158.3–dc22

                                        2013012020

A catalogue record for this book is available from the British Library.

Cover image: Ladder to the sun © Mehmet Salih Guler / Getty Images
Cover design by Richard Boxall Design Associates

Set in 10/12.5pt Galliard by SPi Publisher Services, Pondicherry, India
Printed in Singapore by Ho Printing Singapore Pte Ltd

Contents

About the Author   vii
Foreword to the First Edition *by Stephen Palmer*   ix
Preface to the Second Edition   xiii
Acknowledgements   xvii

1   Introduction   1

2   The Coming of Age: Coaching Psychology,
    Coaching and Mentoring   9

3   Philosophy and Theories of Learning Applicable to Coaching
    and Mentoring: Positive Psychology and the Learning Process   23

4   Definitions: Coaching Psychology, Coaching,
    Mentoring and Learning   53

5   Leadership and Organizational Coaching and Mentoring:
    Becoming a Learning Organization and Learning Community   63

6   Developing a Universal Integrative Framework
    for Coaching and Mentoring   91

7   Techniques and Tools   119

8   Continuing Professional Development, Learning Resources
    and Practical Exercises   153

9   Case Studies   175

10 Evaluation   203

11 Conclusion, Discussion, Future Research and Development   219

References   237
Index   253

About the Author

Dr Ho Law is an international consultant and practitioner psychologist, Health and Care Professions Council (HCPC) registered occupational psychologist, Associate Fellow of the British Psychological Society (BPS), Fellow of the Chartered Management Institute (Chartered Manager), Fellow of the Higher Education Academy, Fellow of the Royal Society of Medicine, and BPS Registered Coaching Psychologist, Chartered Scientist, Chartered Psychologist, and Registered Applied Psychology Practice Supervisor. Ho has had over 25 years of experience in psychology and management consultancy. He has delivered numerous workshops and conference seminars, and carried out consultancy work in the UK and abroad (both in the East and in the West). Ho values diversity in people, respects their cultures, and believes in equal opportunities for all. He was one of the first equality advisers to the Assistant Permanent Undersecretary of State in the Home Office; he was also the Deputy Chair of the BPS Standing Committee for Promotion of Equal Opportunities. Ho is passionate about helping people to develop their talents and achieve their full potential through coaching and mentoring. Ho is a founding member and the former Chair of the BPS Special Group in Coaching Psychology; he is also founding director and treasurer of the International Society for Coaching Psychology. He has published over 40 papers and received numerous outstanding achievement awards, such as the Local Promoters for Cultural Diversity Project in 2003; the Positive Image (Business Category) in 2004; and Management Essentials Participating Company in 2005. He was also winner of the first Student Led Teaching Award (2013) – Best Supervisor. He is the Head of Profession in Coaching Psychology, the founding director of Empsy® Ltd and the president of Empsy® Network for coaching (www.empsy.com). At the University of East London School of Psychology, Ho is a Senior Lecturer, Co-Programme Leader in the MSc Coaching Psychology programme, Admissions Tutor, and Leader Tutor in the distance-learning programme (http://www.uel.ac.uk/programmes/psychology/postgraduate/coachingpsychology-dl.htm). Ho is currently supervising two part-time students' PhDs at the University of East London, and the students are working in the United Arab Emirates.

Foreword to the First Edition

Stephen Palmer

The psychology of coaching, mentoring and learning is an exciting and rapidly expanding area. However, psychology's contribution to particular fields is often overlooked; and the field of coaching and mentoring is no exception. For example, many coaching courses teach students how to coach by using a basic model or structure on how to hold a conversation with a client. One example is the GROW model, the name of which is a useful acronym standing for Growth, Reality, Options and Will (or wrap-up). In addition, courses usually include a range of listening and communication skills. Yet the whole programme is often taught within a psychological vacuum, as little or no psychological theory or research is covered that underpins coaching practice. We could conclude that most coaching practice is belief-based. Brent Rushall at San Diego State University describes belief-based coaching as

> a common and traditional form of coaching. Its guides for practices are usually a mix of personal experiences, some limited education about sport sciences, selected incomplete knowledge of current coaching practices, and self-belief in that how coaching is conducted is right. Changes in coaching practices occur through self-selection of activities. The accumulated knowledge of belief-based coaching is subjective, biased, unstructured, and mostly lacking in accountability. Belief-based coaching also includes pseudo-scientific coaching. Pseudo-scientists attempt to give the impression of scientific knowledge but invariably their knowledge is incomplete resulting in false/erroneous postulations. Belief-based coaching is normally the foundation of most coaching development schemes. Organizations are closed (isolated) systems resisting intrusions of contrary evidence that might alter the constancy of the beliefs and social structure. Logical (knowledge) entropy increases with time in these structures. (Rushall, 2003: 1)

This excellent description of belief-based coaching highlights how often practitioners do not necessarily underpin their practice with psychological theory and academic research. Is there an alternative? Fortunately there is. In academic institutions and within coaching-related professional bodies there is a gradual trend towards evidence-based practice. Rushall (2003) describes evidence-based coaching as a restricted and relatively rare form of coaching. Its guides for practices are principles derived from replicated reputable studies reported by authoritative sources in a public manner. Often there is consideration of objective studies that do and do not support principles. Evidence-based coaches have fewer guides for practices, but what are included are highly predictive for accomplishing particular training effects. The accumulated knowledge of evidence-based coaching is objectively verified and structured. However, evidence-based coaching principles are developed in a fragmented scientific world. It could be somewhat difficult to gather all the relevant knowledge into an educational scheme. Organizations are open systems structured to constantly accept new knowledge and concepts. Logical (knowledge) entropy decreases markedly as order is established. (Rushall, 2003: 1)

Applying evidence-based practice is the challenge facing the profession of coaching and mentoring, as we need more research to inform our practice. However, in recent years, with the launch of relevant coaching, coaching psychology and mentoring academic and practitioner journals, researchers and psychologists are in a better position to publish their research findings. These journals include the *International Coaching Psychology Review*, *The Coaching Psychologist*, and the *International Journal of Evidence Based Coaching and Mentoring*. What has been noticeable is the gradual increase in the number of published papers showing the effectiveness of using solution-focused and cognitive behavioural coaching approaches with non-clinical populations. There are plenty of published research papers highlighting how effective these approaches are with clinical populations; but the real challenge has been to prove that they are effective with non-clinical populations.

But, of course, it could all be down to the coaching relationship, and not to the approach to coaching. This has been the argument we have heard so often in the field of psychotherapy. Grbcic and Palmer (2006) decided in a research study to dispense with the coach (or therapist) and just test the cognitive–behavioural methodology on managers by using a manualized, self-coaching approach to stress management and prevention at work. Did it work? If it was largely down to the practitioner–client relationship, then it should not have worked! In this randomized controlled trial, statistically significant results were obtained indicating intervention effectiveness regardless of the frequency of work stressors and lack of organizational support remaining unchanged. The control group remained the same, unlike the self-coaching group, which showed measurable improvement. Hence, in a short period of time, of about six years, researchers are already making substantial progress and building up data that can make a positive impact upon evidence-based practice.

It should not come as much of a surprise to learn that recent surveys have found that the most popular approaches being practised by UK-based coaching psychologists are the facilitation, solution-focused and cognitive–behavioural approaches (Whybrow and Palmer, 2006). This is relevant as the meteoric rise in popularity of coaching psychology in the UK has led to more research being undertaken by postgraduate students on university courses or doctorate programmes. This exciting development parallels the creation of the Coaching Psychology Forum in 2002 and the subsequent launch of the British Psychological Society Special Group in Coaching Psychology in 2004. Dr Ho Law was one of the key figures in the setting up of both groups.

Unlike this book, the early literature on the psychology of coaching and on coaching psychology focused on the psychology of sports coaching (e.g. Griffith, 1926; Lawther, 1951; Gaylord, 1967; Tutko and Richards, 1971; Wilt and Bosen, 1971; Llewellyn and Blucker, 1982). This book adds to evidence-based practice by attempting to unify psychological theories that underpin coaching, mentoring and learning. The core element of the book is based on three years of research and development in the psychology of coaching, mentoring and learning. The research and practice provided a foundation to develop a universal integrated framework that should be applicable across cultures. This book is a welcome addition to the literature and will inform the fields of mentoring, evidence-based coaching and coaching psychology.

References

Gaylord, C. (1967). *Modern coaching psychology.* Iowa: W. M. C. Brown Book Company.

Grbcic, S. & Palmer, S. (2006). A cognitive–behavioural self-help approach to stress management and prevention at work: A randomized controlled trial. Conference paper presented on 24 November 2006 at the Joint Association for Rational Emotive Behaviour Therapy and the Association for Multimodal Psychology National Conference in London, UK.

Griffith, C. R. (1926). *Psychology of coaching: A study of coaching methods from the point of view of psychology.* New York: Charles Scribner's Sons.

Lawther, J. D. (1951). *Psychology of coaching.* Englewood Cliffs, NJ: Prentice Hall.

Llewellyn, J. H. & Blucker, J. A. (1982). *Psychology of coaching: Theory and application.* Minneapolis, MN: Burgess Publishing Company.

Rushall, B. S. (2003). Coaching development and the second law of thermodynamics [or belief-based versus evidence-based coaching development]. Downloaded on 8/11/06 from http://www-rohan.sdsu.edu/dept/coachsci/csa/thermo/thermo.htm

Tutko, T. A. & Richards, J. W. (1971). *Psychology of coaching.* Boston: Allyn and Bacon.

Whybrow, A. & Palmer, S. (2006). Shifting perspectives: One year into the development of the British Psychological Society Special Group in Psychology in the UK. *International Coaching Psychology Review,* 1.2, 75–85.

Wilt, F. & Bosen, K. (1971). *Motivation and coaching psychology.* Los Altos, CA: Tafnews Press.

Preface to the Second Edition

The engagement in coaching, mentoring and learning is part of life itself. Like life, it continuously evolves and changes. Since the publication of the first edition of this book, a lot has happened in the coaching psychology world. For instance, from 1 July 2009, professionals who are practising psychology in the UK are required by law to register with the Health Professions Council (now Health and Care Professions Council) as practitioner psychologists. While at present coaching and mentoring remain unregulated, the debate on their standards and practices continues. The first edition of this book reported the development of the British Psychological Society's (BPS) Special Group in Coaching Psychology (SGCP), which was formed in 2004; in 2012 the BPS set up a Register of Coaching Psychologists, in acknowledgement and recognition of those practitioner psychologists who have specialist expertise in coaching psychology.

I was saddened to learn the tragic news that Michael White, my teacher in narrative therapy, died from a heart attack on 4 April 2008 in San Diego, aged 59. We last met only a few months before, at the Narrative Conference in Norway, where we discussed with enthusiasm (as always) how we could transport narrative practice into reinvigorating other people's lives, hopes and dreams. I hope the second edition of this book serves to honour Michael's contributions to people's lived stories, including mine.

As for the three authors of the first edition, our lives have changed too. Since the publication of the first edition, we have gone our separate ways. Sara Ireland left her job in the healthcare sector and furthered her professional development. Zulfi Hussain continues to develop his other business engagements. Both Sara and Zulfi resigned from their positions as directors at Morph Group Limited in 2008. The company remained dormant for a few years and eventually was dissolved on 3 April 2012. In 2009 I became Senior Lecturer at the University of East London (UEL), helping to lead its coaching psychology programme. I have been dividing my time between my academic engagements and business consultancy ever since.

In this edition I have continuously advocated a vigorous scientific approach towards coaching and mentoring processes, their theories and practices. This demands an evidence-based evaluation, taking into account the output and outcome as well as the stakeholders' experience of the coaching intervention. The concept of a 'journey' is used as a metaphor for coaching and mentoring. For many of us, it is a journey of discovery and rediscovery, one full of surprises. Most of all, the journey has been punctuated with magical moments in coaching and mentoring engagements, as in life. I continue to take pleasure in sharing some of these surprises and experiences in writing this book, which started another journey of its own.

The 'writing journey' was punctuated by the loss of my father, who passed away in Hong Kong on 9 May in 2012. I had to travel to and fro between the UK and Hong Kong and I was particularly touched by all the support I received during this period. My colleagues at UEL from both the BSc and the MSc programme teams stepped in at short notice to do the necessary student supervision, marking, and double-marking of the assignments, within a very tight schedule; their support has made me feel part of the team and of the community in which I feel blessed. There is a Chinese proverb saying that it is easy to add icing on the cake, but it is difficult to give support to someone in destitution. It is the times of hardship that test true collegiality, fellow-feeling and friendship. I thank my colleagues for making such great teams.

My father went through a proper traditional Chinese funeral. The ritual and its procedures were quite novel to me (as I have been out of touch with my own culture for so long). They offered me and other members of my family, especially my mother, a scaffolding for grieving. My father, aged 96, had witnessed a lot of changes during the wars and cultural revolution in China before he moved to Hong Kong. On reflection, though, he enjoyed a long and happy life, especially in his later years, seeing all six of his children grow up and achieve their aspirations – and starting to see the same in the grandchildren. He left no unfinished business. So, in his case, the funeral was truly a celebration of the completion of his life, even though sometimes there is still a kind of strange, lingering sense of loss…

My father's middle and first names are Kai Sin; they mean 'showing' and 'kindness'. These words resonate with the spirit of coaching and mentoring. I shall hold onto this spirit, keep it dearly in my heart and attempt to manifest unconditional kindness in everything I do.

In all my engagements I have continued to be active in teaching, learning, research and development – all in coaching psychology. The preparation of this second edition reflects my ongoing commitment to the development of coaching psychology as a discipline. And I keep my conviction that coaching psychology is a scientific discipline, yet there is a magic to its art.

Following the same structure as the first edition, this edition contains the essence of that book. While both Sara and Zufi contributed to the development of the initial universal integrated framework (UIF), I have further refined the framework through ongoing research and development. Thus I have taken care to update all the chapters and to ensure that they remain current, coherent, and consistent as a whole. The key additions are:

- the results of the Global Coaching Survey commissioned by the International Coach Federation (ICF) and the latest discussion on the Coming of Age: Coaching Psychology (Chapter 2);
- updated literature on learning theories, including social learning theories and narrative practices (Chapter 3);

- recent business case studies and the agile coaching approach in developing a learning organization (Chapter 5);
- an updated UIF model, including systems approach and alternative representations of the model across cultures (Chapter 6);
- new case studies in coaching and mentoring (Chapter 9);
- an up-to-date discussion on coaching and mentoring, their standards and their supervision (Chapter 11).

The online tool that was developed in the first edition is now further refined to measure an individual's cultural and social competence (CSC) as a self-assessment questionnaire (SAQ). This is now available at http://www.uelpsychology.org/csc/ and readers can contact me to gain access to using the tool.

So, whatever your interest in the process of coaching or mentoring, I hope this book takes another step forward in widening your access to its practice through the psychology of learning. For aspiring individuals everywhere who have experienced the benefits of coaching or mentoring directly, I hope that you might feel just a little closer to understanding some of the theories behind how this process works. And for those still looking in from the outside, I hope the approach presented in this book encourages you to get involved.

> There is a time for everything,
> and a season for every activity under the heavens:
> a time to be born and a time to die,
> a time to plant and a time to uproot.
>
> (Ecclesiastes 3: 1–2)

Now it's time to learn and to get involved in coaching and mentoring...

Acknowledgements

As happened in the first edition, there are, inevitably, many names to acknowledge, including those of family members and friends, who have been taken for granted while this book was being written; and there are also many unintentional omissions. So, without mentioning every possible individual, I shall list some of those who have continued to inspire me as well as some of the contributors – the unsung heroes and organizations within the context of my journey of preparing this edition.

Thanks go to:

- Dr Carla Gibbes, Senior Lecturer at the University of East London, for her kindness and support;
- Liz Hall, for communicating the concept of narrative coaching to wider professional communities via *Coaching at Work*;
- Trevor Hall, OBE, CBE, who has continued to inspire me in championing equality and diversity in my cross-cultural journey, in my career, and in life;
- Professor Stephen Palmer, for his continuous support and for updating the Foreword;
- Kaemorine Prendergast, for her kindness and righteousness in championing equality;
- Aquilina Reginald, my former coaching student, for helping me to introduce coaching to nursing and for contributing to the case study on leadership coaching in the healthcare sector in Malta;
- Dr Donald Ridley, principal lecturer at the University of East London, for his support and guidance;
- Christine Stocker-Gibson, for contributing to the case study on Community Coaching Café;
- Michael White, Dulwich Centre, who inspired and trained me in narrative approaches from down under: his spirit will continue to manifest itself in my narrative coaching.

Organizations that have provided me with support and information for this edition are:

- the Association for Coaching;
- the British Psychological Society's (BPS) Special Group in Coaching Psychology;
- the Chartered Management Institute (CMI);
- the European Mentoring and Coaching Council (EMCC);
- the International Coach Federation (ICF) – which gave me permission to publish the results of its Global Coaching Study (ICF and PricewaterhouseCoopers, 2012)
- the International Society for Coaching Psychology.

Most of all, I would like to thank all those whom I came across in my coaching or mentoring journey, in many spaces and places, starting with the place where I live: people in Peterborough and the neighbouring areas within Cambridgeshire. It was here that a number of coaching and mentoring programmes took place – for communities, for individuals, for private and public organizations. It was here that some of the case studies have been consolidated. It was here that the universal integrated framework was developed, through our lived experience.

And from the place where I work, in particular, I would like to thank all my colleagues in the School of Psychology, University of East London, where the 2012 London Olympics and Paralympics took place. The place truly embodies the spirit of the games, which is to inspire individuals to achieve their highest potential; for this is the spirit of coaching and mentoring too!

There are many more of you out there who have contributed to my understanding. To you, perhaps the unacknowledged, I offer my thanks.

Ho Law
Peterborough, England

Disclaimers

The views expressed in this book are those of the author, and not those of the publisher, or Empsy Ltd, or UEL or anyone else. This is in no way affected by the right reserved by the author to edit the cases published. Owing to the requirement for confidentiality within our code of ethics, the context and stories of some case studies may have been adapted and individual identities kept anonymous. If the case studies documented in this book have omitted any partners' contributions, this is entirely unintentional.

Any constructive comments and suggestions for future editions of this book are welcome. Please write to:

Ho Law PhD CPsychol CSci CMgr MISCP(Accred) AFBPsS FCMI FHEA
PO Box 696
Peterborough PE2 9YQ
England, UK
Email:
Personal: ho.law@ntlworld.com
Company: ho.law@empsy.com
http://www.empsy.com/

Twitter: @empsy
www.twitter.com/empsy
University: law2@uel.ac.uk
http://www.uel.ac.uk/psychology/staff/hochunglaw/
Internet: drholaw@gmail.com
Ho Law

1

Introduction

This book is about the psychology of coaching, mentoring and learning. There are many books about learning and mentoring; there are even more about coaching. However, there are very few books that bring together these important, diverse and growing fields, making them intersect. The title of the book reflects the value I place on diversity in the emerging discipline of coaching and how the latter can be enriched by being continuously expanded so as to include mentoring, while it remains grounded in the solid foundation of the psychology of learning.

Aims

The aim of this chapter is to help readers gain a rapid understanding of the nature of the book and find easily the information it offers. It provides a rationale for the book, together with a résumé of its overall structure and a brief description of each chapter. It also suggests how readers working at different levels can use the book to make it meet their interests, experience and professional competence.

Whom Is It For?

The purpose of this book is to show how individuals and organizations can apply the theories and principles of psychology in coaching, mentoring and learning. To this end, the book is written for the following groups:

- coaches, mentors and trainers who would like to learn the general theories and principles of psychology that underpin coaching, mentoring and learning;
- psychologists who want to apply their experience to the coaching, mentoring and training of individuals and organizations;

The Psychology of Coaching, Mentoring and Learning, Second Edition. Ho Law.
© 2013 John Wiley & Sons, Ltd. Published 2013 by John Wiley & Sons, Ltd.

- senior executives and managers responsible for the use of training budgets, who would like to realize their potential benefit and understand how to design and evaluate effective training programmes for their organizations;
- students of psychology who would like to consider their future career in coaching, mentoring and training.

I am aware that the emerging field of coaching and mentoring, coupled with the popularity of psychology in the UK, will attract a very wide readership. Thus my intended readership is not limited to the categories described above. Readers may well include teachers, instructors and anyone involved in coaching, mentoring, training or supervision.

   With the rapid development of coaching and mentoring as an industry, much confusion exists between the psychology of coaching and mentoring and the psychology of counselling and psychotherapy. In comparison to the development of psychotherapy as a discipline, we have found in our disciplines a lot more sharing of practices, which has been promoted by various coaching and mentoring organizations (see Chapter 2).

How This Book Differs from Others

There are many books on coaching and mentoring in the market. However, this book differs from others in the following aspects:

- As far as I am aware, in its first edition, this has been the first book in the UK to attempt to bring together the psychological theory that underpins coaching, mentoring and learning. It embodies a number of developments in coaching and mentoring, as well as in coaching psychology. It traces the development of the Special Group in Coaching Psychology within the British Psychological Society, which addresses coaching psychology as a discipline.
- It reflects the latest thinking, research and development in coaching psychology through high-level theories, principles and practical applications. This second edition ensures that the research and development are up to date.
- It applies psychology to *both* coaching/mentoring *and* learning, thereby blurring the boundaries between these disciplines and yet addressing the differences between them.
- It contains cross-cultural elements that make the theories universal and applicable across different cultures.
- It applies, to coaching and mentoring, the general psychology of learning rather than psychotherapy (Chapter 3).
- It demonstrates the know-how and exercises with step-by-step instructions, as well as with case studies from diverse organizational and community contexts (Chapters 7–9).
- It includes a chapter on evaluation that demonstrates the effectiveness of applying the psychology of learning to coaching, mentoring and learning (Chapter 10).

Working terminology

Before you get going, this section offers some pragmatic working definitions to those of you who have no knowledge of coaching, mentoring and learning. These definitions will be further refined in Chapter 4. Broadly speaking, the book talks about processes and activities that support learning. In this context, 'learning' can be defined as a cognitive process of acquiring skill and knowledge. 'Coaching' is often described as a process of offering support to an individual; this process is performance-focused and goal-centred and it results in action. A 'mentor' – a term used in mentoring – is a critical friend who oversees the development of another. All these processes are learner-centred and learner-driven. A theme running throughout this book is the cross-cultural application of coaching and mentoring. 'Culture' is broadly defined as the predominant attitudes and behaviour that characterize the functioning of a group, community or organization; we typically apply it to a whole range of contexts: countries, ethnic categories, professions, workplaces. The term 'cross-cultural' refers to the interaction between people or entities from two or more cultures. Theories, concepts and techniques will be tested cross-culturally, so that we can see if they are transferable to other contexts and hence valid beyond the original application setting.

Towards the integration of terms

The material provided in this book represents the fertile ground of interaction between coaching, mentoring and psychology (in particular, learning). This triangular relationship can be represented in a simple Venn diagram (see Figure 1.1).

However, as the research and coaching or mentoring journey unfolded, one would discover that there are actually increasing overlaps between the three disciplines. Thus one could see the three circles of influence in Figure 1.1 gravitating towards each other (see Figure 1.2). The next question then becomes clear: How much overlap is there between the three disciplines in practice?

The three are in fact interwoven. Chapter 2 shows that coaching and mentoring are coming of age. It considers market forces, the development of the coaching/mentoring

Figure 1.1 The ground of fertile overlap between coaching, mentoring and the psychology of learning

Figure 1.2   Increasing the area of overlap between coaching, mentoring and the psychology of learning

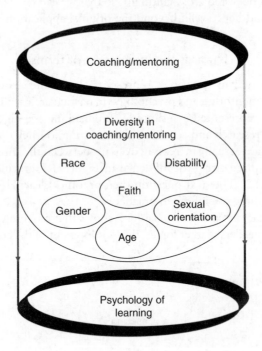

Figure 1.3   Working with a 3D model of coaching, mentoring and psychology of learning

industry and the global market place, and their roles in shaping practice. In order to bring the model of coaching/mentoring and psychology of learning to life, the orientation of this book can be rearranged as a three-dimensional (3D) working model (see Figure 1.3).

In this model, coaching and mentoring are viewed as an interchangeable continuum. Sometimes they may even be regarded as the same thing, depending on the context. For simplicity, the terms coaching, coach and coachee are used to mean coaching/mentoring, coaches/mentors and coachees/mentees respectively (unless their specific meaning is stated explicitly). Whatever the context, due regard should be given to the diversity of all participants in this process. This understanding extends to their appreciation of sensitivities and of the respect that each one should have for the others' values, beliefs, faith, gender, sexual orientation, social barriers, disability, and racial and cultural backgrounds. To understand the universality and diversity of coachees within a diverse setting, it is important that coaches learn more about the principles and techniques grounded in the psychology of learning and applicable across cultures.

Content in a Nutshell

Coaching and mentoring are different disciplines. Organizations and groups have been set up specializing in coaching and/or mentoring. These include the Association for Coaching, the British Psychological Society's Special Group in Coaching Psychology, the European Mentoring and Coaching Council, and the International Coaching Federation (see Chapter 2). Coaches and mentors come from diverse backgrounds. While you may not need a degree in psychology in order to be a coach and a mentor, for coaching and mentoring to be effective, you need to understand the psychological principles on which the practice is based. Without this understanding, coaches and mentors risk not achieving their intended outcome.

Drawing on the comprehensive literature in the psychology of learning, this book focuses on linking theory to practical application. The core principles of positive psychology and learning are described in Chapter 3. The same chapter provides a literature review as well as highlighting the philosophy of positive psychology and the learning theories that are useful in coaching and mentoring practice within the tradition of epistemology. (When we refer to epistemology, we mean to question the nature of what we know: fundamentally, epistemology asks what knowledge is and how we distinguish it from our internal thoughts and beliefs.) Chapter 4 addresses key definitions of coaching, mentoring and learning, which are grounded in the psychology of learning from the previous chapter. Once we revised the psychology of learning and established our own key definitions within the intersecting domains of coaching, mentoring and learning, we set out here on a journey of enquiry, and we proceed logically to guide the reader through the chapters that follow. Chapter 5 describes how coaching and mentoring can be used as a vehicle to help organizations become learning organizations. From the consolidation of theory into coaching and mentoring practice in diverse settings, a universal integrated framework (UIF) is developed; and its revised version, the integrative learning system (ILS), is described in Chapter 6. The major classes of techniques and tools are described in Chapter 7. Chapter 8 supplements them with relevant practical exercises; I hope readers will find them useful. Chapter 9 provides a number of case studies in terms of the UIF and a reflective learning process to demonstrate that these theories and exercises work in the real world, in various organizations as well as in diverse communities. One of the major criticisms of the emerging coaching industry is that most theories and practices lack rigorous, evidence-based evaluation. Chapter 10 meets this challenge by providing an impact evaluation of the UIF linked to a case study. Finally, Chapter 11 describes perceived future directions and work by incorporating the following key themes:

- matching between coaching/mentoring pairs;
- coordinator role;
- emotional intelligence cross-cultural competency;
- evidence-based research and impact assessment;
- supervision;
- training;
- coaching/mentoring standards, codes of conduct and ethics.

Book Research Approach

Writing this book has been like riding two horses. I would like to ensure that it is easy to read and accessible to a diverse readership without compromising its academic rigour. Thus, wherever possible, the writing style is straightforward. Academic references are only noted at specific points in the text. They reflect the wide range of literature reviewed from online sources and the information obtained by attending international workshops and conferences – in the UK, Europe, Australia and Hong Kong. While the literature review casts the research net very widely, it also focuses on the deliverables that this book represents – that is, on useful guidance for learners and practitioners in the field of coaching psychology, coaching, mentoring and training. Although the UIF developed here is grounded both in established psychological theories of learning and in evidence-based evaluation for its effectiveness and efficacy, it has been continually refined and revised for this new edition.

Why Coaching, Mentoring and Learning?

As globalization leads to more intense competition, organizations need to continue to recruit, develop and deploy the best people in order to stay ahead and survive. We have seen rapid and unprecedented change in our organizations and communities across the globe. This has taken place in the fast-growing communications industry as well as in public organizations. Repeated reconfigurations in search of service improvements have meant that leaders are required to work at the furthest bounds of their capability. Corporate leaders have begun to realize that traditional training methods may not be able to cope with the pace of change. Hence organizations have turned to coaching and mentoring to help develop their people, to deepen their talent pool and to enhance their organizational learning capability. Mentoring and coaching go beyond industry. Individuals from vulnerable communities need to be channelled to effective routes, towards learning in trusted partnerships; isolated groups need a mechanism for breaking down barriers and reaching out to mainstream communities; and any people who want to learn more about themselves, or increase their knowledge in targeted areas and in the wider environment, can benefit.

How to read this book

Owing to the philosophy that underpins this book, the following terms are used interchangeably throughout this book:

- you and readers;
- coaches and mentors;
- coachees and mentees;
- learners, trainers and supervisors.

Each chapter is intended to be independent in terms of its topic and content. You may pick and choose which chapters are relevant to you. Nevertheless, throughout this book you will find that the chapters are interwoven, and some are clustered more closely around a topic than others at a certain juncture in the coaching journey. It is recommended that the chapters be read consecutively in pairs. For example, if you are a learner or a student who would like to know more about coaching and mentoring and about how they link to the psychology of learning, you should read Chapters 2 and 3. If you are a busy chief executive or a training manager who wants to find out about the relevance of coaching and mentoring to organizations, you may like to read Chapter 5. For experienced coaches and mentors wishing to refer directly to the techniques and exercises, Chapters 7 and 8 can be read together. Chapter 8 provides a things-to-do list for coaching; in addition, the exercises are organized in a systematic way, so that readers can refer back to the principles described in Chapter 7. Whether you are a beginner or an experienced coach or mentor, you will find these two chapters useful, as they provide pointers for you to begin your continuous professional development or to fine-tune what you already know. Readers who are interested in concrete examples, case studies and the evidence-based evaluation of coaching and mentoring programmes can go directly to Chapters 9 and 10. Throughout the book, each chapter highlights, through cross-referencing, concepts and ideas that are interwoven. In this way I hope that our 'conversation' will provide a sense of continuity as the story unfolds and will encourage a dramatic re-engagement with many of your experiences that may fill some of the gaps in this book. To help readers apply the theories to reflective practice, each chapter is written to a standard format. It begins with an introduction designed to outline its content and ends with a chapter summary and reflection, which summarizes the key concepts and reflects on practical implications.

2

The Coming of Age
Coaching Psychology, Coaching and Mentoring

Introduction

This chapter describes the developments in coaching psychology, coaching and mentoring. It provides an up-to-date review, drawn from various disciplines that underpin coaching psychology, coaching and mentoring. Through the discussion of the literature, it will trace the 'journey' of development in coaching psychology, coaching and mentoring. This journey will involve many disciplines: science, social science and various branches of psychology: educational, social, behavioural as well as business psychology; also sociology, business studies, management systems and economics. The chapter will then explain how coaching psychology, coaching and mentoring are interrelated. The discourse leads to the convergent integration of coaching and mentoring through learning, which provides a bridge between two emerging fields in psychology: positive psychology and community psychology.

The Coaching Psychology, Coaching, Mentoring and Training Market

The coaching, mentoring and training market has been in a state of flux. In 2004, when the first edition of this book was being written, our initial estimate of the average turnover of companies that would offer coaching was £8 million, with £500,000 pre-tax profit. This figure was found to be conservative. As the coaching and mentoring industries continue to grow exponentially, the total turnover is now estimated to exceed many billions of dollars (on a global scale).

Each month, in papers and coaching magazines, we have been bombarded with news about companies and organizations using coaching or mentoring to leverage

---

The Psychology of Coaching, Mentoring and Learning, Second Edition. Ho Law.
© 2013 John Wiley & Sons, Ltd. Published 2013 by John Wiley & Sons, Ltd.

their business performance. For example, the Medical Research Council applied coaching to develop its organizational strategy (Whiteley, 2006); the United Kingdom Atomic Energy Authority (UKAEA) coached 130 employees in its leadership programme; Armagh College, Northern Ireland, developed a coaching culture by undertaking the Centre for Excellence Learning's 'Leaders as Coaches' programme; Greater Manchester Police has developed internal coaches to strengthen its leadership (Hall, 2006a). Mentoring has also enjoyed financial backing from business tycoons. For example, a £200 million mentor fund was set up in 2001 in West Coast Capital, Scotland, to invest in high-growth businesses across the UK. A survey of 109 coaches in 2004 showed that many practitioners offered more than one area of coaching. The majority of respondents were from business applications (over 60 per cent); others were from career, executive and leadership coaching (Palmer and Whybrow, 2004). For the past few years, coaching psychology took off around the world – six international congresses were held, in London (UK), Dublin (Ireland), Barcelona (Spain), Stockholm (Sweden), Pretoria (South Africa) and Sydney (Australia).

In 2012, PricewaterhouseCoopers conducted an online survey commissioned by the International Coach Federation (ICF) as part of its Global Coaching Study. It received 12,133 responses from 117 countries. The results of the survey indicated that there were around 47,500 professional coaches worldwide. In other words, we had approximately 7 coaches per 1 million population. Of these, 87 per cent (41,300 coaches) were actively engaging clients, with an average annual revenue of $47,900. This generated a global income of $1,979 million in total. The majority of the coaching services were in consulting (62 per cent) and/or training (60 per cent). Most of the professional coaches (76 per cent) were in the high-income regions of the world: North America (33.2 per cent: 15,800), Western Europe (37.5 per cent: 17,800), Australia and New Zealand (5 per cent: 2,400). But the survey also showed that there was rapid growth in emerging economic regions, especially in Asia (7 per cent: 3,300), the Middle East and Africa (4.3 per cent: 2,100). Despite the economic climate of the time, the majority of coaches – 55 per cent, and mostly in the emerging economic regions – reported an increase in income, compared with 15 per cent, who reported a decrease. As we can see from the ICF report, the coaching industry is in good health as a whole and professional coaches can look forward to the future with confidence.

Within both the private and the public sectors, there exists a diversity of services, ranging from technology to education, some suppliers operating within one business sector while others offer coaching and training across a wide spectrum. The majority of providers who specialize in coaching and mentoring are very small, employing no more than six people. Despite its diversity, we attempt to categorize the industry into four types:

1   academic and professional institutions;
2   business and management consultancies;
3   independent practitioners;
4   internal coaches and mentors.

In what follows I shall expand on each type, discussing its scope and development.

Academic and professional institutions

This category includes colleges of further education, institutions of higher education and business schools, as well as professional institutes such as the British Psychological Society (BPS), the Institute of Directors (IoD), the Chartered Management Institute (CMI) and the Chartered Institute of Personnel and Development (CIPD). For example, the BPS has a formal process of accrediting psychologists through its chartership. The CIPD has a membership of more than 120,000 and runs a wide range of training courses, including in coaching, the psychology of management, learning and development. Furthermore, participants on the courses have access to its web-based learner support site, which is designed to provide additional resources and to enhance and extend their learning.

The coaching and mentoring programmes in these organizations tends to be run by their in-house staff or members. Sometimes the academic and professional institutions also offer external training programmes and courses on coaching and mentoring. These may range from tailor-made short vocational courses to formal academic studies leading to a diploma, a master's degree or a doctoral qualification.

Professional organizations for coaching psychology, coaching and mentoring

In recent years a number of professional organizations have been developing that specialize in coaching psychology, coaching and/or mentoring. Some are entirely new (new in the sense that they were founded less than 20 years ago). The relatively new organizations include:

- the Association for Coaching (AC);
- the Association for Professional Executive Coaching and Supervision;
- the European Mentoring and Coaching Council (EMCC);
- the International Coach Federation (ICF);
- the International Society for Coaching Psychology (ISCP).

Even established professional organizations such as the BPS and the CMI have also developed new coaching or coaching psychology subsystems within their organizations. These subsystems include:

- the British Association for Counselling & Psychotherapy (BACP) Coaching Division;
- the BPS Special Group in Coaching Psychology (SGCP);
- the CMI Coaching Division.

I shall describe some of this development in greater detail in the next sections.

BPS SGCP
The British Psychological Society (BPS) is a well-established professional society. It was founded in 1901. In 2011 it celebrated its 110th anniversary through a number of initiatives aimed at promoting excellence and ethical practice in the science, education and application of psychology. However, the Special Group in

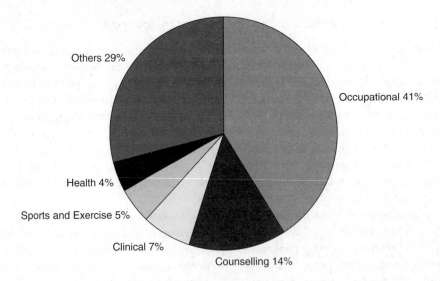

Figure 2.1   The BPS SGCP membership in 2011

Coaching Psychology (SGCP) is a relatively new development within the BPS. As this development is most relevant to the psychology of coaching, I shall describe its history briefly here.

On 18 May 2002, at the BPS Division of Counselling Psychology (DCoP) Annual Conference in Torquay, a workshop about coaching psychology was convened by my colleague, Professor Stephen Palmer. It was attended by 29 members. Initially Stephen intended to create a Coaching Psychology Special Interest Group (SIG) within DCoP. However, at that time DCoP did not have a constitution that allowed the formation of a SIG (there was some politics underneath the process, but I will not go into the details here). As a way forward, an Internet Coaching Psychology Forum was established. To promote the Forum and its membership, the first article for the introduction of coaching psychology was published in *The Occupational Psychologist* – the bulletin of the Division of Occupational Psychology (Law, 2002). The article generated a surge in the membership, which accounts for the majority of membership in the Forum coming from the Division of Occupational Psychologists. This trend continues within the BPS SGCP. On 21 February 2003, a Coaching Psychology Forum meeting was held in London and a proposal was made to set up a Special Group within the BPS. Looking back, it was quite a long struggle with the organizational process and politics within the BPS structure to get the proposal through. To cut a long story short, the SGCP was finally formed, and on 15 December 2004 it held the inaugural meeting in London. Since then, the membership has continued to grow and consolidate. In 2011 SGCP had around 2,300 members, and it is the fourth largest Member Network within the BPS. Figure 2.1 provides a breakdown of the membership.

ISCP
The SGCP held the International Forum for Coaching Psychology on 18 December 2006, at the 1st International Coaching Psychology Conference, which was held at City University, London. Twenty delegates from around the world discussed the possibility of creating an International Association, Society or Forum for Coaching

Psychology. It was pointed out that there were at that time international associations for coaching, but none was specifically dedicated to the field of coaching psychology. There was a need for an international association or society with a remit to promote and develop coaching psychology around the world. In April 2008 the Society for Coaching Psychology was launched. The Society aimed to promote coaching psychology around the world and to encourage the development of theory, research and practice in this field. On 18 July 2011 the Society was granted permission to change its name to that of International Society for Coaching Psychology (http://www. isfcp.net/).

CMI

The CMI (the former British Institute of Management) was founded in 1947 and awarded a Royal Charter in 2002. It is a mature professional body. The accreditation required the re-design of the module specifications that map onto the learning outcome of its Qualifications and Curriculum Framework (QCF). This has already been done in the CPD (continuous professional development) module specifications for a short course award (CMI, 2012). Such a course would offer students more scope in terms of employability and credibility. It would provide an information centre for job opportunities. Recently the CMI incorporated the Institute of Consulting. This move offers CMI members a diverse scope in terms of further development and employability.

Business and management consultancies

More and more business and management consultancies offer coaching services – as well as training for coaches – as part of an overall consultancy package or separately.

In general, business and management consultancies use coaching as part of personal and management development. Their aim is to help organizations to improve:

- return on investment (ROI);
- bottom-line profit;
- human capital;
- relationships;
- conflict resolution;
- work–life balance;
- career development.

Independent practitioners

These include large companies as well as sole traders who offer coaching or mentoring as their main activity. There is a significantly large number of independent practitioners in coaching and mentoring. Their background ranges from training or personnel to business and management consultancy or marketing. In particular, many individuals who claim to be 'a life coach' tend to be sole traders who may or may not have another job to supplement their income. Although many sole traders often have a low profile, they do provide quite a competitive market, as their costs and fees are relatively low. The presence of such a large number of individual private coaches and mentors in an unregulated industry does pose concerns in terms of ethics and standards. These issues will be further discussed in Chapter 11.

Table 2.1   Coaching and mentoring marketing matrix

	Internal	External
Corporate	Academic and professional institutions Internal coaches and mentors	Business and management consultancies
Private	Private arrangements	Independent practitioners

Internal coaches and mentors

Internal coaches or mentors provide services similar to those of their employer's staff. For example, a lot of colleges and universities have developed internal mentoring procedures: each new member of staff may have a mentor assigned to him or her, and the mentor may or may not be the mentee's line manager. The issues arising from the debate whether the mentor should or should not be the mentee's line manager will be discussed later. Internal coaches or mentors are also competing in the market, as their professional rates tend to be much lower than those of the external consultants. They present distinct advantages in that they understand their clients and the context of the organization.

External and internal managers can be mentors and coaches. For good practice, it may be better to use external coaches or mentors, in order to ensure confidentiality and to give reassurance to those in more challenging and demanding positions. In a mixed economy of external and internal coaches and mentors, using managers this way offers an opportunity to share good practice within one framework.

To summarize, the above types of coaching and mentoring providers can be classified into the matrix in Table 2.1.

There are some overlaps between categories in the above matrix. For example, larger corporate companies and institutions may employ both internal coaches and mentors and external consultants who operate as independent practitioners. Technology is another factor to add to the complexity of the above matrix. For example, online coaching and mentoring programmes and training packages may be available on the Internet. These offer a significant amount of information and knowledge at a fraction of the cost. They can be stand-alone as well as tailor-made, so that they can be integrated into the internal corporate coaching and mentoring programme. For example, Chapter 9 presents a case study in applying an online tool in the coaching and mentoring programme within the National Health Service in the UK, and another in a transatlantic coaching pilot project between the Association for Coaching (UK) and Rice University in Houston (USA).

Coaching and mentoring play a big part in developing human potential and in improving performance both for individuals and for organizations. There is a variety of types of organizations as well as of styles of coaching and mentoring, ranging from a direct instructional approach to non-directive, facilitative techniques. Some of these techniques will be explored further in Chapter 7. In this book we do not intend to preach that there is a right way of coaching and mentoring, but we argue that, for coaching and mentoring to be effective and applicable across different contexts and cultures, they are to be grounded in the psychology of learning. The rest of this chapter provides a literature review relevant to this important area and explains how the psychology of learning interrelates with coaching and mentoring. As we shall see later, the psychology of learning can be regarded as a starting point in understanding the coherent framework of the diverse practices in coaching and mentoring.

Coaching

From our observation, most people believe that coaching is beneficial for them and good for their business. Out of 36 executives who received coaching in South Africa, 97 per cent reported that coaching delivered return on investment (ROI) to their organization (Hall, 2006c). The perceived average benefit of ROI from 43 respondents was reported to be 5.7 times the initial investment in the UK's study (McGoven et al., 2001). Sue Holland reported that executive coaches from different parts of the world had found coaching to be useful in helping them to calibrate what was a cultural norm and what was individually unique at Unilever (Whiteley, 2006). Coaching enables people to create space to think and reflect upon their learning.

Mentoring

There is a lot of misunderstanding around the concept of mentoring. For example, with recent media coverage and the emerging development of various associations and groups dedicated to coaching and coaching psychology, many people thought the mentoring market was not as high-profile as coaching. This is apparently not so. Articles about mentoring stories are published by various magazines and journals. For example, one reads that, 'from Tom Hunter to James Dyson, British business tycoons are opening their minds to the next generation of entrepreneurs as mentoring programmes flourish...' – as was published by the Institute of Directors in its magazine *Director for Business Leaders* (Magee, 2006). There are a number of associations, new and established, which regard mentoring either as their core business or as part of the approaches embedded in their services: for example, Eastern Mentoring Forum and the Prince's Trust. The European Mentoring and Coaching Council, as the name suggests, regards both mentoring and coaching as its core organizational activities.

Another myth about mentoring is that it takes place only in the world of business and that mentors are usually more experienced persons who help their 'protégées' get up the corporate ladder. This is not necessarily the case. Many mentoring programmes are set up in public sectors, including educational institutions such as colleges and universities, as well as in large organizations, for instance the National Health Service (see Chapter 9 for our case studies).

In this book, as we have already explained, we use the metaphor of a journey. The context of coaching may be very different from that of mentoring – the former may be on improving the performance of an organization while the latter may be about one's own career progression; yet coaching and mentoring are actually very close together. Viewed from this perspective, mentors appear as trusted guides, who understand the theory of personal development and have had experience of translating it into practice (see, for example, Daloz, 1999). Mentors are not simply providing mentees with a road map and travel tips, but also walk some of the journey together with them. The collaboration (co-journeying) enables both mentors and mentees to develop; and they experience a new journey that is full of surprises.

Coaching Psychology

Historically, coaching as used in sports was based on the psychology of sports and exercises. This embraces both cognitive and behavioural psychology. Sir John Whitmore, former international racing driver, has followed this path of development in his coaching career, and is now widely regarded as one of the pioneers of the coaching industry. As he said: 'I think [the coaching] principles are universal and it will eventually be common in all aspects of life – such as parenting' (quoted in Hilpern, 2006).

The above statement has two important implications. First, the nature of mentoring is implicit in parenting. This reinforces our view on the interwoven relationship of coaching and mentoring. Second, and more importantly, the statement represents a widely held belief that there are common strands of psychological principles that can be readily adopted and applied to coaching and mentoring. By the same token, the same principles can be readily applied across different contexts, be that in sports or in the activity of international business corporations. Although the coaching practice advocated by Sir John and his sports coach Timothy Gallwey – the so-called 'inner game' – had been rooted in the psychology of coaching sports such as tennis and skiing, from our perspective it was no surprise that the practice was soon drawn into the business world. Sir John continues his personal development in humanistic psychology and more recently he has rediscovered the link between transpersonal psychology and his new style of coaching. As he commented in *Coaching at Work*, 'even the most pragmatic of coaching interventions, such as daily task performance, are enhanced if the coach holds a transpersonal perspective' (quoted in Hilpern, 2006). More importantly, Sir John links transpersonal coaching to the value of corporate social responsibility – the so-called triple bottom line (profit, people, and environment) that chief executives and managing directors should take on board, coaching and being coached throughout their organizations (see Chapters 7–9 for some of the theories and practices developed along this line).

Following the first edition of this book, my colleagues Stephen Palmer and Alison Whybrow (with whom I and other colleagues co-founded the BPS) edited *The Handbook of Coaching Psychology*, which was published in December 2007. The Handbook consists of a collection of chapters and offers a wide range of coaching approaches contributed by psychologists in the field. David Peterson (2009) criticized the coaching approaches included in the Handbook as mostly based on counselling psychology and therapeutic practice – while coaching should be rooted in positive psychology and non-clinical practice, as advocated in our first edition. We shall explore this foundation further in the next chapter.

On using therapeutic-based coaching approaches, Douglas McKenna and Sandra Davis (2009) argued that psychotherapy and coaching are similar and thus can be generalized when applying therapeutic approaches to coaching (and vice versa). They pointed out that psychologists (especially occupational and organizational psychologists) tended to overlook psychotherapy as a source of information (especially in terms of the outcome of its research). Indeed the evidence-based practice that is routinely used in psychotherapy and in clinical and counselling psychology can yield invaluable information for coaching practices. I shall describe in detail some of the methods for evaluating the coaching outcome in Chapter 10.

On the basis of thousands of studies, McKenna and Davis identified four 'active ingredients' that account for most of the variance in the successful outcomes:

1   client factors (40 per cent);
2   the relationship or alliance (30 per cent);
3   placebo or hope (15 per cent);
4   theory and technique (15 per cent).

McKenna and Davis (2009) also suggested that psychologists have training and experience that would enable them to leverage these active ingredients in coaching. However, there are certain areas in coaching where psychologists may need to have further training and continuous professional development experience. In this book I shall explore the active ingredients further and show how they can be integrated in the coaching practice.

When writing the first edition, I wondered whether coaching psychology was coming of age in 2007. Alison Whybrow (2008) also questioned if coaching psychology was indeed coming of age. She asked:

- What does it mean to be a 'coaching psychologist'?
- What has enabled coaching psychology to progress to the current state so quickly?
- What is the scientific basis for coaching psychology?
- What do coaching psychologists do?
- How do coaching psychologists serve their clients?
- How do psychologists and coaches become coaching psychologists?
- What might that mean for this emergent professional area of psychological practice?

Whybrow argues that, to answer these questions, coaching psychologists would need to make their framework explicit and to share the standard of practice. She also strongly argued that coaching psychologists do clearly articulate their framework of practice.

The debate on the coaching psychology continues. Michael Cavanagh and David Lane (2012a) asked: 'What does coming of age, or "growing up" in this world look like for us as practitioners, researchers and as a profession?' Drawing from the work of Ralph Stacey (1996) on strategic management and organizational dynamics, they highlighted the challenges we face today in the messy world of complexity; and they discussed the implications of these challenges for the practice of coaching and for coaching psychology – the profession and the research. The discussion generated quite a bit of debating, with responses from the academic world and from practitioners in the field. Debates seemed to be around the following issues:

- coaching models;
- professionalism;
- evidence-based practice.

Coaching models

On coaching models, Cavanagh and Lane (2012a) advocated systems thinking to inform coaching practice. In particular, they borrowed Stacey's certainty/agreement matrix as a way to handle complexity. Like a *cynefin* (Snowden and Boone, 2007), this matrix provides a 'map' (that is, a spatial representation) to show how agreement and certainty interact. A boundary was drawn around the buffer zone (the grey area) – the interface between stability/instability and high/low agreement (so-called 'the edge of chaos'). Within this grey area, one could not rely on rational approaches (such as mathematic modelling) to help decision making. Unfortunately one would never be able to predict the zone within which a decision for action has to be made. Furthermore, even within the zone of high stability/high agreement, a small fluctuation might escalate into unexpected chaos (this is known as 'the butterfly effect' – a systems property). This renders the certainty/agreement matrix totally useless as a decision-making tool. Moreover, as a result, the matrix misrepresents the complexity of the real world and very often gives its users a wrong sense of security, making them believe that they are in control and could mobilize all sorts of decision-making techniques, depending on which zones they are operating in. These concerns were pointed out by Ralph Stacey himself in response to Cavanagh and Lane's proposal (Stacey, 2012).

As for coaching approaches, Drake advocated the narrative approach as a psychological framework for coaching, since it provides a structure and function that would help coaches to make sense of the coachee's action within the system's context (Drake, 2008b).

In response to the debate on complexity and systems approaches, Drake (2012) questioned its implications for coaching practice, and research, for instance by asking:

- What does 'complexity' mean for coaches in practice ('when they are sitting in front of their coachee')?
- How would one apply the systems approaches in coaching?
- What are the implications for coaches' conceptualizations, applications of evidence and research?

Chapters 7 and 8 present a range of coaching techniques and practical exercises that include the narrative approaches within the systems framework.

Despite all the disagreements and competing concerns, Cavanagh and Lane (2012b) argued that systems thinking provides a valuable contribution to coaching. One thing that the scholars do agree upon is the role of coaching:

> The process of *exploring* stories *in all situations* requires mindful, reflective responsiveness rather than reactivity. The task here is for the coach and the client to notice and reflect on the qualitative themes present in the client's situation, and to think through together the possible trajectories of outcome that any action might precipitate. This is not to suggest that the coach or client should seek to predict with any degree of certainty, what might unfold. Rather, the task is to hold those multiple possibilities in mind and take action that maximises the ability to respond flexibly as outcomes emerge. (Cavanagh and Lane, 2012a: 82; reiterated with emphasis by Stacey, 2012: 95)

This is all about us exploring, thinking and reflecting together, as 'reflective practitioners'; and it is regarded as 'the hallmark of the expert practitioner' (Schön, 1983, 1991 and Stacey, 2012 respectively). This book will explore reflective models and practice further.

Professionalism

On the issue of professionalism, Dr David Drake introduced the term 'postprofessional' as a frame for the future development of coaching psychology (Drake, 2008a). Looking from the psychodynamic perspective and citing the work of Donald Winnicott (1971), he regarded the role of coaches as one designed to provide 'holding environments' – a 'container' or 'eco-system' that holds the coachee's anxiety; thereby both the coach and the coachee can create more adaptive responses in complex and chaotic environments. Here coaches would take a 'de-centered' position. Drake regarded 'agency' as an important function in the coachee's development, in leadership and in decision making in complex environments (he is citing Weick, 1995, as an example).

Evidence-based practice

Like many good coaches and coaching psychologists, Cavanagh and Lane (2012a: 88) cleverly posed their recommendations as questions to the reader. From reading the debates, with contributions from various colleagues as well as my own, it seems that, in order to respond to today's challenges, coaching psychologists need to develop:

- a new interdiscipline ('a new sort of psychology') that embraces diversity and 'cross-disciplinary engagement' (Cavanagh and Lane, 2012a: 88);
- research approaches that have rigour beyond the traditional methods;
- training that enables coaching psychologists to be competent while working within the ambiguity and uncertainty of complex systems;
- a profession that can help us to work within the complex and chaotic contexts of today's world.

I hope that this book will contribute in some way to the above developments.

e-Coaching and Mentoring

With the development of the Internet, and in response to the rising oil price, online options have been increasingly adopted by companies and organizations as alternative means of communication. Purple Insight, a software company in Gloucestershire, UK, was spending £2,000 a month more on travel in 2005 than in the previous year. When the company switched to web conferencing, it saved £1,500 a month in travelling expenses. As the company grew, the saving was expected to grow to many thousands, as reported in *Director* (Higgins, 2005). Under the current economic condition in the UK, many institutions in the higher education sector are also expanding their distance-learning programme via virtual learning environment (VLE) software such as Moodle. For instance, the University of East London has been offering postgraduate coaching and coaching psychology programmes via distance learning since 2010. Other programmes and institutions are following this trend.

From the author's experience in leading the distance-learning modules, this virtual environment seems to be well received by the students. According to a student's feedback, 'the VLE provided the students with opportunities to share their experience and engage in conversation on the discussion forum, which was useful and aided understanding of the material'.

The e-mentoring has also been generally well received. This was highlighted by Hunt (2005: 7), who pointed out that 'little is still known about the e-mentoring approach.

> Some organizations have flirted with e-mentoring but few have come close to emulating the successes that have been achieved in the areas of business-to-business in the UK or business to university in the USA' and this may be due to our lack of understanding of e-mentoring's key features and benefits. He thus concluded that, 'any e-mentoring program should be professional in its approach and design, be confidential for the partic- ipants, be convenient enough that it fits in with the day-to-day work, be easy for partici- pants to join and actively participate, be flexible and add value' (Hunt, 2005: 10).

The convenience and flexibility of e-mentoring allows for regular informal communi- cations between individuals or groups, enabling asynchronous (email) or synchronous exchanges (messenger or text). David Clutterbuck (2004: 164) proposed that a blend of methods and technologies could improve the mentoring process:

> As technology becomes more sophisticated it is reasonable to assume that there will be much broader and more intelligent use of technologies. There will in particular be more use of video conferencing through desktop PCs and web cameras. In the future it seems likely that the majority of relationships will be hybrids of face-to-face remote and asynchronous textual exchanges. The evidence suggests that this has great potential to enrich the dialogue between mentors and mentees. Mentoring scheme co-ordinators will have to include the effective use of these technologies as an integral part of mentor and mentee training.

With the development of the Internet and e-messaging, we have also noticed that some companies offer e-coaching or e-mentoring either as a stand-alone or as part of their training programmes. Much of the research has compared face-to-face with computer-mediated communication. Some of the results highlighted the danger of depending entirely on the technology. For example, people were found to be more aggressive and hostile over email than they were face to face (Kiesler, Siegel and McGuire, 1984). This led to concerns about the potential impact of loss of account- ability in online communication, where individuals feel more distant from the target person and thus less careful and sensitive about how the communication will be received. In the 1990s such concerns diminished, as evidence of hostility was low. Several theories have been prominent in developing our understanding of how online communication differs from face-to-face communication.

There has been a range of studies indicating that trust may take longer to build in online relationships to begin with, but that final trust ratings are the same over time. For example, Tidwell and Walther (2002) have queried whether communicating face to face would actually be more personal and productive than communicating via electronic means. However, synchronicity might need more time to 'cover the ground', and that has been rarely factored in in studies where researchers have been looking at the same time controls in both comparison sets, for instance in face-to-face versus online ones.

Other researchers have found that online relationships were moderately inter- dependent, deep, committed (Parks and Floyd 1996), and gave a sense of predictability and understanding (Swann, 1990). It has also been shown that those who already network socially are more likely to add the Internet to the media they already use to socialize with, rather than to replace, them. Shy people have found it easier to open up on the Internet, and initial disclosure is higher on the Internet than in face-to-face situations (Bargh, McKenna and Fitzsimons, 2002).

More recent developments in online chatting have the benefit of immediacy. In many corporate teams working internationally members are in online meetings throughout the day and may even be in more than one meeting at a time, so the rate of communication in any one minute might be very productive. Many such teams now describe these simultaneous meeting routes as highly productive, but different from face-to-face meetings. For example, SGCP carried out most of its committee meetings via teleconferencing. It achieved significant cost savings. The practice was recommended by the Council of the BPS, which encouraged other committees to conduct their meetings using teleconferencing methods more often.

Chapter Summary and Reflection

To summarize, the coaching and mentoring industries have enjoyed a relatively high profile in recent business developments. Although most news and articles that were sampled reported a perceived positive outcome and business benefits, there has been very little objective evidence that helps us to predict enduring social and work partnerships in every aspect of coaching and mentoring, or diverse coaching and mentoring relationships across all people and situations. Encouragingly, there is some universality about aspects of the process that are positive from the reports gathered. Positive psychology offers some pointers to the further development of frameworks for coaching and mentoring. We need to ensure that the growing coaching and mentoring practice remains aligned with sound psychological principles and that diversity is represented in all the forms of research methodology and sampling. We shall describe how the coaching and mentoring framework and programme can be implemented in Chapters 6 and 9 respectively.

I argue that, in order for a coherent generic framework to be to developed, the approaches have to be grounded in the psychology of learning. This forms the core topic of the next chapter. When coaching is grounded in psychology, it is perceived as the cutting edge, and there is a string of business cases for the proposed model (see Chapters 5 and 6). I hope that readers understand by now, from this chapter, not only the relationship between coaching, mentoring and psychology, but also their bene-fits (both as commodities and as social responsibilities) for individuals and their communities.

Coaching and mentoring can be understood from the perspective of positive psy-chology in terms of one's positive emotion within the present and future domains.

Using the 'journey' metaphor for coaching, one focuses on the present – the here and now – as a primary concern and regards the future – the aspiration – as if it were real (see Figure 2.2). Another metaphor is that of playing chess. There are many options (say, within the GROW model) in the middle game. This book aims to equip readers with some useful techniques and strategies for playing the middle game in coaching and mentoring (this will happen in Chapters 7 and 8). Both the systems

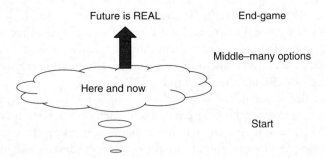

Figure 2.2 Coaching and mentoring paradigm

approach and the research on learning (discussed next) suggest that the effective development of coaching psychology as a discipline requires an interdisciplinary enquiry into the relevant theories and techniques.

A multicultural perspective has increasingly become a dominant ethical imperative for individual behaviours and for organizational practice. Multiculturalism is a moral movement with its own agenda, which is related to enhancing individual dignity, human rights and the recognition of marginalized groups (Fowers and Richardson, 1996: 609). It resonates with the recent development in community psychology, which is beyond the scope of this book. However, Chapter 9 provides some examples of community coaching.

Coaches and mentors must decide how to deal with the influence of culture and socio-historical aspects of our time within their diverse communities. The concept of positive development must therefore be defined in terms of five dimensions (Jørgensen and Nafstad, 2004):

1 motivation;
2 action;
3 goals;
4 context;
5 socio-temporal elements.

These dimensions offer us some direction towards furthering our research and developing a universal framework that is cross-cultural. While to translate the positive psychology of optimal experience into coaching practice so as to enable everyone to enjoy a flow experience may be Mihaly Csikszentmihalyi's dream, there are some key practical questions that require our attention. These are:

- How do we guide coachees and mentees to achieve their optimal experience (the experience of flow)?
- What are the techniques?
- What are the measurements?

We shall explore some of the possible answers to these questions in our coaching/mentoring journey of this second edition.

3

Philosophy and Theories of Learning Applicable to Coaching and Mentoring
Positive Psychology and the Learning Process

Introduction

This chapter describes the philosophy and theories of psychology that are applicable to coaching and mentoring. Positive psychology is identified as the philosophy that underpins coaching and mentoring. Numerous learning theories that are relevant to coaching and mentoring are reviewed. First, the chapter will introduce the philosophy of positive psychology as a foundation for coaching. It will then give an overall discussion based on the general review of literature on the psychology of learning. Finally, some of the more generic learning theories are singled out for further development. These will form a building block in our development of a dynamic coaching and mentoring model and of a universal framework that is applicable across cultures.

Positive Psychology

Following his introduction to the 2000 edition of the *American Psychologist*, Martin Seligman (with his colleague Mihaly Csikszentmihalyi) published 16 articles on the topic of positive psychology (Seligman and Csikszentmihalyi, 2000). The themes broached in these articles ranged from questions such as what enables happiness, what are the effects of autonomy and self-regulation, how optimism and hope affect health, or what constitutes wisdom to expositions on how talent and creativity come to fruition. For example, Mihaly Csikszentmihalyi (1991) introduced the concept of flow to describe the optimal experience: the fact that people could improve the quality of their life by focusing on improving their experiences. This conscious attempt could be applied to all areas of one's life: work, everyday experience or the search for meaning. The authors outlined a framework for a *science* of positive psychology. They had an optimistic view that this paradigm shift would enable us to understand and build the factors that allow individuals, communities, and societies to flourish in this new century.

The Psychology of Coaching, Mentoring and Learning, Second Edition. Ho Law.
© 2013 John Wiley & Sons, Ltd. Published 2013 by John Wiley & Sons, Ltd.

In the UK, an exploratory workshop entitled 'A Positive Agenda for Occupational Psychology', hosted by Pearn Kandola at Oxford on 28 April 2005, described the emergence of positive psychology as 'the scientific study of well-being and fulfilment' and claimed that it 'opens up new perspectives for occupational psychology. Bringing together theory, research and practice from disparate fields, it offers the possibility of an integrated and well-founded approach to enhancing the quality of working life and organizational effectiveness' (quoted from the PowerPoint presentation at the workshop).

From our review of modern literature in psychology, which is not limited to learning theories, we have noticed that positive psychology is directly relevant to coaching and mentoring. Positive psychology is also concerned with the improvement of performance and well-being (Linley and Harrington, 2006). It shares a similar paradigm shift from a pathology-orientated understanding to a perspective of growth and positive development. The shift is exemplified by Christopher Peterson and Martin Seligman's (2004) presentation of their book *Character Strengths and Virtues* as a 'Manual of the Sanities', in direct contrast to the 1994 *Diagnostic and Statistical Manual of Mental Disorders* sponsored by the American Psychological Association.

So we see positive psychology providing us with a possible foundation to improve quality of life, as well as coaching and mentoring practice. If this discipline were applied in the clinical setting, it would offer a promise to prevent illnesses and the sense of hopelessness and meaninglessness – and it would do it in a different way from how it's done in classic psychotherapy and clinical psychology. More specifically, the European psychotherapeutic approach has been criticized as 'culturally blind', non-universal, and biased in its over-emphasis on the pathological model (Law, 2004a, 2004b). As a result of this approach, we live inherently in a culture that lacks positive features such as aspirations, wisdom, creativity, future-mindedness, courage, spirituality, responsibility, perseverance, hopes and dreams that make our lives meaningful and worth living.

Although positive psychology has been perceived as a new movement in modern psychology, its linage can be traced back throughout European psychology to Maslow (1968), Rogers (1963), Allport (1961), Jahoda (1958), Jung (1933), and as far back as James in 1902 (James, 1960); see Linley and Joseph (2004a, 2004b). Philosophically and culturally, it has a resonance in the Platonic and Aristotelian tradition, which is shared by all Western philosophies.

There are three 'pillars' of positive psychology in relation to the concept of a more positive and fulfilling life:

1   positive emotion – the pleasant life;
2   positive character – the engaged life;
3   positive institutions – the meaningful life.

A positive emotion such as happiness can be classified within three domains:

1   the past (satisfaction, contentment, fulfilment, pride and serenity);
2   the present (joy, ecstasy, calm, zest, ebullience, pleasure and flow);
3   the future (optimism, hope, faith, trust).

Coaching (and mentoring) can be understood from the perspective of positive psychology (Kauffman and Scoular, 2004; Linley, 2004). Positive psychology covers enquires into human conditions such as happiness, wisdom, creativity, and human strengths. It has considerable potential for benefit – and this benefit extends to coaching, so in this section we provide a detailed account of their area of overlap.

Sponsored by the Values in Action Institute, Peterson and Seligman (2004) conducted some research by means of a survey designed to measure human strengths. They found 24 'signature strengths', which were clustered into six dimensions:

1   wisdom and knowledge (creativity, curiosity, open-mindedness, love of learning, perspective): cognitive strengths that consist of knowledge acquisition and its application;
2   courage (bravery, persistence, integrity, vitality): emotional strengths that involve the exercise of the will to accomplish goals in the face of challenges, dangers, difficulties, fears, obstacles, pains or threats;
3   humanity (love, kindness, social intelligence): interpersonal strengths that involve 'tending' and 'befriending' others;
4   justice (citizenship, fairness, leadership): civic strengths that underlie a healthy community life;
5   temperance (forgiveness and mercy, humility and modesty, prudence, self-regulation): strengths that protect against excess;
6   transcendence (appreciation of beauty and excellence, gratitude, hope, humour, spirituality): strengths that forge connections to the larger universe and provide meaning.

The 24 elements of strengths (with their sub-elements in the bracket) are as follows:

1   Creativity (originality, ingenuity): produce adaptive and original ideas or behaviour that have a positive contribution to your life or others'. Think of novel and productive ways of doing things. This strength covers artistic achievement but is not limited to it. We extend it to contributions to the organization, community and society.
2   Curiosity (interest, novelty seeking, openness to experience): explore and pursue novelty, variety and challenge; seek experience for its own sake (for its intrinsic interest).
3   Open-mindedness (judgement, critical thinking): search for evidence against your favoured belief, plans, goals, and weigh such evidence fairly when it is available. Think the situations through and examine them from all sides, without jumping to conclusions.
4   Love of learning: be positively motivated to acquire new skills and knowledge or to enhance existing skills and knowledge. This also associates with the strength of curiosity but goes beyond it to describe one's tendency to learn systematically and improve what one already knows.
5   Perspective (wisdom): take a long-term view on the basis of your knowledge and experience. Provide wise counsel to others; look at the world that makes sense to yourself and to other people.
6   Bravery (valour): do what needs to be done voluntarily, despite fear in a dangerous situation. Speak up for what is right even if there is opposition; act on convictions even if they are unpopular.

  7   Persistence: finish a task despite obstacles and take pleasure in completing it. 'Get it out the door.'
  8   Integrity (authenticity, honesty): tell the truth and present yourself genuinely, but take responsibility for your feeling and act without pretence.
  9   Vitality (zest, enthusiasm, vigour, energy): feel alive, have enthusiasm in what you do, even in difficult circumstances. Approach life with excitement and energy. Live life as an adventure.
 10   Love: reciprocate, develop and value emotional relationships with family members, friends, colleagues, coachees and mentees.
 11   Kindness (generosity, nurture, care, compassion, altruistic love, niceness): be compassionate, helpful, nice to others. Do favours and good deeds for others; help them; take care of them.
 12   Social intelligence (emotional intelligence, personal intelligence): be aware of the emotion of other people and of your own. Process emotion (so-called 'hot information'). Know what to do to fit into different social situations, and what makes other people tick. See Chapter 6 for more discussion about this element within our universal integrated framework.
 13   Citizenship (social responsibility, loyalty, teamwork): identify with a common goal that is above your personal interests and includes the group of which you are a member. Do your share and work well as a member of a group or team. Be loyal to the group.
 14   Fairness: treat all people equally and without bias. Give everyone a fair chance.
 15   Leadership: inspire group members to do what they are supposed to do, and at the same time keep a good relationship and high morale: this is the so-called transformational leadership (Tichy and Devanna, 1986).
 16   Forgiveness and mercy: let bygones be bygones instead of being negative. Forgive those who have done wrong. Give people a second chance instead of being vengeful.
 17   Humility and modesty: let your accomplishments speak for themselves. Acknowledge your mistakes and imperfections.
 18   Prudence: consider carefully the consequences of your actions in order to achieve long-term goals effectively.
 19   Self-regulation (self-control): exercise control over your emotions and responses in order to achieve a desirable outcome.
 20   Appreciation of beauty and excellence (awe, wonder, elevation, transcendence): appreciate and enjoy the experience of beautiful things such as art, music, foods and drinks and so on.
 21   Gratitude: have a sense of thankfulness in response to gifts. Be aware of and thankful for the good things that happen. Take time to express thanks.
 22   Hope (optimism, future-mindedness, future orientation): think about and work towards future outcomes positively. Expect the best in the future and work to achieve it. Believe that a good future is something that can be brought about.
 23   Humour (playfulness): laugh and tease; bring smiles to the faces of others skilfully. See the light side. Make (not necessarily tell) jokes.
 24   Spirituality (religiousness, faith, purpose): have a coherent belief about the higher purpose and meaning of the universe and one's place in it. Have beliefs about the meaning of life that shape conduct and provide comfort.

By examining the common characteristics of the elements of strength (thematic analysis), Peterson and Seligman (2004) set up ten criteria for inclusion. The items listed above satisfied most of them. The ten criteria are:

1   being fulfilling for individuals (for the self and others);
2   being morally valued in its own right;
3   not diminishing others when displaying a strength;
4   having a non-felicitous opposite;
5   being trait-like;
6   having distinctiveness;
7   being a paragon;
8   being expressed by prodigies;
9   contrasting with the strengths of others (those who do not have such a strength);
10   being nurtured by institutions and rituals.

The optimism of positive psychology represents an attitudinal shift in psychology from its focus on individuals as asocial to individuals as socially, culturally and ethically responsible beings. Positive psychologists regard this as a fundamental cornerstone for meeting the challenge for change in our multicultural societies and in the face of globalization. For more recent developments in the research and applications of positive psychology, see for instance Hefferon and Boniwell (2011).

Linking Learning to Coaching and Mentoring

Many coaches and mentors argue that coaching and mentoring would function as a powerful lever to promote leaning and change. In this book we argue that, while coaching and mentoring offer such an opportunity for learning, this outcome could not be guaranteed as a 'given'. For learning to take place, coach and coachees, mentors and mentees must actively engage in the learning process during the coaching and mentoring journey. So this epistemological position provides a starting point in asking more questions:

- What is the 'right condition' for learning? What condition could lead to an 'Ah ha!' experience?
- How do coaching and mentoring sessions provide the condition for learning?
- What factors does this condition consist of – for example, what assumptions, beliefs, ideas and values – and how do we establish them?

Coaching and mentoring as a learning process

Coachees and mentees as well as coaches and mentors are all learners. We thus regard coaching and mentoring as learning processes. While the learning condition includes both physical and social aspects, there are likely to be many barriers in the process of learning. Most of these barriers are psychological (the so-called 'inner game': see Gallwey, 2000). These inner barriers may have developed from individuals' negative experiences in the past. Many people had negative experiences with learning, and this may prevent them from learning further, new materials. This in turn forms a negative feedback loop, which hinders future learning. On the other hand, positive learning experiences can help coachees to develop their capacity for further learning. This in turn forms a positive feedback loop. For example, participants in coaching programmes were asked to list:

1   the negative experiences they have had in the past, which may stand in the way of change;
2   the attributes of a poor coach;
3   the attributes of a good coach.

In response, many of the participants responded with memories of their own teachers and lecturers.

From all this we learn that the essence of learning, be it in teaching, training, coaching or a mentoring context, seems to be universal. To learn, one must embrace (internalize) a new set of values, attitudes, skills or knowledge that one did not have before (for child developmental learning, see Kegan, 1982, 1994). In this context, the learner's task is to internalize the *socio-cultural-temporal surround* of the new situation (Jarvis, 1987).

The coach's task is to help learners bring to their awareness what was internalized in the past. The process is known as mapping the landscape of action on the landscape of consciousness, in a narrative approach (see Chapter 7 for techniques and tools).

Clients tend to focus on learning that connects to the context of their workplace, in particular in executive coaching. It is therefore helpful to provide a number of case studies that may help readers to identify their own context.

The Psychology of Learning

Historically, the study of learning was divided according to two ways of thinking – epistemological and experimental:

1   Epistemology questions the nature of what we know, asking what knowledge is and how we distinguish it from our own internal thoughts and beliefs.
2   Experimental approaches derive theories by conducting scientific experiments.

There are three kinds of learning theories within the epistemological tradition. These are:

1   *Objectivism* Reality is external and independent from the learner. Knowledge is acquired through sensory experience.
2   *Pragmatism* Reality is both external and internal. Although reality exists, it is provisional, as it cannot be known directly. Knowledge is interpreted through signs and negotiated from experience and reason.
3   *Interpretivism* Reality is internal, relative to individuals' frames of reference. Knowledge is constructed by the learner through thinking.

Experimental approaches have generated four major learning theories:

1 *The principle of association* One learns ideas by direct association. This was demonstrated in 1885 by Ebbinghaus (1850–1909) through the famous verbal learning experiments of nonsense syllables, which produced the classic forgetting curve (Ebbinghaus, 1913). Ebbinghaus argued that meaning did not influence learning and that the prior knowledge we store in our memory has no effect on what we continue to learn.

2 *The law of effect* One learns by associating sensation/impulse to action (proposed by Thorndike, 1874–1949).

3 *Classical conditioning* One naturally generates a response (*unconditioned response*) to a stimulus (*unconditioned stimulus*). An example would be the secretion of saliva when food is presented. The same response can be produced by pairing the unconditioned stimulus with a neutral stimulus. Over time, the neutral stimulus alone can elicit the same response. The stimulus and response are now called *conditioned stimulus* and *conditioned response* respectively (this theory was advanced by Pavlov, 1949–1946).

4 *Gestalt theory* originated from the perception of motion from flashing light (the phi phenomenon). Gestalt psychologists propose that knowledge acquisition requires the learner to actively impose organization (*gestalt*) on sensory data in order to derive insight (insightful learning).

According to gestalt theory of insightful learning, there are five stages of learning:

1 The learner goes through a period of trial and error.
2 The learner completely grasps the solution. This seems to occur suddenly (an 'Ah ha!' moment).
3 The learner produces a smooth error-free performance.
4 The knowledge is long-lasting.
5 The learner can apply the same principle to solve a similar problem in a new context.

Psychological research has indicated that there is a lot we can do to optimize our chances of achieving effective outcomes when we act as learners, having exchanges in purposeful relationships designed to bring about new knowledge and skills. Self-determination, autonomy, participation and choice underpin many studies about learning participation (Spreitzer, 1995). Social learning theories, and particularly the reinforcement affect model, continue to influence our understanding of learning in collaborative settings (Clore and Byrne, 1974). In short, this model assumes that we like anyone who or anything that makes us feel good and dislike anything that or anyone who makes us feel bad. Rewards in relationships can include attention or being attended to, praise and positive interaction. As learners, we will do better when we are in a receptive environment where we feel attended to and supported. In a different kind of setting the transferability of these theories is limited. Self determination, autonomy and choice are often, in certain cultures, preferred values for a range of behaviour, and the interpretation of positive inter-action may vary from setting to setting. For example, autonomy might be very valued in one company but be considered averse to teamwork in another, which prefers compliance with a procedural framework.

Another commonly cited element in learning success in developmental relationships is goal setting for learners (Locke, Shaw, Saari and Latham, 1981). Goal setting has been a Western preoccupation and may not be automatically meaningful across all cultures and situations. Even in studies in Europe, where coaches have been asked to work in coaching relationships without clear goal boundaries, coaching participants have evidenced no negative outcomes as a result (Law, Ireland and Hussain, 2005). Increasingly over the years, practitioners have started to talk more about emergent learning, unstructured learning, informal learning and the idea that all this may be more exploratory and less rigidly goal-restrained than was previously thought.

Likewise, our fixation with linking evaluation to development has meant that we have used traditional goal-based structures to facilitate evaluation processes, which have gained credibility through the hard core of scientific data from research. New developments, in particular the wider acceptance of looser structures for evaluation in social science, such as appreciative enquiry, have liberated us from some of those constraints. Appreciative enquiry is more able to address relative and individualized progress within the context of operation rather than progress against preset targets.

On the basis of the principles of positive psychology described earlier, we can identify what we are already able to do but need to do more of. We can also identify areas where our capabilities are weak and where we need to update our skills and knowledge. We can check our motivation to achieve our goals and our levels of self-efficacy (Bandura, 1982).

The self-efficacy concept comes from social cognitive theory. It is a belief in one's own capacities to achieve a given goal (Bandura, 1997). Self-efficacy also links expectation to action/behaviour and outcome. There are three possible types of outcome that one could expect (Bandura, 1986, 1997):

1   physical effect as a consequence of one's direct action (e.g. pain or pleasure);
2   social effect (e.g. approval, recognition etc);
3   self-evaluative effect (reflective).

While outcome expectancies refer to the perception of the possible consequences of one's action, self-efficacy expectancy refers to personal action, control or agency. A person who believes in being able to produce a desired effect can conduct a more active and self-determined life course. This 'can do' thinking represents a sense of control over the environment. It reflects the belief that you can control challenging environmental demands by means of taking adaptive action. Individuals with high self-efficacy choose to perform more challenging tasks, anticipate optimistic scenarios and are active in identifying knowledge and skill sets that can help them overcome barriers and achieve their learning goals. According to Bandura (1977, 1982, 1997) there are four ways to influence one's self-efficacy:

1   by providing feedback on learners' own capabilities (*enactive mastery experiences*);
2   by providing comparative information about the attainments of others (*vicarious experiences*);

3   by telling learners what others believe them capable of achieving (*verbal persuasion*);
4   by letting learners judge their own ability to engage in the task at hand (*physiological states*).

Four conditions for continuous motivation and self-regulation (known as the ARCS model of motivational design) are proposed by Keller (1984). These conditions are:

- to gain and sustain *attention*;
- to enhance *relevance*;
- to build *confidence*;
- to generate *satisfaction*.

To summarize, to design a coaching and mentoring process may involve the following steps:

1   analysing the coachees and mentees;
2   defining motivational objectives;
3   designing a motivational strategy;
4   implementing the plan of action;
5   evaluating and reviewing.

There are numerous motivation theories that can be applied to the study of the motivation of learners. Maslow (1954, 1968) put forward a model of hierarchical needs. People are motivated to satisfy their psychological, safety, belonging, self-esteem and self-actualization needs. These needs represented conditions that learning partners might seek to establish in order to maximize learning outcomes. Psychology has traditionally recognized the power and role of beliefs in shaping reality. Theories have been put forward with belief systems in the mix, or where beliefs alone are central to understanding behaviour. Merton (1948), in line with the latter tradition, introduced the concept of self-fulfilling prophecy, to refer to a false belief that leads to its own fulfilment. Such beliefs are associated with under-achievement, social stereotyping and discriminatory behaviour. In learning situations, individuals with low expectations and beliefs about themselves – which are perhaps the result of what others have communicated to them (e.g. 'you won't do well') – tend to deliver according to expectation, so they don't perform well. When negative and limiting expectations are extended to the stereotyping of groups, under-achievement might follow.

This individualized self-fulfilling prophecy approach has been criticized, because recent studies show that the impact of self-fulfilling prophecy is low and other factors are more significant in determining behaviour and outcomes. The self-fulfilling prophecy has been used to explain the under-achievement of minority groups. It conveniently places the problem of under-achievement in the lap of the minorities themselves. It suggests that there is a real deficit in their belief systems, which results in their under-achievement and indirectly limits their successful engagement in processes that would help them be successful. Extensions to an inter-group perspective recognize that the false beliefs may be communicated and maintained by the majority culture. However, there is less financial sponsorship dedicated to re-aligning the beliefs of majority cultures. Secondly, individual minority success (which defies predictions using this model) is rarely celebrated in ways that are likely to shift majority opinion.

Vroom (1964) has been credited with creating the expectancy valence theory, where there needs to be positive correlations between efforts and performance, favourable performance results and desirable rewards. Rewards satisfy important needs, and the desire to satisfy the need is strong enough to make the effort worth while. This approach has been criticized for a lack of inclusion of normalized and routine behaviour, which is particularly embedded in cultures.

Many Western psychological concepts are seen as the absolute 'truth', when in fact they are limited in their scope when it comes to describing and predicting behaviour across the diverse communities in which people engage in learning. Learning goes beyond concepts of individual difference, and particularly beyond our modern fascination with self-management. Learning might stem more from the interplay between the individual learner and the environment in which he or she operates.

Even the nurture–nature debate appears in a different light in a world of diversity, where science and technology are interacting before we are born, determining the core of our being. For example, genetic research and the standardization of aspects of nurture such as the core educational curriculum wrap around care and national standards to ensure the homogenization of nurture in institutional settings. Conceptually, the whole debate is limited by the primary assumption that nature and nurture are elements that are completely separate from each other and can be judged in terms of the independent and distinctive influence of each on the subject learner. But there are many counter-assumptions that we are indistinguishable from our environment and that nature and nurture are entwined in such a fundamental way that no valid measurement could be used to isolate the contribution of one independently from the contribution of the other. Secondly, this debate has often failed to recognize that we are changed by our environment while we are also an agent of its change, and that learning comes from the experience of the interplay between these two sides of the coin.

The context of operation and an appreciation of the other players are key to our learning success. At times the context in which we operate has fixed elements, which may limit our learning goals or the methods we employ, and at other times it is something we can shape entirely. However, this context is rarely as fixed as we presume, and the learning starts by ensuring that we are able to accurately construe our environment, to define the culture and its players and to be clear about what is fixed and what is fluid.

Naturally, the environment is ever changing, and we are also always changing adaptively, in light of our emerging learning and insights. We need therefore to integrate our own learning into new goals (if applicable), at the same time as keeping up with the contextual and cultural changes that affect our relationships and purpose.

Our perception of fixed elements and fluid elements in the culture of operation is also impacted by such things as the perceived locus of control (Rotter 1956). In the locus of control model (which is part of social learning theory), there is a general expectation that one's behaviour is or is not directly related to the outcome. Depending on their perceptions, individuals attribute the source of the power to change particular life events to internal factors, to external factors or to chance. Hence one person might see more elements in his or her environment as fixed beyond his or her control than another. Such impressions may impact on our learning strategies and styles.

Locus of control theory is also problematic in terms of how it explains cross-cultural differences. Control tends to be a Western higher order priority, which is not always transferred globally. Destiny and fatalism, reticence, putting others' needs before one's own, and reflection may have a lower value than a 'think can do quickly' approach endorsed in Western contexts.

Learning Theories Revisited

This section combines the pragmatic and interpretive approaches described in the earlier section and aims to re-examine the key learning theories within this tradition, both past and present, which inform coaching and mentoring practice. From the literature review, a whole family of theories emerge that are relevant in this context (e.g. Belenky, Clinchy, Goldberger and Tarule, 1986; Loevinger and Blasi, 1976; Perry, 1970; Kegan, 1982, 1994; Kolb, 1984; Mezirow, 1991, 2000; Freire, 1992; Lave and Wenger, 1991; and Wenger 1998). These include:

* the learning process;
* reflective learning;
* constructive–developmental theories;
* social learning theories.

The learning process

Learning, like coaching, is a process that has a beginning, a middle, and an end (and we can use journey as a metaphor here too). It is like a wheel (Figure 3.1), as in Kolb's (1984) learning cycle, except that some of the positions of the elements have been changed in relation to coaching and mentoring. As a starting point,

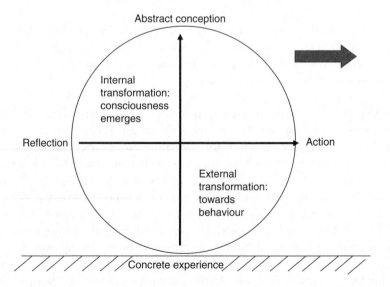

Figure 3.1   The learning wheel (modified from Kolb's (1984) learning cycle)

learning is grounded in a concrete experience when learners and coach interact (the point of social engagement).

Our learning wheel consists of four stages of learning:

1   concrete experience;
2   reflection;
3   abstract conception;
4   action.

Concrete experience   For learning to take place, first the learners need to experience an event. This provides the individuals with a starting point in understanding how they experience the situation and handle any problems or challenges in relation to the world.

Reflection   The value of reflective practice has been well recognized as a framework for our professional learning and development in coaching and psychology (for example, for coaching in sport psychology, see Anderson, Knowles and Gilbourne, 2004). After experiencing the event, learners also need to appreciate the nature of their experience and to take time to reflect upon it (Merriam, 1994). It would be desirable to think about the lessons learnt (how and what). This involves comparing the present event with the past experience and thinking about the future possibilities (this is pattern matching within the schema structure). It is also important for learners to reflect on themselves as learners. Learning is 'a way of being' (Vaill, 1996). Reflection is viewed by a lot of practitioners in education as an important part of learning. It is also an essential element in leadership development as well as in the development of coaches and mentors, so we shall devote the next section to exploring this stage in greater detail.

Abstract conception   Through reflection, this is a process designed to translate the experience into a meaningful concept. (See the later section on meaning.)

Action   We define the term 'action' quite broadly (in contrast to Kolb, who narrowly refers to the end stage of the learning cycle as an active experimentation). Action may include a decision arrived at through reflection and evaluation of an event. Thus action could include an option not to act.

For the wheel to roll forward in the learning process, two forms of transformation are required: upward and forward. The upward movement reflects an internal transformation from concrete experience to the formation of a new consciousness (abstract conception). The forward movement indicates a behavioural shift from internal reflection to external action.

Knowledge, resulting from this process, is a combination of grasping the everyday experience and transforming it into an abstract concept. From our experience, we have also found that there are considerable individual differences among coachees and mentees in terms of their strengths and weaknesses in the learning process. Some are good at producing knowledge (thinkers), while others are quick to act (actors). Some enjoy engaging in actual events and learning from experience (sensors), while others prefer to reflect upon their experience (evaluators). The four modes of learning – as

Table 3.1   Learning styles

	Internal Transformation	*External Transformation*
Internal Cognition	Thinker	Evaluator
External Perception	Sensor	Actor

sensor, thinker, evaluator, and actor – define an individual's learning styles (see Table 3.1).

Moreover, learners who are internally focused on their locus of control are more likely to focus on goal-setting for themselves and on the development of self-efficacy (evaluators and thinkers), whereas externally focused individuals are more likely to be receptive to external feedback and sensitive to the environment around them (actors and sensors). People who attribute causality to chance or fate might be more passive in their engagement with causality. Those who have achieved the mastery of all four learning styles are known as *reflective practitioners*. Reflective practitioners are able to grasp the concrete experience and transform it into action through reflection and conceptualization. In coaching and mentoring (and also in many learning professions such as education and psychology), we aim to develop learners' competence so that they may become reflective practitioners. As the term suggests, reflection is an important element in this learning process. We explore this further in the next section.

Reflective learning

In its simplest form, learning can be viewed as having the potential to transform. This may be achieved through reflection and action (*praxis*), whereby a new consciousness emerges (*conscientization*: Freire, 1992). Through this learning process, individuals become free from their limiting beliefs and arrive at an informed and reflective decision (*emancipatory learning*: Mezirow, 1996).

As seen from the previous section, reflection is an important driver for transformation within the learning process according to Kolb's (1984) learning cycle. For, without reflection, people would not learn from their experience; they would continue to experience the world in which the same emotion and perception occur in a 'self-confirming loop' (Brookfield, 1991; Jarvis, 1992). From the above assertions we can clearly conclude that reflection is a cognitive function that may occur even when the individuals are away from the situation where the event has taken place. It may occur from memory, by remembering the experience. We thus define reflection as *a cognitive process that involves both thinking and feeling about an experience (past or present): from this thinking and feeling a new consciousness emerges with a new appreciation, understanding and insight about that experience.*

Our definition resonantes with the opinions of many other scholars in the field (see Brookfield 1991; Boud, Keogh and Walker, 1985: 19). The definition implies that reflection is a metalevel of information processing where individuals interpret their thinking, learning and understanding, paying attention to their own assumptions, beliefs and values, which might shape their conclusion. Reflection is effectively a form of internal self-assessment, which could be made explicit by disclosing it to others verbally, in a coaching session, or through writing – in the form of an essay, letter or

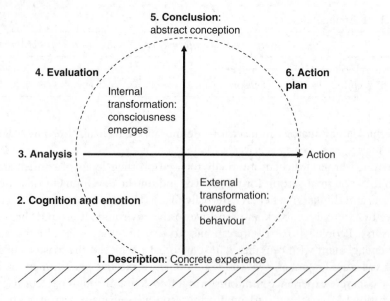

Figure 3.2   Six substages of reflection (combined models from Kolb, 1984, and Gibb, 1988)

diary (see Chapter 7). Such disclosure, known as a *reflective account*, is beneficial for both learners and coaches: it helps them to understand their own experience and draw conclusions or a plan of action from it.

The reflection stage within the learning wheel can further be expanded into a sub-loop with six finer stages, as shown in Figure 3.2 (see, for example, Gibb, 1988):

1   Description: describe what happened during the concrete experience.
2   Cognition and emotion: reflect on your thoughts and feeling. What were you thinking/feeling during the engagement/incident?
3   Analysis: try to understand what happened and draw meaning from the experience. What sense can you make of the experience?
4   Evaluation: assess the pros and cons, benefit and cost of the outcome of the experience.
5   Conclusion: summarize the meaning and the lessons learned; look for improvement. In the light of what happened, would you have done it differently? What else could you have done?
6   Recommendation/action plan: recommend a future plan of action for further learning and improvement. If a similar situation arose again, what would you do? What are you going to do to further improve and develop yourself/performance?

We have modified Gibb's six-stage model of reflection, as we felt that analysis is closely linked to the conclusion but should be its prerequisite. As the saying goes, 'don't jump to conclusions' without an analysis and without making sense of the experience. Conclusions should follow logically from the evaluation, with possible recommendations for future action. This framework also fits well within our dynamic coaching/mentoring/learning model, with meaning as an intervening variable (to be discussed later).

In making a critical reflection of the coaching process itself, coaches and mentors would experience a dialectic tension, in the sense that, on one hand, the experience in coaching and mentoring is usually rich in physical motion and emotion, while on the other a reflective account is always anchored around 'levels of cognitive engagement'. These levels of cognitive engagement may be aligned with Haberman's (1971) three levels of cognitive interest, as follows (Gilbourne, 2006):

1   Technical cognitive interest: relates to a limited form of reflection such as accountability, effectiveness and efficiency.
2   Practical cognition: valuates and reviews the consequences of actions and their underlying meaning for practice.
3   Intuition: associates with emancipatory processes and ethics (in this case, with a transpersonal spirit – a spirit that is beyond oneself).

In practice, the three levels overlap. Level 3 may act as an overarching reflective scaffolding from which one may choose to climb up or down. The form of self-assessment given above is part of a critical reflection that involves individuals in making authentic, objective judgements about themselves (Boud, 1995; Marienau, 1999). In the process, learners would gain a greater appreciation of the influence they have on their own learning and future possibilities. Self-development becomes a natural outcome of the reflective process.

Constructive–developmental theories

Constructive–developmental theories link developmental growth to meaning construction (Perry, 1970; Loevinger and Blasi, 1976; Belenky et al., 1986; Kegan, 1982, 1994). As the name of the theories suggest, many advocates of this approach link the theory of learning to the child development process (Piaget, 1954; Loevinger and Blasi, 1976; and Kohlberg, 1981). Constructive–developmental theories are essentially cognitive development theories within the paradigm of constructivism. Constructivism assumes that knowledge is constructed from our experience of the world, with many signs and symbols (hypermedia), through a critical discourse. In this section I shall highlight some of the major theories that may be relevant to coaching and mentoring.

Piaget's theory of child development
In European counties and generally in the West, Piaget's proposed stages of child development have been widely applied over the past few decades in the design of the educational curriculum. His views continue to attract the interest of teachers, students and parents. Within the context of coaching and mentoring, Piaget's theory of stages may have implications for mentoring in school and for parenting of children and young people. These stages of cognitive development are briefly outlined below:

1   *Sensorimotor* (from birth to age 2) This stage is linked to the development of sensory perception and the ability to respond via motor reflexes (grasping and sucking during the first eight months are examples of such responses). Gradually children develop an awareness of the world around them; for example, they

become aware of hidden objects (object performance), and they actively explore objects for their own pleasure (for example, they manipulate objects to seek attention, or they imitate the behaviour of others – the role-models; and this includes deferred imitation – that is, imitation that takes place even after the role models have gone).

2   *Preoperational* (ages 2–7) Children acquire language and develop an ability for thinking in terms of symbols or symbolic representation (for example 'X = apple') and for imagination with mental imagery. At this stage children would only see the world from their own perspective (they are egocentric), and they hold a relatively static view of the world (centration).

3   *Concrete operations* (ages 7–12) Children develop an ability for logical reasoning applied to concrete objects and events; they also develop or acquire multiple viewpoints (for example, they realize that the same object may have different appearances – the conservation concept).

4   *Formal operations* (ages 12–25) Young people are able to perform abstract reasoning and make hypotheses to predict outcomes.

One should note that the above stages are somewhat theoretical and abstract. In practice, the boundaries between them are blurred. There are various deviations from this abstract model of developmental stages among children across the world. Social–cultural influences on child development should not be underestimated. For the application of coaching and mentoring in education, see work by Pask and Joy (2007) and van Nieuwerburgh (2012).

In coaching and mentoring we argue that development does not stop in adulthood. Given the right conditions, most adults continue to learn throughout their lives. Theories of adult development would be more applicable to most coaching and mentoring in and outside the workplace.

Levinson's life structure theory
On the basis of results from the interviews of 40 men aged between 35 and 45 and using the metaphor of seasons, Levinson, Darrow, Klein, Levinson and McKee (1978) identified the following life stages:

1   spring (childhood and adolescence: from birth to the age of 16)
2   summer (early adulthood: 17–40)
3   autumn (middle adulthood: 41–60)
4   winter (late adulthood: 60+)

Each stage represents a period of transition that is characterized by the development of hopes and dreams, consolidation, evaluation in the face of challenges, further change in life (e.g. identity crises and self-doubts) and re-evaluation in relation to the reality of one's world view. For instance:

1   *Early adult transition* (17–22) As one enters adulthood, there is a sense of excitement about establishing independence in relation to one's own parents. One opens up to a new world of ideas, embracing its uncertainty about where one stands in relation to one's own aspirations. One has choices to make: entering

further or higher education, entering a career or establishing a family. At such a critical juncture, one may experience self-doubt about one's own ability to cope with the change in responsibility, as one senses the world's expectations and demands (Who am I? What kind of person do I want to become?).

2 *Provisional adulthood* (22–28) This is a period of establishing one's competence at being independent along one's chosen path of development.

3 *Age 30 transition* (28–33) Around this age, one is likely to settle down with a job and develop one's career. However, one may sometimes question one's own commitment to one's organization or to the relationship one is engaged in (Is this what I really want to do, to become? Whom do I want to be with?). One has choices: to leave the job and change one's circumstances; or to end a relationship.

4 *Settling down* (33–40) This is the time to grow roots and reap the fruit of earlier efforts.

5 *Mid-life transition* (40–45) Around the age of 40, one may recognize one's own unfulfilled ambitions (lost hopes or broken dreams). One may feel tired of what one is doing and begin to question one's own commitment again, asking deeper questions (What is the meaning of life? What is it all about?) This critical moment is often called mid-life crisis.

6 *Restabilization* (45–50) At this stage, one is likely to settle down with an established career. It is the time to bear fruit, develop still further and mentor others.

7 *Age 50 transition* (50–55) This is another critical moment for self-reflection (perhaps the result of another lost hope or broken dream); at the same time one feels somewhat out of touch with what is going on out there in relation to the younger generation; one has a sense of loss and regret for opportunities missed in the past (What have I achieved? What do I really value?).

8 *Middle adulthood* (55–60) One's inner calm is restored. One may realize one's limit, experience uncertainty about one's own longevity and realign one's priorities, in life and in relationships. One can afford to make choices in accordance with one's own value and sense of identity. One may develop still further and make one's assets grow; alternatively, one may choose to disengage from work or re-engage in new work or in a new enterprise.

9 *Late adult transition* (age 60–65) This probably represents the final stage of transition, during which one may need to plan ahead for the remaining years. Further reflection may take place, and hopefully one can enjoy the rest of life.

Later on, Levinson (1997) interviewed 45 women aged 35 to 45 and found that, although women may go through similar life stages, the rhythm of change tends to be different and they tend to be more concerned with the family and social aspects of life. Again, we need to be cautious about applying the life stages theory presented above too rigidly when we assess one's development. The theory was developed on the basis of a study of a small number of people within the American culture. It could not accommodate the diversity of human development. In particular, it does not pay heed to different life stages, which mark the rites of passage for people of a different sexual orientation, race, culture, religion and belief. For instance, the 'late adult transition' phase (60–65) usually represents the stage of retirement, construed in relation to the normal retirement age in Western societies. However, even in the West, the situation is now changing as a result of recent employment legislation, which in turn responds to changes in life expectancy and economic conditions.

The social constructive paradigm and cognitive–developmental theories:
Vygotsky's zone of proximal development
Within the constructive paradigm, among the cognitive–developmental theorists, there are two forerunners whose ideas are relevant to learning, coaching and mentoring: Lev S. Vygotsky (1896–1934) and Jerome Bruner (b. 1915). Both regarded the role of culture as instrumental to cognitive growth and as an *amplification of human intellectual power*.

Central to Bruner's theory is the idea of knowledge representation and how the representation of knowledge is used by children and adults to assist them in their understanding of the world. Bruner (1964) regards the process of learning as consisting of three specific stages of knowledge representation:

1   *Enactive representation* The knowledge is represented in the physical action. Although one may not be able to describe the knowledge, one is able to explain it through action, as if the muscle has its own memory (motor responses) – for example, by pointing out a direction.
2   *Iconic representation* This is a spatial–temporal imagistic representation of the perceptual input, and it is based on the experience of events in the world.
3   *Symbolic representation* This is the expression of learning to use signs and symbols – for example, language, to describe an experience of the world.

Through a number of experiments in which children were introduced to a series of problem-solving tasks of progressive difficulty, Vygotsky (1962, 1978) revealed the existence of a learning gap between an 'actual developmental level' and a higher level of 'potential development' under the guidance of, or in collaboration with, more sophisticated peers. This gap is called the *zone of proximal development*, and it is relevant to our discussion of the coaching definition (as exemplified by Tony Grant; see Chapter 4). People consult coaches and mentors when they face barriers that prevent them from improving their performance at work or from fulfilling some aspiration in their lives. In other words – they 'got stuck'. In these situations people tend to reproduce the problem solutions or the behaviours that are familiar to them from past experience. Adopting Vygotsky's developmental method, this gap between the known and familiar, and what is possible to know and do, can be understood in terms of the 'zone of proximal development'.

Although Vygotsky's research focuses on child development and childhood learning, in our coaching and mentoring context the concept of a zone of proximal development is also relevant to adult learning. We could regard coaching and mentoring as a form of social collaboration. In this collaboration the skilled coach or mentor provides supported learning tasks, which are within the reach of the coachees or mentees but require the investment of significant effort. Through this social collaboration, with the help of a set of goals, challenges and actions, coachees and mentees have the opportunity to distance themselves from their immediate experience of the world and to move towards what might be possible to know.

This development of complex thinking provides a foundation for the development of 'concepts'. The development of a concept presupposes more than unification. To form a concept it is also necessary to abstract, to single out elements, and to view the abstracted elements apart from the totality of the concrete experience in which they are embedded.

This conceptual development provides a foundation for the learner to intervene in the shaping of his or her own actions and life. The learner is now able to operate with these concepts independently, according to the demands of the task, and with an awareness of these operations, understanding them to be processes of a certain kind. It is this development that leads to self-mastery. This concept of development is the foundation of deliberate attention, logical memory, abstraction, and the ability to compare and to differentiate (Vygotsky, 1962). This development of conceptual thought is the foundation of personal agency. It is by developing concepts and personal agency that learners begin to inhabit their own lives.

In this scaffolding of proximal development, coachees are supported in performing manageable learning tasks, called 'distancing tasks', as they incrementally and progressively 'travel' from one zone to another. According to Vygotsky, there are five levels of distancing tasks:

1 Low level: tasks that encourage people to characterize specific objects/events of their world (characterization of initiative; description).
2 Medium level: the development of chains of association ('complexes') by establishing relations between these objects and events (relation: initiative in relationship; analyses/pattern matching).
3 Medium to high level: tasks of reflecting about, realizing, and learning about specific phenomena from the chains of association (evaluation).
4 High level: tasks that abstract the reflection, realization and learning from their concrete and specific circumstances in the formation of concepts about life and identity (understanding, making judgements and decisions).
5 Very high level: tasks that formulate the planning for and the initiation of actions; tasks that predict the outcome of specific actions founded upon this concept development (conclusion/recommendation).

Vygotsky's learning theory and narrative coaching

Vygotsky's idea of constructing a scaffolding to help the learner create a bridge between zones of proximal development has been embedded in narrative therapy (White, 1997, 2000, 2006). When I first introduced the narrative approach to one of the community coaching programmes in the UK during 2006, narrative coaching was a relatively novel application (Law, 2006b; Law, Aga and Hill, 2006; Hall, 2006b: 10; see also the case study in Chapter 9 for an example of the application). Similar developments of narrative coaching have also been advocated by David Drake (2006, 2007, 2008b, 2009) in Australia and by Reinhard Stelter (2007, 2009) in Denmark. While my collaborators and I ground coaching in narrative approaches, these developments have evolved quite independently. The theoretical foundation of Drake's approach seems rooted in the psychodynamic tradition, which has different implications for the practice. The theoretical foundation and the methodology that are advocated in this book are grounded, respectively, in social development theories of learning and in narrative–collaborative practice. They embody Michael White's approach and represent further synthesis as a result of further narrative collaboration (Stelter and Law, 2009, 2010).

There are two central foundations of the narrative approach:

1   a societal/cultural foundation, which consists of conversation as a reflective space and self-created meaning making and uses the metaphors of the coachee's own culture (e.g. Turner, 1967; Myerhoff, 1982);
2   a learning foundation, in which learning functions as process of co-creation of knowledge – this is Vygotsky's (1962) proximal development – and as a situation and part of a community of practice.

In many situations learning is integrated into the social process and becomes part of it. The knowledge generated in this way is a joint 'product', evolved from the social negotiations of the community of practice. Thus learning has an important influence on one's self and identity development. Learning takes place when the individuals or groups are 'disturbed' from their routines in such a way that their habitual modes of thinking and understanding can no longer be applied to solving specific problems or challenges. Thus learning is also part of a self-created discovery.

To summarize what has been said about learning so far, learning is essentially a process that always starts from specific experiences in a concrete social and material environment. This process builds on two interrelated dimensions:

1   individual meaning making;
2   social interaction → co-creation of meaning.

In the narrative practice, dialogue between coach and coachee is an essential vehicle in helping the coachee to construct knowledge and meaning. According to Hounsell (1984), there are two kinds of dialogue:

1   surface approach: direct interpretation from dialogue into 'text' – as for example in learning by rote;
2   deep approach: further processing of the textual information to extract meaning from it.

Individual meaning making

Meaning is an important element in constructive–developmental theories. Against Ebbinghaus' assumptions discussed earlier, we argue that meaning has an important role in learning. Kegan (1982) regarded meaning making as the irreducible 'primary human motion'; and indeed its activities take place at three levels of interaction:

1   at the physical level (or more accurately at the psycho-sensory level) – that is, at a perceptual and cognitive level – in that it consists of (1) grasping the concrete experience through the sensory perceptors; (2) processing the information internally through a set of sensory and neuro-networks; and (3) making sense of the perceived experience (I refer this as the internal transformation in the learning cycle in Figure 3.1);

2   at the social level, in that it requires others and their social interaction;
3   at the level of survival, in that it is something one lives for.

At the cognitive level, meaning, perception and processing are two essential components in learning. For example, David Ausbel (1968) proposed that the 'cognitive organization' and 'processes of meaning' are two key elements in his 'meaningful reception learning theory'. According to this theory, the information we hold in our memories (*cognitive structure*) is stored in a *hierarchical form*: knowledge that is more general (or common knowledge) can be remembered more easily and stands at the top in this representation, whereas more specific knowledge stands at the bottom and is difficult to remember. This structure forms the basis for learning, and new ideas are integrated within it. The specific and relevant ideas that the learner already has (Ausubel called these 'anchoring ideas') help learners to interpret meaning derived from their new experiences/information by providing this meaning with *a point of entry* in the existing cognitive structure. It is possible to integrate the new knowledge into the existing structure at three levels (according to the *assimilation theory* of meaning processing):

1   Subordinate (*subsumption*): New ideas are integrated *below* the existing cognitive structures of the learner. One learns a new concept either by adding it to an existing structure (as a *derivative*) or by modifying/extending the existing structure (as a *correlative*).
2   Coordinate (*combinatorial learning*): This is the learning of information that does not relate specifically to pre-existing knowledge but aids learning in other general areas.
3   Superordinate: New information is learnt that is integrated *above* existing cognitive structures of the learner. This happens for example when one comes to know a phenomenon across many instances of it, then learns its name, thereby unifying all these occurrences.

Our understanding of Ausbel's meaningful reception learning theory can be improved by incorporating Bartlett's (1932) notion of schema or *packet of knowledge* (hence the so-called schema theory; see Anderson, Spiro and Anderson, 1978) and by understanding how knowledge is represented there. A schema is 'a data structure for representing the generic concepts stored in memory' (Rumelhart, 1980). Schemata, like a set of variables, theories or procedures, form our mental model for a particular situation, place, person, or event (e.g. in terms of formal logic: $Z = X + Y$, with an instance: $c = a + b$). We access these schemata when trying to make sense of a situation by filling in gaps of what we are experiencing (instantiating the missing variables with the default values, for example $c = a + ?$ – where $? = b$). Therefore our mental model directs our learning and affects our performance (Johnson-Laird, 1983; Norman, 1983). Formal logic can explain why one could infer the fact that a canary has wings, and therefore can fly, from the higher schema stored with the instance that a canary is a bird and that birds have wings and can fly (Collins and Quillian, 1969). The knowledge acquisition and representation are updated flexibly in order to accommodate new facts and exceptions – for example, 'the ostrich is a bird, but it cannot fly'. The adaptive updating of schemata is referred in Anderson's ACT (adaptive control of thought) model (Anderson et al., 1978).

Learning must permanently alter our schemata, so that they continuously guide us towards managing new situations in the light of new experience. This is done through the following processes (see Rumelhart and Norman, 1978; Rumelhart 1980; Vosniadou and Brewer, 1987):

- accretion – which happens when new information is added (*instantiated*) into a schema, 'filling gaps' in our existing knowledge (e.g. Y = b);
- tuning – a process of refinement; prior knowledge is modified with new information, and the schemata evolve to become more consistent with experience (Rumelhart and Norman, 1978);
- restructuring – or the creation of new schemata to replace or modify existing ones (Rumelhart and Norman, 1981). This involves a degree of trial and error, in that we use an existing schema to help interpret the new situation. If the old schema is correct – in other words, if it fits in with the new experience – we are likely to incorporate it in our newly created one. But if it is incorrect we will replace it with our more up-to-date experience (what we have learnt).

Meaning is formed through our actual experiences and through the knowledge that the individual implicitly acquires from them in different life contexts. To make meaning, first one needs to make sense of an experience (Mezirow, 1990). According to our discussion so far, this is essentially a reflective process, which is influenced by individuals' assumptions, beliefs and values as well as by the culture (Cranton, 1996). We ascribe our actions, our experiences and interactions with others, and our life and work to specific values. These values evolve in the interplay between our acting, sensing, reflecting and telling specific stories – about ourselves and about the world we live in. These stories become meaningful. Through stories we begin to understand our own way of thinking and acting. Meaning is a central concept in a narrative approach.

Social learning theories

Like Vygotsky, Jean Lave and Etienne Wenger (1991) locate learning within the social context of conversation – a co-participation they called 'legitimate peripheral participation' (LPP). Learning emerges from a kind of social practice that facilitates LPP. Wenger's (1998) social learning theory regards social interactions (such as everyday conversations) as part of the human condition – namely processes in which we learn and become who we are (we acquire self-identity). Social learning theories regard learning as:

1 part of human nature (it is not a specific process that can be separated from everyday lives);
2 a form of meaning production, in other words an ability to discover, construct and negotiate new meanings (learning is not a mechanical process);
3 an emergent property that creates structures (Wenger regarded the 'community of practice' as part of 'the social learning structure');
4 social experience;
5 a process of transformation or identity development, insofar as it transforms practices, communities and one's identity;

6   a process related to the development of histories (or 'trajectories of participation', which do develop histories) – personal as well as communal (or collective);

7   a form of personal/social development and management of personal boundaries (we may have multiple forms of membership in relation to our participation and identity – for instance, one may be a mother, a teacher, a student, a friend… depending the situation and social context);

8   a part of social energy and power, namely as a process related to power relationships, economies of meaning and membership in society (this resonates with Myerhoff's (1982) notion of membership as a metaphor for self-identity, where life (in this case society) is regarded as a 'club'; therefore one is free to choose and manage one's membership or the membership of one's own 'life club');

9   a part of our social engagement, and one of our opportunities to enter (or acquire membership in) particular communities of practice, which enable such engagement;

10   a part of our imagination – of one's identity in a wider context;

11   a form of alignment;

12   an interplay between local and global contexts within and between which a community of practice operates.

According to Wenger (1998), social learning theory is in fact an embodiment of a number of interrelated theories:

1   Theories of social structure: these emphasize the community or the organizational structure, its norms and rules as the primary object of study; social patterns and structures should be accounted for because they determine the actions of individuals who live in them.

2   Theories of situated experience: these value individuals' experience and action – and the notion of agency – as the primary object of study. Studies of human–environmental interactions are a good example.

3   Theories of practice: these focus on the social activities that produce and reproduce the practice – the local culture – of a given community.

4   Theories of identity: these examine the formation of self-identity from social and cultural perspectives – for example, from the perspective of social categories such as age, class, ethnicity, gender and so on.

In addition to these four types, Wrenger (1998) adds:

- Theories of power, which question the conceptualization of power rather than following the status quo.
- Theories of subjectivity, which explain how subjective experience emerges from social interactions.
- Theories of meaning, which examine the production of meanings and culture socially rather than philosophically – namely how meaning is produced through social participation and how it is owned by individuals in relation to power.
- Theories of collectivity, which examine how groups or communities are formed and sustained. These groups range from local ones (families and villages) to global communities (states, the global network, or global movements). These theories

also attempt to explain how social actions are produced and reproduced, for example as culture or social cohesion.

What kind of social experience constitutes learning? More specifically, '[l]earning can be defined as a realignment of experience and competence, which pulls the other. It is therefore impaired when the two are either too distant or too closely congruent to produce the necessary generative tension' (Wenger, 1998: 227).

Wenger's (2009) later work outlines four fundamental components of social learning in terms of social system and learning capability:

1　social learning spaces: meeting places that allow genuine conversation and active engagement among learners about their experience;
2　learning citizenship: a code of ethics of learning that ensures substantial commitment from the participants, their willingness to participate rather than to be imposed upon;
3　social artists: people who provide inspiration to learners and address the 'social dynamics' at work in the complex system;
4　learning governance: learning is part of wider social systems that require some principles of 'governance' to guide the configuration of the social learning space and of its processes in order to optimize the learning capability of the system (the 'system' being the community).

The components of learning presented above reflect a shift in the way we focus on learning. Understanding, meaning making and learning are situated in a social context and emerge as a result of interpretation rather than developing a fixed cognitive structure (knowledge representation). Placing emphasis on them represents a shift in the learning paradigm, from the cognitive to the social. For educators, researchers, coaches and trainers, Wenger's social learning theory raises new questions about learning, for example:

• What kind of social interaction provides the optimal condition for learning?
• What social context can best facilitate such interaction?
• What are the forms and structure that enhance (rather than hinder) learning?

In mentoring (and in coaching), although the mentee is the one who benefits most from the mentoring process, the context that best facilitates their interaction is the whole social context in which both of them, mentor and mentee, act as expert performers in their own right within their own domain of knowledge; as a result, both benefit from such collaboration. Viewed from the social learning perspective, coaching or mentoring provide a form of LPP in which learning would take place (for both participants).

Applying Psychology of Learning to Develop a Coaching and Mentoring Framework

As we have seen from the review of some key learning theories in psychology, the learning process is a developmental process and the coach–coachee interaction is crucial in the transformation that leads to development.

Three essential elements of learning theories emerge from the above literature review:

1 experience;
2 reflection;
3 meaning.

Reflective learning theories overlap with constructive development theories in terms of knowing how learners understand. Both kinds of theories emphasize the contribution of past experiences to present and future engagements. The self-agency for change anchors on an internal discourse – seeing the world through one's reflective lens. It shapes the future direction with the intention of reframing one's understanding.

The paradigm of coaching and mentoring as reviewed in Chapter 2 focused on the future (see Figure 2.1). However, coachees and mentees usually do have psychological barriers to moving forward, towards a future destination. The goal exists in the form of hopes and dreams in a 'here and now' state. The barriers may be based on unexamined beliefs – for example, 'the future looks too foreign and threatening'. On the other hand, if the coaching condition that the coach or mentor created were too familiar, the coachees or mentees could not move forward, as they would be directed to dwell on the past: the learning wheel would 'get stuck'. There is also the matter of the inevitable challenge of learning in a metaphorical comfort zone, where more elements are fixed and familiar, rather than in an uncomfortable or out-of-comfort zone, where more areas are fluid and ambiguity is commonplace. A very fixed perception of the environment in which we operate helps us sustain and perhaps 'freeze' change and learning in exchange for security and safety; but a fluid environment is conducive to exploration and reflection, and safety is sacrificed for the sake of learning. The fixed world is a convenient perception, perhaps based on stereotypical thinking and past experience, and it leaves us without due appreciation for the distinguishing features of the environment we now operate in and for the players we are relating to. Thus coach and mentor need to create a transitional state – a condition that is neither too new nor too familiar for the learner to rise up to the occasion. See Figure 3.3 (also Figure 3.1).

There are problems with some of the early work in this field, which presupposes that homogeneity generates better learning relationships. People tend to seek relationships where there is a high rate of point-by-point correspondence; this facilitates easy empathy. Research into interpersonal attraction has shown that similarity in attitudes, political beliefs and religiosity predicts attraction. Byrne and Nelson (1965), Festinger, Schachter and Back (1950) and Allport (1954) described prejudice as a faulty and inflexible generalization, namely negative regard for another group. So, when we experience difference in our relationships with others – either at a personal level or in the environment of operation – we might negatively transfer an attitude directed at a group to one of its individual members. Further, the representation of difference as something generating discomfort – something to be 'overcome' rather than savoured, assimilated and desired – is prejudicial in itself.

The greater the differences we perceive between ourselves and others within our cultural context, the greater the perceived unfamiliarity. This results in discomfort within ourselves, which may cause negativity towards individuals who are different

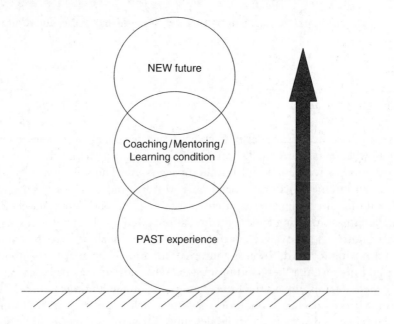

Figure 3.3   Upward transformation in the coaching/mentoring/learning paradigm

from us. This may include a range of attitudes, behaviours and characteristics. This is the leap many writers have taken when communicating the metaphorical comfort zones for learning in a cross-cultural paradigm. In coaching and mentoring, as in learning, this notion of belief needs to be questioned.

We hear that success in leadership is demonstrated by working successfully across traditional boundaries (working in new areas, with new clients, with new partners, in new ways) – in other words, through the ability to move regularly beyond boundaries and fixed positions or zones. Those who want to learn know that they will only be stretched if they engage with someone who has a different perspective – at least in one dimension; and the greater the number of different zones they bring to the 'party', the greater the number of new possibilities for learning. Thus if we map the learning wheel and the coaching and mentoring paradigm onto each other (i.e. if we overlay Figure 3.3 onto Figure 3.1), we have a dynamic coaching/mentoring model that is based on learning (Figure 3.4).

If we look from the framework described above, we can see the six substages of reflection described in the earlier section effectively overlapping the three realms of the learning wheel: past experience → meaning → new future.

The movement towards the new future destination becomes a resultant force (from the upward and forward transformations). This diagonal upward force defines the rolling mechanism. As some coaches would say, 'let's get the ball rolling'. Towards the end of this rolling or learning cycle or process, the coachees' or mentees' internal consciousness emerges, which is reflected in their behaviour – and this is equivalent to Schön's notion of thinking in action.

In practice, the resulting progression from past experience to future aspiration may not be straightforward – either in the coaching and mentoring arena or in the real world. In fact to a lot of coachees and mentees, from junior managers to chief

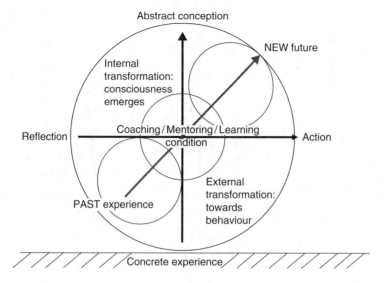

Figure 3.4   Models matching: Learning wheel and coaching/mentoring paradigm

executives at the very top, the journey of living the dream could be extremely challenging. One of the barriers usually cited is the difficulty of adapting to a new culture. For some individuals, whether they are company directors or new immigrants, adapting to a new culture produces loss of meaning: somehow meaning is lost during this journey. The cause may be the lack of social references, or perhaps the challenge of a new experience. The phenomenon is well known from the new imigrants' experience of alienation. However, as far as chief executives and senior managers are concerned, it may be equally true that 'it is lonely at the top', as the saying goes. While these people may well have experienced how meanings are formed in their earlier journey of career and life, they may also have suffered from the experience of how those very meanings were challenged and lost. One of the challenges for coaches is to find a way to sustain and revitalize the coachees' personal meaning at that juncture of their lives; for meaning making involves feeling and thinking. To understand someone's meaning is not like understanding an idea or an abstract concept – something that can be bought off the shelf – but to experience it deeply and personally within the context of a shared culture.

Like good teachers, coaches and mentors would need to acquire skills in order to unpack the process of meaning making (for example, narrative approaches mentioned earlier and some of the exercises described in Chapters 7 and 8) and to help learners to form or rediscover their own meaning and take responsibility for it. Thus meaning making is an important intervening step in our equation of the internal transformation. Mapping this new substage onto our dynamic coaching/mentoring model in Figure 3.4, we have a more complete model (see Figure 3.5).

Understanding the above framework, we could appreciate how a concrete experience in coaching or mentoring could be transformed into a personal development and extended into broader commitments, meanings and purposes. To use Mentkowski's apt phrase, 'the distance, future, and past can seem immanent in the lived moment, making such moments pregnant with meaning' (Mentkowski, 2000).

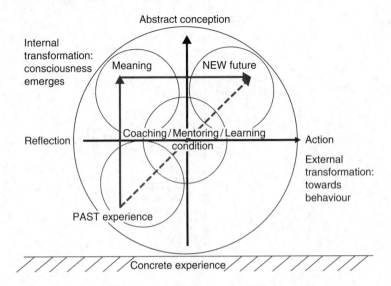

Figure 3.5   Dynamic coaching/mentoring/learning with meaning as an intervening variable

There may also be a precursor stage in the learning journey in a wider socio-cultural context, where individuals need to be clear where they are and to feel secure in their own identity before they can explore new dimensions, stimulated by different perspectives and angles but not based on core empathy. Core empathy might be achieved by high similarity with one's learning facilitator on the key defining elements of identity. In the course of developing a framework that is both universal and applicable across different cultures, we aim to unpack some of these key elements (as will happen in Chapter 6). The dynamic coaching/mentoring model discussed so far is grounded in the psychology of learning. We have found that it is very useful, as it could be readily applied to many coaching approaches such as cognitive behavioural therapy (CBT). Chapter 7 shows how CBT could embed the dynamic model in practice.

Chapter Summary and Reflection

I started this chapter by first describing the development of positive psychology as a philosophical foundation for coaching, then reviewing a range of learning theories and identifying their contribution to a universal framework for coaching and mentoring. From reading this, you may find that some of these theories do not always support your practice and some areas may have more utility than theoretical insight. In this rapidly changing global market, the ability to learn quickly, in transition, outside of an established (and over-programmed) framework, is increasingly important. Working across different contexts with different people is a matter of positive curiosity, not of discomfort. Here discourse means open and objective dialogue, which challenges biased or distorted beliefs and assumptions (Mezirow, 1996).

Our discussion of a positive psychology framework in coaching, mentoring and learning has also highlighted its departure from psychotherapy. We hope that readers will understand the reasons why certain psychotherapeutic approaches might not be applicable in coaching, mentoring and learning and why in these arenas there might be a risk of inappropriate application of psychotherapeutic approaches, in particular in the context of cross-cultural diversity.

Taylor, Marienau and Fiddler (2000) summarized the common features of the learning process outlined in various theories by describing it as a process of 'resolving contradiction in dialectical fashion'. In this process, the following characteristics are identified:

- increase in awareness;
- new possibilities;
- multiple perspectives;
- new ways of viewing the world and oneself;
- active responsibility for the world.

To sum up, here are the factors that underpin the learning process and are relevant for coaching, as they may have a significant impact upon the learner's experience and upon the learning outcome:

- action – doing (some social activities);
- barrier (this may be transformed into a set of bridging tasks);
- becoming;
- change;
- culture;
- champion – a leader, a facilitator, coach or mentor (Wenger called this kind of person a 'social artist');
- community – social system;
- conversation;
- discourse – open and objective dialogue, challenging biased or distorted beliefs and assumptions (*meaning schemes*, Mezirow, 1996);
- ethics – learning citizenship;
- governance – learning governance;
- meaning and purpose;
- practice;
- space – social learning spaces;
- self-identity – sense of belonging.

4

Definitions

Coaching Psychology, Coaching, Mentoring and Learning

Introduction

In Chapter 1 you have learnt about a generic working description of coaching and mentoring, as a developmental process of support offered to an individual, which results in action. I hope that this has been enough to get you started in your exploration. Against the background of our discoveries so far, the present chapter provides a critical review of the definitions of coaching psychology, coaching, mentoring and learning, which come from different traditions. A succinct definition of a universal approach to the psychology of coaching, mentoring and learning will be given at the end.

The Meaning of Mentoring

The word 'mentor' comes from a character in Greek mythology portrayed in Homer's *Odyssey*: Mentor. Mentor was actually Athena, the goddess of wisdom, in disguise, entrusted to educate Telemachus, the son of Odysseus. In China, one would regard Confucius (孔子) as the first mentor (see Figure 4.1).

The traditional image of a mentor perpetrated the misconception that mentors are usually more mature and experienced people, who pass on their knowledge and skills to help their protégés up the corporate ladder. This notion fixes the roles into a learner–teacher hierarchy and counters our value of equality and the idea that the process is mentee-driven.

More recent historical literature reviews (e.g. Louis Antonine de Caracciolo's *Le véritable mentor ou L'éducation de la noblesse*, or the work of Levinson, Darrow, Klein, Levinson and McKee, 1978, mentioned in Chapter 3) seem to suggest that mentoring is closely related to the process of development (Garvey, 2011) in three main respects:

The Psychology of Coaching, Mentoring and Learning, Second Edition. Ho Law.
© 2013 John Wiley & Sons, Ltd. Published 2013 by John Wiley & Sons, Ltd.

Figure 4.1   Athena and Confucius: the first mentors? *Source:* Athena: Stephane Mallarmé, *Les dieux antiques, nouvelle mythologie illustrée* (Paris, 1880). Confucius: © sinopics / istockphoto

- psychological (cognitive and emotional): for example, through self-awareness and emotional intelligence;
- social: for example, through social development – both one's own and that of the other (Sheehy, 1976, 1996; Levinson et al., 1978);
- professional: for example, through career development (Clutterbuck, 2004).

Daloz (1999) spoke about 'mentors as trusted guides, who understand theory of personal development and have experience in translating it into practice'. The European Mentoring and Coaching Council (EMCC) defines mentoring 'as a developmental process which may involve a transfer of skill or knowledge from a more experienced to a less experienced person through learning dialogue and role modelling, and may also be a learning partnership between peers' (EMCC, 2011: 4). In consequence, by comparison with coaching, mentoring seems more concerned with a longer term personal/career development. Many of the single-strand mentoring definitions derive from corporate settings, and phrases such as 'overseeing' or 'outside the line of management' do not make them appropriate for the different context of mentoring. One may simply define mentoring as a social interaction between at least two people, in which the knowledge, experience and skills of one (or of both) are shared through a process that leads to psycho-social or professional development – in the form of personal growth, self-awareness and understanding (insight). This definition resonates with the recent practice of the East Mentoring Forum in the UK.

Are there differences between coaching and mentoring?

Following these traditions, some practitioners (e.g. Parsloe, 1995) draw clear boundaries between coaching and mentoring. Viewed from this tradition, mentoring can be defined as a personal, development-centred approach, primarily embracing career issues – whereas personal development and coaching are more performance-centred. Mentoring becomes a long-term relationship, which continues through job changes, while co-coaching (in which coaches coach each other) may be of a relatively short term and linked to a project or performance issue. In practice, coaching may take place in the line relationship in specific areas, but co-coaching is always outside the line and a manager experienced in some aspect of improvement is undertaking the supervision.

Some practitioners and organizations do not draw a distinction between coaching and mentoring. For example, the Chartered Institute of Personnel and Development (CIPD) describes both coaching and mentoring as 'helping behaviours' that are used 'to support personal development over shorter and longer periods respectively' (CIPD, 2012).

The EMCC regards both coaching and mentoring as 'activities within the area of professional and personal development with focus on individuals and teams and relying on the client's own resources to help them to see and test alternative ways for improvement of competence, decision making and enhancement of quality of life'. It considers both the coach and the mentor as 'an expert in establishing a relationship with people in a series of conversations with the purpose of serving the clients to improve their performance or enhance their personal development or both, choosing their own goals and ways of doing it' (EMCC, 2011: 3).

Pauline Willis (2005) suggests that coaching and mentoring are similar activities and processes. Coaches and mentors often share the same skills and practices. In this book I advocate the overlapping and interchanging nature of a coaching–mentoring continuum, not only because it is grounded in a common psychology of learning, but also, and more importantly, because it is more fluid, flexible and adaptable to an individual's changing needs over time across contexts and cultures.

Definition of Coaching

The term 'coach' has a double meaning in English. As a person, a coach is usually understood to be an instructor or a trainer in sport. This is one of the reasons why coaching psychology has its earlier roots in sport psychology. However, coach also literally means 'carriage' – a vehicle to transport people from A to B. In the past, a coach used to be a horse-drawn carriage (see Figure 4.2). Nowadays we have the image of a modern vehicle, which takes us on a journey from where we are now to where we wish to be (destination). This play on words (the double meaning of 'coach') was first used in William Thackeray's *Pendennis* in 1849 – as Garvey (2011: 12) observes in the course of drawing a history of coaching.

This actually resonates with the metaphor I use for coaching – which is that of a journey. Thus the role of a 'coach' is to act as a vehicle that carries (transports) the coachees from where they are (here and now) to where they aspire to be (in the future). The historical perception mentioned earlier, which has defined mentoring,

Figure 4.2   A Coach?

also helped shape the early definitions of coaching. Coaching has been defined by a number of scholars and practitioners as the art of facilitating the performance, learning and development of another (Downey, 1999); one is directly concerned with the improvement of the coachees' performance and the development of their skills. This may be carried out in the form of a conversation, tutoring or instruction (Parsloe, 1995).

The above resonates with the classic definition mostly spoken about by coaches, coined from Timothy Gallwey in John Whitmore's (2002: 8) *Coaching for Performance*: 'Coaching is unlocking a person's potential to *maximize* their own *performance*. It is helping them to *learn* rather than teaching them.'

My colleague Dr Christian van Nieuwerburgh (2012: 17, cited in *Coaching in Education Study Guide*) defines coaching thus:

> A one-to-one conversation focused on the enhancement of learning and development through increasing self-awareness and a sense of personal responsibility where the coach facilitates the self-directed learning of the coachee through questioning, active listening, and appropriate challenge in a supportive and encouraging climate.

To summarize, coaching activities have the following characteristics (Law, 2002):

- They unlock people's potential to maximize their own performance.
- They help people to learn rather than teaching them (they have a facilitation function).
- From an instructional point of view, they are directly concerned with the immediate improvement of performance and the development of skills through a form of tutoring or instruction.
- They enhance performance in the domains of work and personal life, and this is underpinned by models of coaching grounded in established psychological approaches.

Each professional coaching body has its own definition, too. According to the International Coach Federation (ICF), coaching is a 'partnering with clients in a thought-provoking and creative process that inspires them to maximize their personal and professional potential' (ICF, 2013). Similarly, the EMCC describes coaching as a 'partnering with clients in a thought-provoking and creative process that inspires them to maximize their personal and professional potential' (EMCC, 2011: 5) and claims that this is a process 'facilitating the client's learning process by using professional methods and techniques to help the client to improve what is obstructive and nurture what is effective, in order to reach the client's goals' (p. 3).

The Association for Coaching (AC) provides a comprehensive range of definitions for coaching in terms of the following domains (AC, 2012):

- Personal/Life: 'A collaborative, solution-focused, results-orientated and systematic process in which the coach facilitates the enhancement of work performance, life experience, self-directed learning and personal growth of the coachee' (citing the definition by Anthony Grant in Australia).
- Executive: 'personal coaching [...] is specifically focused at senior management level, where there is an expectation for the coach to feel as comfortable exploring business related topics, as personal development topics with the client in order to improve their personal performance.'
- Corporate/Business: 'the specific remit of a corporate coach is to focus on supporting an employee, either as an individual, as part of a team and/or organization to achieve [sic] improved business performance and operational effectiveness.'
- Speciality/Niche: 'the coach is expert in addressing one particular aspect of a person's life e.g. stress, career, or the coach is focused on enhancing a particular section of the population e.g. doctors, youths.'
- Group: 'the coach is working with a number of individuals either to achieve a common goal within the group, or create an environment where individuals can co-coach each other.'

As mentioned in Chapter 2, there are diverse styles of coaching and mentoring, ranging from the direct instructional approach to non-directive, facilitative techniques. There is no agreement on which is the best approach. It usually depends on the individual client, coach or mentor, and the contextual situation the stakeholders bring into the space of engagement. However, there is a common agreement among coaches and mentors that they work with their clients to help them to discover and maximize their strengths for their own benefit and/or that of their organizations. Typical statements from coaches and mentors include:

> [...] the intention of helping people to achieve a breakthrough in their lives and then helping them beyond that breakthrough. (Breakthrough and Beyond Ltd., participant in the workshop)

> [... to help] people to communicate better, to help them understand other people's perceptions, and indeed their own too, and to become much more effective in everything that they do. The ultimate aim is to enable organizations to be more efficient, to increase their retention of good staff and to be profitable. However the programmes are also about personal development, so that participants can take away learning and experiences that will help them in their private, as well as their working lives ... It seeks to make learning fun to enable individuals to take learning back to their work and lives [...] develop a person's capacity to learn and grow in such a way that they continue learning long after a course ends. (Learning to Inspire Ltd., participant in the workshop)

The above observations represent a diverse spectrum of approaches, ranging from facilitation at one end to instructional approaches at the other. According to the

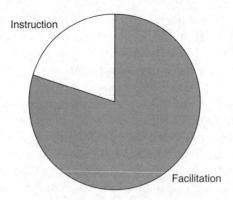

Figure 4.3 Facilitation versus instructional approaches in coaching

Special Group in Coaching Psychology (SGCP) survey, the facilitation style is the preferred approach, being favoured by more than 70 per cent (see Figure 4.3). In a universal approach, there should be in-built sustainability and renewal. Potentially, everyone can be a coach to support others who are engaging in the process.

Definition of Learning

In this book it is argued that coaching and mentoring should be anchored in the psychology of learning; and the book adopts Marcy Driscoll's definition, as she has successfully brought together different strands of psychology and used them for practice by reflecting on her accumulated knowledge and years of experience in teaching undergraduates and new graduates in education.

According to Driscoll, learning is a *persisting* 'change in performance or performance potential that results from experience and interaction within the world' (2005: 9; emphasis added). According to this definition, learners take the input from their experience and produce a permanent change in their performance. While the definition also implies that the focus should not always be on short-term, readily measured performance improvements, performance does matter and needs to be a point of focus in any development process, at least for some of the time.

A key question is: what are the exact factors that cause the permanent change? From Chapter 3, you have learnt that this is a complex process and involves many factors. Learning theories aim to unpack some of those factors. They usually look at the concept of learning through four areas (Figure 4.4):

1 Input: what (and who) is needed for the process of learning to occur? Answer: some action (doing some social activities); a facilitator; the presence of barriers (where the facilitator needs to design a set of bridging tasks to help the learner to overcome them); and a code of ethics (learning contract).
2 Means: how does it occur? Answer: in the form of a conversation; in space (which is a social learning space); by developing a community (social system) and a learning culture; through governance and practice.

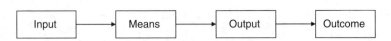

Figure 4.4 Defining a learning process

3 Output: what are activities generated from the learning process? Answer: the performance of the learnt task.
4 Outcome: what changes take place? Answer: the co-creation of meaning; a sense of purpose and self-identity (sense of belonging).

Applying the definition of learning to instructing, coaching and mentoring

Applying the psychology of learning to the definition of instruction, Marcy Driscoll connects learning theories to instruction for trainers (which has a similar implication for teachers, coaches and mentors). She defines instruction as 'any *deliberate* arrangement of events to facilitate a learner's acquisition of some *goal*' (2005: 23; emphasis added).

Definition of personal strength: contribution from positive psychology
According to Linley and Harrington (2005: 13), positive psychology is '[t]he scientific study of optimal functioning, focusing on aspects of the human condition that lead to happiness, fulfilment, and flourishing'; they also lead to strength, construed as '[a] natural capacity for behaving, thinking, or feeling in a way that allows optimal functioning and performance in the pursuit of valued outcomes'.

From these two definitions, coaches and mentors can expect that understanding more about psychology will help coachees and mentees achieve their optimal functioning and performance in the pursuit of valued outcomes. Let's see how this compares with the definition of coaching psychology.

Definition of Coaching Psychology

Coaching psychology aims to enhance well-being and performance in the domains of personal life and work *with normal, non-clinical populations*, and it is underpinned by models of coaching grounded in established adult learning or psychological approaches (Grant and Palmer, 2002: 8; emphasis added).

Note that the above definition emphasizes the application of psychology to coaching for *normal, non-clinical populations* only. It brackets out the potential population of clients who may benefit from coaching. Moreover, the line to draw between clinical and non-clinical within the continuum of a normally distributed population is both arbitrary and difficult. It is also probable that clients who seek a coaching intervention may suffer from psychological problems such as stress, trauma and depression. It is argued that coaches have a duty of care in their practices if their clients enter the consultation with clinical problems (Spence, Cavanagh, and Grant, 2006).

While Grant and Palmer's definition was initially adopted by the Coaching Psychology Forum in May 2002, the above issues were discussed in a number of meetings as the Forum evolved into the established Special Group in Coaching Psychology. It was decided that the phrase '*normal, non-clinical*' be deleted from the definition, in order to make it more inclusive. Thus coaching psychology is defined as being 'for enhancing well-being and performance in personal life and work domains underpinned by models of coaching grounded in established adult learning or psychological approaches' (Palmer and Whybrow, 2006: 8).

More recently, in 2006, the SGCP definition has removed the term 'adult', as coaching psychology can also be applicable to children's learning (e.g. to parenting). Thus coaching psychology is for enhancing well-being and performance in personal life and work domains, being underpinned by models of coaching grounded in established psychological approaches.

Definition of Intercultural Coaching Psychology

As mentioned in the introduction, valuing diversity and applying coaching across cultures are essential criteria in successful coaching in the modern global communities – be it in international business or in a multicultural society. We thus pay particular attention to redefining coaching psychology in a way that is applicable across cultures.

Intercultural coaching psychology enhances the well-being and the performance of individuals from different cultural backgrounds or with dual cultural heritage in their personal life and work. Cross-cultural coaching is subtly different from intercultural coaching. It is a form of coaching individuals who come from different countries, and hence have different cultures. We advocate in this chapter that it would be useful for the psychological approaches that underpin both forms of coaching to be based on cultural anthropology. However, the traditional emphasis on culture as relating primarily to geographical and ethnic variation is not sufficient in a universal model that operates in an increasingly complex, mixed and hybrid world. Nowadays work meets home life, people meet each other, workers with a different ethos work together, partnership between new types of organization and inter-community collaboration in new ways are key to our sustainability. The notion of culture and context need to be fluid enough to encompass the changing micro- and macro-worlds we construct and move between every day.

While our definition is very similar to that adopted by the SGCP within the mainstream, it is more in line with Philippe Rosinski's (2003) proposal that, by integrating a cultural dimension into coaching, we can help our coachees access more of their potential to achieve meaningful outcomes.

Proposal for a Universal Integrative Framework for Coaching Psychology

From the many definitions put forward by many scholars in the field and from our understanding of the psychological theories of learning, a universal integrative framework (UIF) was proposed in the first edition. The framework is 'underpinned by psychological learning theory in a process that is developmental, brings about change and is culturally mindful. It enables flexibility and fluidity in its practice, to extend beyond boundaries' (Law, Ireland and Hussain, 2007: 55).

To this I should add that the 'change' should be relatively permanent and sustainable across the following developmental areas:

- personal: self-awareness and mindfulness;
- social: awareness of social interaction; managing communication, feedback and relationships;
- cultural: appreciation of a cultural environment;
- professional: including learning, supervision and continuous professional development (CPD).

The above four domains will be expanded further in Chapter 6.

Chapter Summary and Reflection

This chapter has provided a list of concrete definitions of the key concepts. The theoretical grounding of coaching, mentoring and learning, and their scientific credentials, have been emphasized. However, readers should be mindful not to subscribe to any specific, narrow approach at the expense of the art of coaching, which is not over-formalized and therefore offers wide possibilities for learning. As a result, a universal integrative framework (UIF) has been proposed – a process that takes people beyond organizational, community and self-imposed boundaries into a new domain. It embodies the spirit of coaching – that is, through coaching, people are moved (transported) out of their comfort zone (their familiar knowledge and known experience) into a new territory of learning (Vygotsky called this the zone of proximal development). Such exposure would increase understanding of the multiple dynamics of any situation and of a complex world. Let's explore this further as our journey unfolds.

5

Leadership and Organizational Coaching and Mentoring

Becoming a Learning Organization and Learning Community

Introduction

In Chapter 3 you have acquired some knowledge about the theories of learning and have become aware of recent developments in positive psychology and their use as a foundation for coaching. Coaching or mentoring programmes are a natural partner of improvement within a learning organization. It works across hierarchies. It extends beyond a relationship of two people, to teams. According to our definition in Chapter 4, coaching is a process that takes people beyond organizational, community and self-imposed boundaries, into a new domain. In this chapter you will continue to explore this territory within the organizational context.

Through a couple of case studies, this chapter builds a case for developing a learning organization via introducing a coaching and mentoring agenda and explains its role in the current economic climate. You will learn how an organization can become a learning organization by implementing coaching and mentoring programmes. The term 'organization' has been expanded to include communities, which reflect diverse practices. You will see why mentoring and coaching are necessary; what their issues and benefits are; and how to start a coaching or a mentoring programme within your organization.

This chapter will also examine learning and change in an organization and community context, the role of structures, technology, engagement and collaboration, perceptions of values and attitudes, and empowerment – all in their contribution to learning community models; you shall also see how coaching and mentoring can support change and how they work within an improvement framework. The chapter will show how coaching and mentoring can benefit organizations; it will bring some specific examples, followed by practical guidance on setting up a coaching or mentoring process.

The Psychology of Coaching, Mentoring and Learning, Second Edition. Ho Law.
© 2013 John Wiley & Sons, Ltd. Published 2013 by John Wiley & Sons, Ltd.

Challenges of the Changing World

Today every organization is seeking to improve its efficiency in response to the changing environment. Boards of directors are looking at the continuous improvement and reorganization brief; governments regularly commission experts to assess strategies for their relevance in the changing context. Organizations are motivated to change to gain competitive advantage, to save money and resources, to increase quality and to incorporate new working practices. New and renewed alliances are the key to timely and efficient deliverables in a bigger marketplace. Outsourcing and partnering in areas where organizations are not competitive make economic sense. Collaborations work well when there is mutual trust and respect, where power is perceived to be equally distributed and ways of working are transparent. Rarely is a complaint investigated that does not change something or some thinking for someone. Many of those complaints fall at the edge of someone's competence, border multiple agency responsibilities, lie between various department functions or are the result of the impact of someone's limited self-belief. Errors also occur when there is no continuity, or memory of what has gone before, to inform what happens next. With virtual social networking systems, more people have access to information; however, that does not automatically transfer into the knowledge to bring about change. The speed of change, the increasing complexity of the environment, the changing marketplace and the role of evolving technology, and the increased expectations and demands of stakeholders all mean that standing still is not an option. In order to survive in a world of upheaval, the organization must continue to learn (Vaill, 1996); and leaders must adopt a new model of practice in this so-called connective era where the connections between diverse concepts and different people within the changing environment are more important than geopolitical boundaries (Lipman-Blumen, 1996). The following examples illustrate what can happen when organizations box themselves in through their past values and do not learn to change.

Enron: unethical corporate leadership culture

Enron Corporation, formed in 1985, was the seventh largest American company in the Fortune 500 in 2001, with a stock market value of $35 billion. However, its leadership and management practices were poor and sometimes unethical. For instance, the 'seagull management' approaches were in common practice throughout the organization (Weissman, 2008). In other words, the managers made a lot of noise, aggressively making sales to the customers, and then they moved on when problems arose. The apparent success of the company was just an illusion created through manipulative devices and contrivances, using dishonest accounting and auditing practice. Different professions (consultants and auditors) were combined within the same company; thus the auditors' obligation of public disclosure was compromised. Enron announced bankruptcy and its chief executives went on trial in January 2006.

Kodak: hard to shift culture

Eastman Kodak, founded by George Eastman in 1881, is an American multinational company for photographic imaging equipment and film products. During the twentieth century the company held a dominant market share (90 per cent) of photographic film sales in the US. Owing to the technological development of digital camera in the late 1990s, the sale of photographic film declined gradually. Ironically, although Kodak invested in the first digital camera in 1975, it was slow to respond to the changing technological environment and reluctant to shift its business focus towards digital technology. The attempt to generate revenues through aggressive patent litigation did not help to save the company: Kodak eventually filed for Chapter 11 bankruptcy protection in 2012. In contrast, its competitor Fujifilm has successfully shifted to digital production and diversified its products.

Learning from case studies

The above stories illustrate the importance of leadership in the rapidly changing environment. While the two companies had a very different ethos, both exemplify the culture that is hardest to shift: the top-down, hierarchical culture, with ritualistic observances of their organizational values. While Enron's unethical accounting and management practice was doomed to fail from the very beginning, Kodak's failure to embrace the new digital technological revolution was due to a mistaken belief steeped in tradition and heritage. The nostalgic value of the so-called 'Kodak moment' – which once represented the cornerstone of the company's success – became the greatest barrier against change. It generated fear that the new technology might kill off the company's traditional film-based photographic market (which was perceived as the company's 'cash cow'). A succession of chief executives were not able to shift the core value of the organization.

Why is it that some organizations have winning cultures, whereas others just have eye-rolling value statements?
Research shows that a strong organizational culture leads to superior performance across a range of measures, whether these are to do with employee engagement, brand or bottom line; so at some point most organizations will have taken some form of culture initiative. However, many fail to deliver much beyond a value statement that never seems to come to life. Only organizations that define values that are meaningful to their people and manage to translate them into every aspect of life at work reap the reward.

To summarize, here are the lessons learnt from the case studies:

1   Past successes often become a barrier against change, leading to future failure.
2   Values, beliefs and attitudes that guide organization and community development need to be owned and constantly changing.
3   Customers want quality at affordable prices, not tradition.
4   Loyalty was not a criterion for purchase.
5   Companies need to recognize change in their customers and their context that influences their buying behaviour.
6   Mutual trust within the senior management team is not enough for successful purposeful engagement.
7   Ethical accounting and management practices need to be embedded as part of the organizational culture.

8   Organizations' ability to gain feedback from customers/users, learn and change is important for their survival.

9   The benefits of an organization have to be relevant to all stakeholders, to achieve a perceived balance of power, to facilitate ownership and to encourage engagement on the part of stakeholders.

10 In the traditional leadership and managerial conception, a lot of activities within an organization are not value-added. This results in low productivity. To improve the performance of an organization, a new working or production philosophy needs to be developed. Lauri Koskela (1992) noted that in the manufacturing industry very little is known about how this new kind of philosophy works.

11 This new way of working requires a shift in mindset and practices at all levels within the organization. Communications and collaborations between teams need to be different, and managers need to be leaders, as the whole organization becomes more flexible in the way it works.

We are not always good at recognizing that it is time to change. As the environment changes, organizations' missions can fall out of step in terms of goals, behaviour and language. They can cease to be legally, ethically or technologically compliant and lose touch with good practice. Organizations can become fixated on semi-permanent frameworks of missions, values and protocols and stay hooked well beyond their sell-by date.

Getting started

The starting point in developing any learning organization is to have a thorough understanding and to make an honest review of the organization's business, its market-place, customers, competitors and suppliers (Verity, 2006). There are various traditional management tools that can help with organizational analysis, such as balance scorecards, SWOT, PESTEL, and the latest developments in cultural social intelligence (CSI), in the universal integrated framework described in the next chapter. Let's first establish what a competent organization should look like; how learning, through coaching and mentoring, can help an organization become a competent one; and how coaching and mentoring may be introduced into an organization as an initiative to help managers and teams to increase their professional competence, learning capacity, efficiency and effectiveness.

A Learning Organization Is a Competent Organization

What does a competent organization look like? From the literature review and the observation of case studies, a competent organization tends to have the following characteristics:

- a sense of direction;
- an ethical value;
- a long-term vision;
- short-term objectives;

- resourcefulness;
- the ability to cope with a changing environment;
- satisfied stakeholders.

These elements are usually captured in the organization's strategy – for example, large organizations have five-year business plans, and sales departments have a strategic marketing plan. Even small and medium-sized companies require business plans incorporating the above strategies if they are to remain competitive. The characteristics are succinctly captured in Johnson and Scholes' definition:

> Strategy is the *direction* and scope of an organization over the *long term*, which achieves advantage for the organization through its configuration of *resources* within a *changing environment*, to meet the needs of markets and to fulfil *stakeholder* expectations. (1999: 10; emphasis added)

For a comprehensive overview of the psychology of strategic management within the context of competent organizations, see Hodgkinson and Sparrow (2002). For an organization to formulate its strategy and implement it through strategic management, at least three sets of issues should arise:

1   Analysis: leads to an understanding of the organization, its strategic position, environment, resources, values and objectives.
2   Choice: formulates courses of action and selects the optimal ones.
3   Implementation: translates the strategy into action via resource planning, organization design and people management.

As in coaching and mentoring, much of the literature and practices in knowledge management and organizational learning are simply repackaging the established tools and techniques of the disciplines of psychology and management. This book seeks to translate these fragmented concepts and 'hypes' into a coherent body of *actionable knowledge* that is applicable both to individuals and organizations. By 'actionable knowledge' (a phrase borrowed from Argyris, 1999), I mean the practical knowledge that is useful to practising coaches and at the same time grounded in a well-researched, evidence-based framework.

Traditionally, there are three schools of thought in organizational learning. These are based on the following sets of imperatives:

1   *Reason* Regard the strategic management (analysis–choice–implementation) as a rational process. Assume that the objectives of the action plan are achievable as long as its rationale is communicated to and understood by the stakeholders.
2   *Evolution* View organizational behaviour as too complex to be understood rationally. Organizations evolve through trial and error, learning by doing. Successful strategies emerge over time, as if the organization had its own memories and remembered the lessons learnt.
3   *Process* Take the middle ground. The strategic frameworks and processes can be rationally designed, but made flexible – adaptable to change and to learning from previous mistakes.

There are various definitions and characteristics of organizational learning and of the learning organization. A learning organization seems to have a process that enables it to:

*   *learn* from mistakes over time; elicit adaptive behaviour; detect and correct error; take collective thinking in action, so-called organizational theory in use or theory in action (Cyert and March, 1963; Argyris, 1977; Argyris and Schön, 1978). These may be achieved by individuals or groups of individuals at the organizational level (Cangelosi and Dill, 1965);
*   *improve* action and outcome through better knowledge and understanding, by making both attitudinal and behavioural changes (Duncan and Weiss, 1979; Fiol and Lyles, 1985);
*   encode inferences from *history* into *routines* that guide current *behaviour* through systematic rules and procedures (Levitt and March 1988);
*   *share* insight, *knowledge* and mental models that build on *past* knowledge and *memory* (Strata, 1989);
*   *learn* and encourage learning in its people (Handy, 1989);
*   synthesize a diverse set of assumptions or beliefs into a commonly *shared understanding* (Ginsberg, 1990);
*   expand the organizational *capacity* to create desirable *outcome* as a result of people learning together continuously (Senge, 1990);
*   acquire useful *knowledge* and *change behaviour* (Huber, 1991);
*   create new knowledge, make tacit knowledge explicit, disseminate it throughout the organization, and embody it into new technologies, products and services (*output*) (Nonaka, 1991);
*   elicit error-free operation (organizational behaviour reflects 'collective minds') and the so-called 'heedful interrelation' (an organization behaves like an intelligent machine) (Weick and Roberts, 1993);
*   create, *acquire and transfer knowledge*, modify its own behaviour to reflect new knowledge and insight; see the world in a *new* light; *learn* from its own *experience and history* and from the experience and best practice of others (Garvin, 1993).

To sum up, a learning organization is an organization that has processes in place to facilitate organizational learning – which is very similar to our definition of the learning process. Organizational learning consists of:

*   input – experience;
*   process – routines and procedures that allow people continuously to learn (e.g. staff competencies framework, personnel training and development plans, and investors in people initiative); to transform experience into new knowledge, insight and understanding; to share and disseminate that knowledge (e.g. interest groups, user forums and communication strategies); to accumulate it into history (e.g. archives); and a mechanism to detect new knowledge, correct errors, change behaviour on the basis of the input experience (e.g. performance management, feedback loop and evaluation);
*   output – changed behaviour, new technologies, products and services, and history (from accumulated experience);
*   outcome – shared understanding and *values*, expanded capacity; improved competencies, action, products/services and customer satisfaction.

Learning organizations are different from the traditional resourced-based organizations in terms of the following task characteristics (Senge, 1990; Arvedson, 1993):

- goal setting – shared visions instead of vision from the top;
- thinking and doing – systemic (thinking and doing at all levels) rather than atomistic (the top thinks, the managers act);
- conflict resolution – setting up dialogue, integrating diverse opinions, sharing understanding rather than mediating politically, through power relationship.

Coaching Psychology and Organization Memories

On 19 December 2006, at the 2nd National Coaching Psychology Conference, in a speech on 'applying existential psychology in a coaching psychology practice', Ernesto Spinelli criticized the over-emphasis on placing the future under focus in coaching philosophy. He pointed out that such an approach in coaching neglects both the past and the present, as if they did not exist. Indeed both the past and the future are important factors that make up our present moment of engagement for change. Organizations that attempt to 'get it right first time' by over-utilizing future technology such as electronic communications and storage run the risk of forgetting their past and falling into organizational dementia, where vital knowledge becomes inaccessible (see the case study of a high technology firm in Blackler, Crump and McDonald, 1999).

The organization's memory, with its embodiment of a collective sense of history and shared values, is key to success and to the delivery of high performance. The first question is: What kind of knowledge should employees share within an organization? Five types of knowledge that need to be shared among members of a team can be identified from our literature review:

- dictionary knowledge (declarative knowledge): definitions and classifications of objects and events; statements that declare *what* should be done (Sackmann, 1991, 1992; Zack, 1999);
- recipe knowledge (procedure/process knowledge): task-specific procedures that describe how a specific task *should* be done, allowing team members to follow the instructions with a shared expectation of the outcome (Sackmann, 1991, 1992; Cannon-Bowers and Salas, 1993; Zack, 1999);
- directory knowledge: task-related descriptions of how tasks are *actually* carried out. This kind of knowledge is usually in the public domain and is commonly possessed by all the existing members, which may place new members in a disadvantaged position (Sackmann, 1991, 1992; Rentsch and Hall, 1994);
- people knowledge: the understanding of each other's competencies within the team, so that members can adapt their behaviour to complement or compensate for others' strengths and weaknesses accordingly. In working as a team or within an organization, one needs to learn who knows what (Moreland, 2000);
- axiomatic knowledge (causal knowledge): knowledge of fundamental attitudes, beliefs and values; these are shared organizational values and team members' attitudes and beliefs, which enable the team to reach consensus effectively and

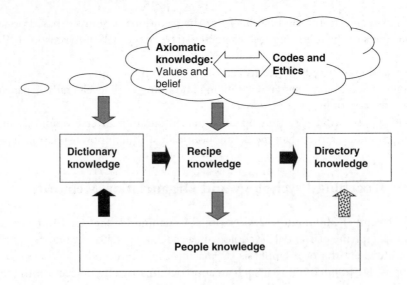

Figure 5.1   Knowledge flows within the organization

efficiently. This kind of knowledge explains *why* people do certain things or behave in certain ways. It shapes and defines an organization's culture (Sackmann, 1991, 1992; Zack, 1999; Mohammed, Klimoski and Rentsch, 2000).

The above types of knowledge are not static entities. They flow between people and process and transform the organization into an effective and functioning one. For an organization to direct employees to reach consensus effectively and efficiently, it is important to translate implicit axiomatic knowledge into explicitly shared values in the form of basic ground rules, ethics, codes and conducts. Figure 5.1 shows how knowledge flows within the organization.

Of course, knowledge would not flow of its own accord. It requires an active and coordinated effort of the stakeholders to ensure that new knowledge is acquired (e.g. through coaching, consultancy, training and development) and that existing knowledge is maintained (e.g. through inventories and storages), as well as diffused and transferred to the new employees (e.g. through induction training and mentoring). These effectively form three clusters: knowledge acquisition and creation; knowledge capture and storage; and knowledge diffusion and transfer (Staples, Greenaway and McKeen, 2001). The process of knowledge management is consistent with our input–process–output/outcome system.

Learning Organization and Psychology of Learning

Within an organization, knowledge exchange requires interaction between people and business information processes. In its simplest form, this interaction requires at least two actors – whether the interaction consists in communications from one person to another or in learning from company handbooks or procedures, which were developed by another person. There are many different ways in which knowledge

Table 5.1 Knowledge transfer matrix

Knowledge	*Implicit/Tacit – in people*	*Explicit – in process*
Implicit/Tacit – in people	**Socialization** (people – people)	**Articulation** (people – process)
Explicit – in process	**Internalization** (process – people)	**Combination/integration** (process – process)

is transferred. According to a Japanese concept of knowledge creation, the approaches can be classified into four types of organizational competence (Nonaka, 1991; Nonaka, Takeuchi and Umemoto, 1996):

- *Socialization* People learn from each other. Within an organization tacit knowledge is directly transferred from individual to individual, through observation and hands-on experience (from tacit to tacit).
- *Combination (integration)* Several separate pieces of explicit knowledge are integrated together into a coherent whole: a set of knowledge and organizational procedures, rules and processes can be combined to form a larger complex system (from explicit to explicit).
- *Articulation* People translate tacit knowledge, giving it an explicit form, and communicate through the organization (from tacit to explicit).
- *Internalization* The declared knowledge, having been communicated, is shared; over time it is internalized in the minds of employees and becomes their own tacit knowledge (from explicit to tacit).

These transfers or flows can be summarized in a knowledge transfer matrix, as shown in Table 5.1.

The organization's learning process described by Nonaka (1991) can be mapped onto our learning cycle as follows:

- from concrete experience to abstract conception, via internal reflection (internalization, from explicit to tacit, process to people transformation);
- from reflection/abstract conception to action (articulation, from tacit to explicit, people to process communication).

Organization learning in the form described above can be expressed as a network of individual learning cycles – via people to people (socialization), people translating their knowledge into business process (articulation) and vice versa (learning from procedures and process, internalization); and the process can be multiplied into a system (combination), and become a learning organization as a whole. Figure 5.2 shows a simplified version of a knowledge network. The network consists of two or more learning cycles where person A can learn from persons B, ... *x* and/or from business processes 1, 2, ... *n*.

The characteristic of the above network model is consistent with cooperative inquiry (Heron, 1981a, 1981b; Reason and Rowan, 1981; Reason, 1988); with naturalistic

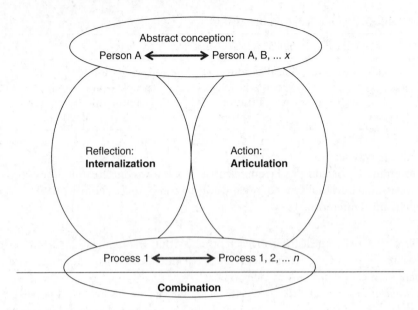

Figure 5.2   Learning cycles and knowledge network

or human inquiry (Lincoln and Guba, 1984; Bell and Hardiman, 1989); and, more recently, with the Agile way of working in teams and project management. In this context, coaching can facilitate knowledge flow within teams and within an organization. The role of a coach here becomes similar to that of a researcher whose objective is to conduct an enquiry into knowledge transfer processes.

While the embedding of the learning cycle into a coaching framework for improving organizational performance might seem to be novel at its first edition, its application to knowledge acquisition and training is certainly not new. As early as 1988, Jill Bell from JB Associates and Bob Hardiman from IBM UK ran a four-day experiential training course entitled 'The Human Side of Knowledge Engineering' in the USA, Germany, Singapore and Brazil, using the human inquiry approach (Bell and Hardiman, 1989). They called their method 'naturalistic knowledge engineering' (NKE). This book has brought the principles of NKE up to date in the context of organizational coaching, which essentially consists of the following processes:

- *Cooperative process* Involves managers, experts, coachees, and other coaches.
- *Natural process* The session should take place in the natural setting where the knowledge is usually applied.
- *Research process* Explores the enquiry with people in the organization.
- *Knowledge acquisition process (articulation)* Finds out the tacit knowledge and puts it into a useful and articulated form.
- *Interactive process* Follows the experiential learning cycle (Kolb, 1984; see Chapter 3).
- *Auditing process* Validates and verifies the knowledge gained.
- *Organizational process* The approach developed needs to be context specific and sensitive to the organizational culture.

Translating Kolb's learning cycle into a knowledge elicitation process, Bell and Hardiman used different interpretations and terminologies, which we expand as follows:

- Collect (concrete experience): one has to collect relevant data, information and knowledge from all possible sources (see Figures 5.1 and 5.2).
- Reflect (reflection): the coach and coachee need to spend some time thinking about what has been learned.
- Theorize (abstract conception): one must record the patterns that have emerged from the coaching engagements, make sense of the data by deriving meaningful knowledge from them, and represent the knowledge in both useful and explicit forms.
- Plan (action): one should plan where one needs to go next.

Role of top team

The management of the knowledge flow process and of the knowledge network within an organization is usually initiated from the strategic cognition in the top management team. Thus the characteristics of the top team would have a significant impact upon the overall organizational performance in terms of its corporate strategic change and strategic consensus. The results from empirical studies over hundreds of large firms from diverse (but mostly private) sectors during the late 1980s and 1990s have demonstrated some significant correlation between top team diversity – in age, demography, educational level, location, management function, tenure and the like – and organizational performance, both in the short and in the long term, with mixed conclusions regarding the intervening variables (for specific research studies, see Murray, 1989; Wiersema and Bantel, 1992; Markoczy, 1997; Lioukas and Chambers, 1998; Miller, Burke and Glick, 1998; Sutcliffe and Huber, 1998, Chattopadhyay, Glick, Miller and Huber, 1999; Smith, Olian, Smith and Flood, 1999).

There seemed to be an optimal level of diversity for the top team to perform effectively and efficiently. We hypothesize that the relationship between the top team, diversity and organizational performance may be in the form of an upside-down U-shaped curve – a shape similar to those produced in stress and performance relationships (see Figure 5.3).

Very little has been known about the exact degree of diversity that produces the optimal organizational performance. This is a subject of research in the areas of measurement of team diversity and team members' attitude towards diversity (see the next chapter for a measurement framework). However, one implication of the relationship between diversity and performance is clear. To maintain a sustainable high performance, diversity within the organization (in particular at the top team level) would need to be harnessed and managed so that the team members can achieve strategic consensus through shared visions, beliefs, values, understandings and insights. Lipman-Blumen (1996) advocates the connective leadership model, in which leaders need to connect their own and others' visions within the team and their groups. One key question is: *What does the top team look like?* To answer such a question would require us to unpack the variables that contribute to management competence. We shall direct our attention to the characteristics of management competence in the next section.

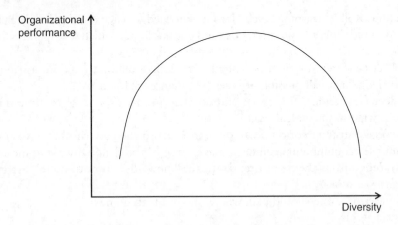

Figure 5.3   Organizational performance versus top team diversity

Managerial and Leadership Competencies

What are the characteristics of a leader in the top team? Leaders in the top team need to communicate with their team members in a way that resonates with their sense of purpose. This requires the leader to have compelling vision that is grounded on ethics. It also requires personal and social awareness – the so called emotional intelligence or EI (Goleman, 1995, 1998). There are many different leadership styles (Burns, 1978; Mintzberg, 1994; Hamel, 1996; Porter, 1996; Bass, 1998; Goleman, Boyatzis and McKee, 2003; Bass and Riggio, 2005; Alban-Metcalfe and Alimo-Metcalfe, 2007; Lee and Roberts, 2010):

- affiliative style: ensures a good working relationship between team members; maintains harmony in the team;
- authentic style: mobilizes people into action undertaken for a personal purpose, and it does so through the leader's charisma and genuineness;
- coaching style: connects employees with the organizational objective by improving their performance;
- democratic style: ensures the commitment of team members by seeking consensus and expressing appreciation of their input;
- engaging style: engages the leader together with others in an organizational mission;
- directive style: commands action; provides a sense of direction and certainty;
- laissez-faire style: takes it easy;
- pace-setting style: sets a standard of high performance for the team by demonstrating the leader's own competence;
- strategic style: provides organizational strategy and plans for action;
- transactional style: intervenes as needed – interferes as little as possible;
- transformational style: energizes people into action carried out with a sense of purpose by raising their consciousness, emotions and awareness about the ethics and meaning that resonate with their needs and values;
- inspirational (visionary) style: inspires team members to share the dream and to move towards a long-term goal.

Different leadership styles are underpinned by different leadership models. For example, the Connective Leadership Model consists of nine leadership styles that are grouped into three sets: direct, relational and instrumental (Lipman-Blumen, 1996). Depending on circumstances, each leadership style may result in a different kind of impact. Simply using a single leadership style would not be effective. To produce a high-performance team, leaders would need to be flexible and to adopt a range of leadership styles, as appropriate. As in the case of diversity in the top team, there is an optimal combination of different leadership styles and an optimal level of using them. Research has shown that the optimal number is around four (Fitzsimmons and Guise, 2010).

Both top and middle management teams would need to develop individual competencies in order to perform a range of leadership roles and styles of response appropriate to different situations. According to the Chartered Management Institute's (CMI) assessment of its Charter Manager's Competence, managers need to demonstrate the following qualities:

- They should lead people – provide a clear purpose and direction; inspire trust, respect and shared values (inspirational and transformational leadership); communicate clearly and succinctly; develop and support individuals and team members (coaching leadership); resolve problems and conflicts with positive outcomes (affiliative leadership); consistently apply strategic thinking (strategic leadership); adapt a leadership style to take account of diverse situations (flexible leadership).
- They should meet customer needs – develop effective customer relationships; create customer-driven improvements to products or services; manage activities to meet customer requirements; work to improve levels of customer service and satisfaction.
- They should manage change – encourage others to be creative and innovative; identify opportunities for change and development; plan and drive change; manage others through the change process; take account of all stakeholder issues.
- They should manage information and knowledge – establish information management and communications systems; provide and use appropriate information to support decision making; develop and exploit organizational knowledge and skills; manage complexity to positive effect.
- They should manage projects, processes and resources – optimize the use of financial and other services; increase operational efficiency and effectiveness; plan and prioritize projects and activities; deliver on time, to budget and to the standard required.
- They should manage themselves – demonstrate resilience in achieving personal goals; use appropriate levels of influence and persuasion; apply good professional and ethical practice; develop effective personal networks.

Leadership and Organization Development through Coaching

From the analyses developed in the previous section, which supports the latest trends in organizational development, we advocate that coaching and mentoring can help leaders and managers to:

- develop their leadership styles;
- improve their awareness of themselves and the others;

- improve their level of professional competence;
- improve effectiveness in their jobs;
- improve their communication and management skills;
- manage and create a high-performance team;
- learn effectively.

In consequence, when an organization has a significant number of middle- and senior-level managers who, through coaching and mentoring programmes, become high performers, that organization will be a competent and learning organization. To achieve this state, we need to establish the link between a competent organization and managerial competencies; and we need to know how coaching and mentoring can be introduced to help improve the competence of the staff and of the organization.

Research into organizational psychology has tended to link managerial competencies with the total sum of cognitive styles and personality traits of which EI is merely a part (Austin, 2008; Mikolajczak, Luminet, Leroy and Roy, 2007; and Smith, Ciarrochi, and Heaven, 2008). These are commonly measured using psychometric tests such as the Myers–Briggs Types Indicators (MBTI; Myers, 1962) and the Embedded Figure Test (Witkin, 1962). The Embedded Figure Test assesses the individual's cognitive ability to separate foreground figures from their background environment (that is, his or her field independence). MBTI operates with four dimensions of personality types:

1   extravert–introvert;
2   sensing–intuitive;
3   feeling–thinking;
4   perceiving–judging.

The learning cycle and the learning styles we developed in Chapter 3 can be used as a measurement of the managers' decision-making behaviour.

The following significant correlations between cognitive styles and decision-making behaviour have been established by Leonard, Scholl and Kowalski (1999):

- concrete experience – associates with feeling and field independence;
- abstract conceptualization – thinking and field dependence;
- active experimentation – extravert;
- reflective observation – introvert;
- analytical decision making – sensing;
- conceptual decision making – introvert.

At the same time, Leonard et al.'s (1999) study also found that field dependence correlates with being intuitive, while field independence correlates with sensing. Given this insight into managers' learning styles, coaching would be a more effective way of helping managers to improve their competence than any generic training. Coaches could tailor their programme of development for coachees individually, by working with their cognitive style and promoting their signature strengths. The key challenge in an organization is the initial barrier to introducing coaching into the organization as part of its culture for change.

Developing a Coaching Culture

To sustain high performance throughout an organization, a learning culture needs to be developed. This can be done by developing a coaching culture within the organization. How do we know that an organization has a coaching culture? An organization with a coaching culture has the following 15 characteristics (Chaplain, 2003; Hardingham, Brearley, Moorhouse and Venter, 2004; Clutterbuck and Megginson, 2005):

1 The organization shows a commitment to develop the learning capacity of its employees.
2 The leadership styles of the organization are predominantly non-directive.
3 People became leaders within the organization according to their passion rather than seniority or position.
4 Developing others and creating a learning environment is part of the managerial role.
5 Coaching and learning are embedded in the organizational process.
6 Members of staff coach and mentor one another at various stages of their career.
7 Coaching is a predominantly cognitive style of leadership, management, and team work.
8 Goal setting is a normal way of working.
9 Teams are organized according to members' interests and expertise.
10 There is a good team relationship.
11 Team members who implement a decision are given autonomy to manage their own goal and make operational decisions.
12 Recognition and rewards are awarded to teams rather than individuals.
13 There are regular performance reviews for both teams and individuals.
14 People throughout the organization value learning.
15 There is a prevalent atmosphere of openness, recognition and respect within the teams and throughout the organization.

To develop the culture described above, first of all, one or more key persons would need to introduce coaching into the organization. You may call this person a learning champion; Wenger (2009) called these people 'social artists'. They may be anyone within the organization, but they would have to gain commitment and support from members of the senior management team.

Introducing a Coaching Programme within an Organization

As with any project appraisal, for a coaching or mentoring programme to be approved by the board of directors within a reasonably sized organization, the coaching advocates would usually be required to make a business case to demonstrate its value for money. A typical business case may consist of the following component cases:

• a strategic case: this sets out the strategy of the coaching programme and how it helps to deliver the organizational objectives as part of the corporate strategy; for example, coaching may facilitate greater use of the organization's strategic intelligence and may lead to widely used management practice;

- an economic case: a project appraisal using techniques such as cost–benefit analysis (see Chapter 10 for framework and details);
- a financial case: this one checks to see if the budget holder could afford the programme;
- a commercial case: this one shows how the programme contributes to the commercial aspect of the organization;
- a project management case: this one demonstrates that the programme is achievable by carrying out scooping exercises and feasibility studies.

As part of the business case, the project manager should also carry out an impact assessment. This aims to assess all the possible impact of the programme upon the organization, its customers and its employees. From the perspective of diversity, the impact assessment should include an equality impact assessment as well as a risk assessment. Targets can be set within a proposed coaching programme to help progress in terms of producing outputs, delivering outcomes and meeting organizational objectives. Targets should be SMARTER, in other words they should be:

- specific – not vague but with enough details for implementation;
- measurable – quantifiable;
- achievable – they should stretch, but within one's capacity;
- relevant/realistic – this is closely related to being achievable, but the targets also need to be relevant to the overall goal;
- time-bound – they should have specific dates (when by);
- evaluative – assessable at the end in terms of their impact and return on investment;
- reviewable – possible to be reviewed at appropriate intervals, to check on progress, and at the end of the implementation, to consider the implications of the impact.

The above could be embedded within a coaching and mentoring programme and could guide the choice of coaching techniques (see Chapter 8).

For the appraisal of a coaching programme to be successful, the following points need to be specified at the outset:

- the availability of coach and other specialist resources that may be needed;
- the cost and benefits of the programme;
- the quality assurance;
- how knowledge from coaching may be transferred;
- a project plan for the programme, setting out key objectives, milestones, resources and coaching streams.

Before any coaching programme is introduced, it is important for the programme owner (budget-holder) to identify a clear need, which is also in the interests of the organization as well as individual staff. Accordingly, a statement of the rationale for the coaching programme should be developed. Key questions for introducing a coaching programme include:

- Is the rationale for the programme clear?
- Is it reasonable to assume that coaching will be cost-effective? In other words, would the benefits of coaching exceed the costs?
- What are we trying to achieve?
- What are our objectives?
- What would constitute successful coaching and mentoring outcomes?
- Have similar objectives been set in other proposals – such as training programmes that could be adapted?
- Are the coaching objectives consistent with the organization's strategic aims and objectives?
- Are the coaching objectives defined to reflect outcomes (e.g. improved performance, stress reduction or enhanced sustainable organizational and personal growth) rather than outputs (e.g. a number of coaching sessions, coaching prosecutions or mentoring matching), which will be the focus of the particular coaching programme?
- How might the coaching objectives and outcomes be measured?
- Are the coaching objectives defined in such a way that progress towards meeting them can be monitored?
- What factors are critical to coaching success?
- What SMARTER targets can be set?
- What targets does the coaching programme need to meet?

Coaching intervention can incur costs and create inspirational distortions from the coachees' perspectives. These must be taken into account when it comes to designing any coaching programme within an organization. For example, a coaching programme may be successful in raising the coachees' aspiration, but some of them might then feel the need to move on; some might even consider the option of leaving the organization that funds the programme. This would involve extra costs for the organization and needs to be taken into account in terms of a psychological contract and contingency plan.

Coaches would therefore need to understand that, to introduce a coaching and mentoring programme, they would need to overcome the following barriers or constraints:

- limited resources: for example, time and budget;
- managers' preoccupation with the resources required and their lack of focus on the benefits;
- preoccupations with the possible problems encountered instead of a focus on solutions;
- too high or unrealistic expectations – for example, a simple solution that will fix all the complex problems;
- resistance from staff – for example, the 'not invited here' syndrome;
- being misled by the 'hype' of coaching and mentoring;

- preoccupations with status: coachees or mentees may want to enhance their status by being mentored by a senior member of staff or coached by a high-profile expert.

In order to identify the scope of the issues involved and the basis for coaching or mentoring, the coach or mentor may need to carry out some research in a form of scooping study that should cover the following:

- the objectives of the coaching or mentoring programme: these should be consistent with the organization's policy, its departmental objectives, and wider micro-economic objectives;
- the result of coaching or mentoring – namely if nothing has changed, or if the change has been minimal;
- the market situation of the organization: would the coaching or mentoring programme help prevent any market failure that the organization might face, or would it improve employment levels?
- current and projected trends and published forecasts of the organization and how the coaching or mentoring can help improve future results;
- potential beneficiaries: those who would benefit from the coaching or mentoring programme should be identified, as well as those who may be disadvantaged (for example, those who could not attend the programme in comparison with their colleagues who could);
- technological developments: for example, e-learning, online tools, and so on;
- whether the coaching or mentoring programme would change in scope or magnitude over time: the effects can multiply as a result of a network of coaches or mentors and coachees or mentees.

From the above analysis it appears that, if a coaching or mentoring intervention were shown to be worthwhile, then the objectives, outputs and outcomes of the proposed new programme need to be stated clearly. This allows the identification of the full range of coaching or mentoring options that an organization may adopt. Examples of coaching or mentoring outputs and outcomes include:

- number of coaches or mentors matching;
- number of coachees or mentees assisted;
- value of extra output, or improvement in the efficiency of the coachees' or mentees' performance;
- development of skills;
- number of coaching or mentoring places;
- number of those who completed the coaching or mentoring programme;
- value of extra human capital and/or earnings capacity;
- exam results (e.g. Master of Business and Adminstration);
- improvement to the productivity of the organization.

Could you identify which of the above are outputs and which are outcomes?

Embedding the coaching and mentoring culture within an organization

A coaching or mentoring programme can be introduced first as a pilot. Once it has been implemented, its stakeholders could then learn from the experience and evaluate the programme in terms of its effectiveness, return on investment and value for money, so that future business cases can be made for a wider implementation (see Chapter 10 for formal methods of evaluation). The wider participation of coaching and learning can spread through organization via diffusion. This is likely to be an evolutionary process that is summarized in Figure 5.4. It would usually have the following six stages (Hawkins and Smith, 2006):

1   Introduction of an individual executive who coaches for a few members of the organization.
2   Development of wide organizational coaching and mentoring programmes to build learning capacity.
3   Support for coaching and mentoring initiatives to ensure their sustainability.
4   Embedding of coaching and mentoring as part of the human resources (HR) and performance management function.
5   Developing coaching as part of leadership styles and management competence.
6   Continued learning and consolidation of the learning culture by gathering the feedback from all stakeholders.

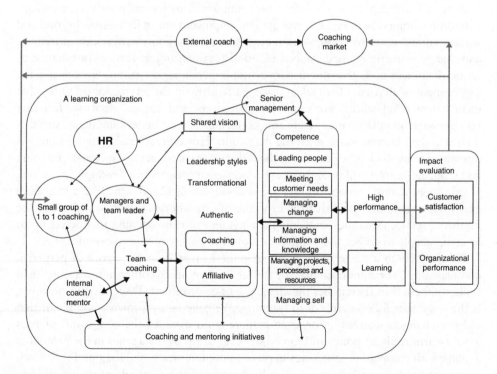

Figure 5.4   Developing a coaching culture

Coaching in groups and team building
As a way of embedding coaching and mentoring within the organization, it may be effective to carry them out as part of the team's activities (for instance, to discuss the concept and planning during the team's day away and to place the coaching or mentoring as an item on the agenda at regular meetings). Techniques for group coaching, such as outsider witnesses and definition ceremony (described in Chapters 7 and 8), would be useful to adopt in the context of the organization.

Widening the Context

The learning organization concept transfers well to communities. Sociology speaks of movements for change in communities; and change is underpinned by learning. Social movements for improvement rely on the realization of a vision, a motivation channelled into positive action that somehow is different from prior attempts to bring about collective change (Eyerman and Jamison, 1991). Only through exploration of old issues in new ways can change be brought about, as individuals have new insights and learning to shape their action. Communicated individual insights are not enough to trigger collective action. Collective action requires the following ingredients: the insight from experience in the context of making a better world, which has transferable significance and resonance for others; the strong association with processes that lead to desired outcomes; and the scope to motivate others to believe that those outcomes are possible through their action (empowerment).

Increased confidence in one's abilities as a result of affirmation and positive relationships with others brings about empowerment. The empowerment of individuals beyond and within existing hierarchies brings new momentum into the context, to release movement and change. Sometimes organizations are good at evidencing lip-service consultation to create document trails that might convey the impression that empowerment and the involvement of all parties have taken place, particularly in the service sector. Often that involvement is superficial. For example, professional and service users may fear that transgressing boundaries may create role confusion or may undermine their expertise. So it is in their interest to maintain the status quo. However, according to our universal integrated framework (Chapter 6) and the case studies based on our experience, listening and challenging roles and boundaries are processes of constructive development as long as risks to continuing service delivery are assessed and managed. One leader in a social enterprise organization said that the expertise of professionals might contribute to the improved service outcomes, but only their wisdom of truly opening themselves up to listening deeply to service users would improve the quality of their experience.

Practitioners in a range of service engagements may describe stories of perpetual complainants. Their motives may be about undermining communities rather than building them, but therein lies the challenge of discernment. Discernment, however, is the stage that follows after deep listening. We have rarely known a complaint that did not change something. For, even if there is no basis for the complaint, there is always learning about policy and forced self-evaluation by the agency in the process of dealing with complaints, structures in place to communicate, the nature of the multi-agency at work or an insight into the background of the complainant that triggers new and unexpected action.

Social support for coaching and mentoring

Providing social support for coaches forms a wider dimension of coaching and mentoring, beyond the traditional mentoring role where a senior person simply supports the less experienced mentees. The looser concept of coaching and mentoring in our universal integrated framework embodied the function of social support, but without some of the hierarchical constraints. This new dimension can be described as constellations of developmental relationships (Kram and Hall, 1996). Access to developmental relationships increases satisfaction. Social support includes emotional support by way of providing reassurance and self-worth, of listening and of showing concern. It also gives appraisal in the form of feedback and confirmation, informational support, instrumental support such as tangible assistance, investment of time and resources. Friendship and caring can play a big role in helping individuals maintain self-esteem (Wills, 1991). While the sponsor's role of mentoring was important for facilitating learning in a career development situation, the psycho-social support of developmental relationships brought about learning and positive change and could reduce stress. This loser concept of lateral and multidimensional mentoring has a place in the development of wider support: it engenders learning in communities such as prisons and schools, support for the ill, and so on. Coaching and mentoring, peer/lateral or group coaching and developmental relationships that are convergent with coaching and mentoring qualities are all vital in building supported communities that are learning and changing.

For some people, the focus on the social support side of coaching and mentoring, underpinned as it is by qualities and skills, represents nothing more than the development of friendships. However, we all know how destructive some friendships can be. Some individuals naturally favour giving advice over listening, criticism over praise and encouragement, and these ingredients might work counter to building self-esteem and empowering individuals. Likewise, the befriended might struggle to move the relationship forward in a purposeful way. So, in this context, we need to work with whole communities to fine-tune their natural befriending behaviour. A combination of busy work and home lives for many, use of and access to technology, increased independence, migrant workforces and diffused families means that there is more pressure on one's time and a tendency to adopt the quick fix approach to problems rather than to develop relationships for their own sake.

It might seem an odd suggestion that we would benefit from returning to some old principles of good listening that might bring about new thinking. No one is pretending that coaching or mentoring is rocket science or something very new. It is often the simplest intervention, with its roots in natural behaviour, that generates the best outcomes. It is in social coaching and mentoring that the benefits are most impressive. For example, in prisons, the mentoring of inmates by outsiders can prepare them for life outside and for re-employment in particular. Organizations such as the National Health Service in the UK and many community groups are beginning to recognize the merits of mentoring inmates with histories of mental illness and addiction as a preventative method, to stop hospital or rehabilitation unit re-admission.

Likewise, mentoring in schools has been particularly effective in working with disadvantaged children. Their learning is often not limited by ability alone; sometimes they lack self-esteem and the confidence to try. For some individuals, the opportunity to sit with an adult 'who is on-side', encouraging and interested in them, is a new experience. The promising results from such encounters have led to region-wide mentoring schemes designed to promote learning for all. Once young people are confident in themselves as learners, they are able to input into the wider learning community in an active way. One of the most powerful examples of mentoring in the community is the situation where those in traditionally powerful roles are mentees to those who have been previously marginalized. Both parties have a chance to explore issues from different perspectives and to gain a new empathy as a result.

The micro-context of coaching or mentoring is entirely congruent with the organizational or community journey to improvement through goal setting, through an exploration of the context of operation and reality of the individual (mapping the environment), through a consideration of the issues from all possible perspectives – including that of tensions in the system and of the move to reconciliation or balance through the generation of options capable of bringing about positive change. Through the process of working beyond traditional boundaries, those who engage in coaching and mentoring are bringing in new ideas and importing best practice into their communities.

The need for collaborative and partnership approaches to learning

The social economic condition in which we operate presents challenges for collaborative working. Within the changing environment, alliances are the key to timely and efficient deliverables. In many cases, outsourcing and partnering in areas where organizations are not competitive may make economical sense. The continued relationship with stakeholders and the customer base is also important. Respect and the positive affirmation of customers and stakeholders are vital to success. Many people can remember the Gerald Ratner case, where he described some of his jewellery products as 'crap', thereby insulting his customers and triggering a downslide in sales and, ultimately, his own resignation. Perhaps that was a bit extreme, but there are many collaborations between organizations and the communities they serve that operate on a subtle undermining of those communities, on gentle ridicule, and on a questioning of their capability to participate in the collaborative process or their judgement as to what is good for them. All of this can create a slightly resentful community or hostile tolerance. To maintain a sustainable partnership, the stakeholders need to develop a learning community.

The need for learning communities

The changing environment also presents challenges to organizations. As discussed in Chapter 2, many coaching scholars have attempted to explain the factors underpinning complexity. Stacey (1996) found that organizations moved between stability, instability and complexity, but the 'frozen' stage described by Lewin was rarely a reality, as change was permanent. In complex environments, social networking becomes essential, as does collaborative work that builds on those connections to ensure seamless processes from customer and stakeholder perspectives.

Knowledge aiming to fuel change is an emergent quality of learning; and informal contexts speed up the availability of knowledge in a timely way, to make the most of the existing opportunities for innovation and change. Formal, controlled and programmed environments generate cautious, orderly activities, which tend to be limited by their structure according to the past experience. Informal emergent and iterative thinking environments generate active experimentation in the present chaos – from which leading-edge thinking derives. This kind of flexible environment is based on Kessels' (1996) corporate curriculum model – enabling participants to develop a tolerance of uncertainty and change.

Consumers are showing more interest in the processes and mechanisms that underpin production and service delivery – be these related to ingredients, technology, or the ethical or unethical nature of production. One key question that learning organizations need to ask themselves is: 'Are we traditional or leading edge, and how does our strategy match our values?'

Organizations need to be clearer about what they are doing, why they are doing it and how they compare with others. We work in organizations and communities where we have to engage with the process of change and in so doing to equip ourselves to be active rather than passive. At the corporate level, the requirement to continue to learn in order to remain at the leading edge is called developing a learning organization – a concept formulated by Pedlar, Burgoyne and Boydel (1991) as a strategy for sustainable development. Throughout all their corporative lives, organizations are required to be active learners, self-modernizers and improvers, reaching out to the changing context in which we all operate. Pedlar et al. (1991) also recognized that organizations need to stimulate, support and challenge people through the process of change by ensuring that they are receptive learners, creative thinkers and implementers. Learning and change go hand in hand. Many situation-based paradigms have emerged that partner active experience (real work) with learning reflection in order to bring about change; such are project-based learning, action learning and coaching or mentoring. The move to become a learning organization takes us away from traditional top-down command into the sphere of involvement, questioning and challenge. We all need to be players rather than observers. If we want to be at the forefront, we have to go beyond participation – to leadership in creativity or innovation and to the implementation of what stimulates them.

There are frameworks to guide organizations in their modernizing. Most models are underpinned by the need to set goals for changes on the basis of a clear understanding of what is to be achieved. Processes of mapping the environment in which organizations operate, processes and flow of activities and analysis and redesign are precursors to improvement action.

Organizations need to know how they will measure the impact of their changes and present the data to others. Improvement strategies at organizational level need to balance the needs of capacity and demand, identify the delays in the systems and bottlenecks, the quality issues that impact on customer experience and the maximization of productivity. To understand these issues, we need to understand stakeholder views at every point in the process and see the range of perspectives. As for moving people forward in change, understanding their views and engaging them in a consultative process early on prepares the ground well. However, there are inevitable human dynamics to manage through the process of change, and hence improvement strategies work to ensure that there are enough skills and knowledge in the system to facilitate change at individual, group and organizational level.

Embedding the change or the improvement at a deeper level, to make it last beyond the life of a funded initiative or flavour of the month initiative, is a real challenge and is aided by ownership, the early experience of benefits, the reflection of personal learning and the spread of the best practice. 'Spread' or take-up of the best practice rarely works when it is a 'must do this way or else' mandate. Success is based on the establishment of a sound methodology (but it should also fit within local planning goals), on detailed environmental mapping and on a committed, locally distributed leadership cohort. Sustainability is increased when all partners and stakeholders have learning mechanisms through which to work in mutually beneficial ways. Developing a community of practice could be one of the learning mechanisms.

Developing a community of practice

The phrase 'community of practice' was mentioned on various occasions (without a proper definition) in Chapter 3, in the context of learning theories. A more detailed discussion is provided here.

The concept of community of practice was first introduced by Jean Lave, an anthropologist, and Etienne Wenger, a researcher; it was based on their observation of five traditional apprenticeship systems. In each situation, a community emerged over time, which in turn served as a 'living curriculum' for the new members who entered the system. The pair called these communities 'communities of practice' (Lave and Wenger, 1991). On the basis of an ethnographic study of a claims processing system, Wenger (1998) developed the concept further, drawing on a social theory of learning that became its foundation (this was discussed in Chapter 3). In recent years, Wenger and his colleagues advocated the notion of 'communities of practice' as a key to knowledge management for leaders in organizations – and this includes the role of stewardship in Internet communities (Wenger, McDermott and Snyder, 2002; Wenger, White and Smith, 2009).

Semantically, the phrase 'communities of practice' is made up of two things: communities and their practice. A community is a collection of individuals who interact with each other and are very often in pursuit of a common goal – be that winning a football match or discussing one's reading of a book in a book club gathering. In pursuing their common goal, these individuals learn how to interact (e.g. by creating or defining the rules of engagement or by observing established social norms). Effectively the social interaction is a process of learning – namely learning by doing (learning how to do something and how to relate with others by doing things together and by gaining experience from it). Wenger (1998: 45) called this social process 'collective learning', and the common goal a 'shared enterprise'.

From the systems perspective, the community of practice is an emergent property: it results from the 'collective learning' of individuals who sustain their pursuit of 'a shared enterprise'; over a period of time, a 'shared repertoire' may be formed. Wenger (2011) simplifies the notion of 'community of practice' still further, defining it succinctly as 'a group of people who share a concern or a passion for something they do, and learn how to do it better as they interact regularly'. To summarize, the defining features of such entities are:

- the domain: a shared learning need (enterprise);
- the community: an entity that evolves from the collective learning;
- the practice: the social interactions and the resources (or shared repertoire) they produce, which in turn affects the practice.

In other words, a learning organization is a community of practice. To develop such an organization or community, one would need first to have a shared enterprise, identify a shared need, develop an environment that facilitates social interactions and provide the resources for collective learning.

Whether this community is a local community interest company, a large international corporation or a virtual community over the Internet, it would need to develop a community of practice and its learning capability. As mentioned in Chapter 3, such a community should have four fundamental components – which are reiterated here and placed within an organizational context. To develop and maintain a community of practice, a learning organization would need to continuously develop:

1   Social learning spaces: it should design its environment so as to make it offer various suitable meeting spaces. These spaces may be meeting rooms for one-to-one coaching or for team meetings, or coffee areas for social interactions. They should allow genuine conversations to take place between peers. There should also be spaces within which team members feel safe to talk about their experiences.
2   Learning citizenship: it should promote an ethics of learning. This may take the form of a code of ethics and good practices. However, to ensure substantial commitment from the staff, such a code needs to be promoted through coaching and mentoring rather than being imposed.
3   Social artists: a learning organization needs to have leaders who are an inspiration for others and address the 'social dynamics' within the organization.
4   Learning governance: it should develop some principles of 'governance' that guide the configuration of the organizational environment in terms of its social learning spaces and processes.

Chapter Summary and Reflection

Collaborations work well where there is mutual trust and respect, where power is perceived to be equally distributed and potential benefits are seen as mutual. Perception and reality are not always the same. For instance, one individual can attribute and interpret a situation differently from another, perhaps on the basis of a prior assumption. The reputation of an organization or agency can continue to operate long after the activity that brought it about has subsided. Authentic relationships between stakeholders and community partners, relationships based on the here and now, can help organizations change their reputations on the basis of the current evidence of their practice. A change of leadership at the top of an organization cannot always bring about change in the way an organization behaves. Leadership in an organization can be working to a very different script from that of the supporting body beneath it, and it can have a very different mission, too. Tacit behaviour and overt behaviour can present some contradictory information to stakeholders about what the real mission is.

There are different types of knowledge that a high-performance team needs to share. These could be explicit, tacit or both. Dictionary and recipe knowledge are explicit, while axiomatic and people knowledge are implicit. Directory knowledge may be either implicit or explicit. The management of these different types of knowledge requires active acquisition or creation, knowledge capture and storage, and knowledge diffusion and transfer. Coaching and mentoring are identified as key vehicles in the facilitation of knowledge acquisition and transfer.

From the discussion of this chapter, we have deduced that the role of a leader in the learning organization is to:

- ensure that a vision exists, maintain and share that vision rather than creating it (inspirational and transforming leadership);
- inspire commitment;
- act as a designer of the organization – a champion or a social artist;
- design learning processes, coaching and mentoring programmes;
- translate implicit assumptions into explicit knowledge, make tacit knowledge explicit and create new tacit knowledge through the learning cycle;
- manage the diversity of the top team and achieve strategic consensus;
- ensure good decision making throughout the organization;
- empower the staff;
- be capable of leaps of abstraction – that is, make inferences from observation and produce valid generalizations;
- maintain a coaching and mentoring culture within which many members act as coaches or mentors.

Novices may be confused when they attempt to distinguish between coach and counsellor. This is partly due to the fact that counselling is an important element in coaching and mentoring. We could not expect coachees entering the meeting as perfect human beings, free from psychological barriers and work and/or life problems (if so, they would not need coaching at all). Most often, they will have psychological baggage, concerns and preoccupations that coaches need to identify and address before the coachees can be set free.

We hope this chapter has made clear that, apart from having counselling skills, successful coaches or mentors within an organization should most likely have the following qualities and skills:

- Awareness: they should be aware of themselves and others, sensitive about their own and others' identity, social needs, and organizational–cultural differences.
- Empathy: they should create a rapport with coachees and mentees as well as with the programme owner, who tends to be a senior manager.
- Extravert personality: they should be friendly and outgoing. The coaches love people, and meeting new people is part of their work. More importantly, they are the people to whom staff at all levels in an organization would like to talk.
- Diplomacy: they should be able to understand the organization's politics and idiosyncratic culture, develop good interpersonal relationships, negotiate a way round the organizational maze.
- Facilitation skills: they should encourage people to talk about their problems as well as guiding them to discover solutions.
- Learning skills: they should be quick to learn who knows what, particularly within a team and an organization.

- Interview skills: they should be able to conduct open interviews and focus on knowledge acquisition from the stakeholders.
- Listening skills: they should listen attentively to what is being said – as well as to what is unsaid – and make people feel valued and respected.
- Management of change: they should be able to initiate, embrace and manage change within an organization.
- Tolerance of ambiguity: they should be able to tolerate the chaos of an organization, where change is constant.

In this chapter we have looked at executive coaching within the context of learning organizations. We have argued the case for coaching as a vehicle for leveraging organizational culture and sharing organizational information; such learning culture is developed and maintained. Thus, apart from performing the role of a 'learner' and that of a 'teacher' or instructor, a coach has also a third role, namely as a facilitator for knowledge elicitation, transfer and management. This implies a new paradigm, which requires the coach to be a quick and flexible learner and to have a professional competence that matches the leadership role, as well as an understanding of diversity and organizational culture. In Chapter 6 we describe this new paradigm with the help of a universal integrated framework designed to show how leadership competence can be developed, and we explore the qualities of coaches more systematically.

6
Developing a Universal Integrative Framework for Coaching and Mentoring

Introduction

In the last chapter I have proposed that coaching or mentoring is a vehicle for developing a learning organization or community. The fact that change has been the trigger for the need to develop a coaching model applicable across diverse cultures is the focus of this chapter. Here I shall further expand on the issues of coaching and mentoring, taking them from personal and organizational contexts into a cross-cultural realm. The context is also enlarged to reveal international and professional aspects of the subject. I argue that, in order for coaching and mentoring to be applicable across different countries, it has to be applicable across different cultures. On the basis of the learning theories that were discussed in Chapter 3, a coaching framework that underpins cross-cultural practice is developed here. The earlier version of a universal integrative framework (UIF) – which was developed in the first edition (Law, Ireland and Hussain, 2007) and also reported in the literature (see Law, Laulusa and Cheng, 2009) – was set within the context of diversity in the UK. In this chapter I shall explore and revise UIF further, taking on board the recent years' experience of applying the framework across cultures.

I shall first extend the discussion of learning beyond the framework of the organization, to individual differences in how we conduct our relationships to stimulate learning. This part builds on some of the theories and research on individual learning in a global context and identifies the role and significance of culture and context for coaching success. Wider influences on learning will be considered, together with the impact of multimedia communications on learning relationships. Communication, feedback and supervision are proposed as means of building collective learning into coaching and mentoring, in order to ensure that both processes are part of a wider learning system. I shall also describe an emotional intelligence framework with an added cultural dimension, which supports the UIF. These features aim to help you to strengthen the way you work in a diverse learning context.

The Psychology of Coaching, Mentoring and Learning, Second Edition. Ho Law.
© 2013 John Wiley & Sons, Ltd. Published 2013 by John Wiley & Sons, Ltd.

Universal Integrated Framework (UIF): Building on the Integrated Universal Elements of Diverse Mentoring Coaching

The idea of building a generic framework – a meta-model – is not new. It is well within the ambition of many leading academics and practitioners in the field – David Lane, in his workshop at the second National Conference of the Special Group in Coaching Psychology, attempted to help participants build their own meta-models (Lane, 2005). Building a meta-model has clear benefits. As Lane points out, it can assist coaches to integrate their coaching processes in terms of:

- frameworks: models can be added into the framework one by one;
- questions: coaching questions can be structured and embedded into the meta-model;
- leadership: the meta-model ensures that coaches have a clear purpose, perspective and process.

The universal integrated framework (UIF) consists of the following unique characteristics:

- learning cycle and supervision, continuous professional development (CPD);
- appreciation of the cultural environment;
- coach/mentor/mentee fluidity;
- integrative continuum;
- cross-cultural emotional intelligence;
- a pragmatic implementation model that embeds all of the above elements;
- communication methods and feedback mechanism.

In the following section I shall describe these features in greater detail and with updated information.

Learning Cycle, Supervision and Continuous Professional Development (CPD)

Implementing the action stage of the learning cycle that was identified in Chapter 3 would complete the learning wheel for coaching (see Figure 6.1). So, as the first step in building the UIF, a dynamic learning model is embedded in the coaching framework.

This constitutes the implementation phase and should underpin each element of the UIF. It also maps very well onto the reflective practice or continuous professional development (CPD) cycle (see Figures 6.2 and 6.3).

The model is consistent with supervision and CPD, which offers coachees the opportunity to review the coaching process and to optimize their learning. Integrating CPD and supervision enables practitioners to achieve excellence, develop talent and ensure the quality of performance.

Supervision is a forum in which coaches and mentors meet their supervisors and talk about their coaching experience with the aim of improving their practice. They

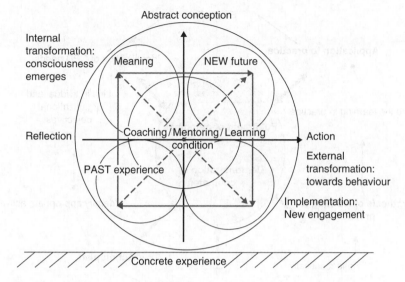

Figure 6.1 Completing the dynamic coaching/mentoring/learning model

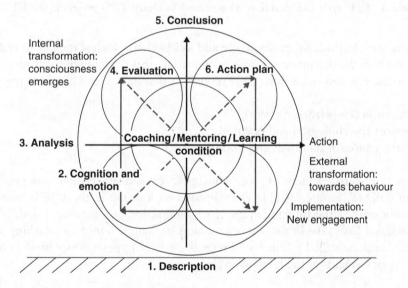

Figure 6.2 Reflective practice and learning cycle

would review the lessons learned from that experience with help from their supervisors, who very often are coaches or mentors themselves. According to Carroll (2006), supervision is a form of experiential learning where the work is reviewed, interviewed, questioned, considered and critically reflected upon – a process in which what he calls 'reflection-on-action' leads to 'reflection-for-action'. So, from the perspective of learning, it makes sense to integrate supervision into the UIF. This enables coaches and mentors to move from 'I-learning' to 'we-learning' (shared learning). The UIF feedback mechanism (which will be described later) may form an integral part of the supervision and CPD process. It can also be used to assess the impact of coaching and

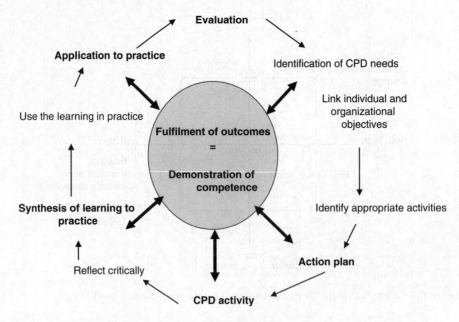

Figure 6.3 CPD cycle (adapted from Department of Health CPD project in the UK)

mentoring on individuals' performance and satisfaction, which is the key to realizing the benefits of the two processes. This would ensure that coaching or mentoring offers value to the business. Kadushin (1992) considers that supervision has three roles:

1   education (knowledge transfer);
2   support (psychological and practical);
3   maintenance (of standards and good practice).

CPD is an essential element of professional practice; and supervision is an important part of CPD (Passmore, 2011). The emphasis on learning in the UIF is consistent with some of the latest thinking in the coaching practice. For instance, Child, Woods, Willcock and Man (2011) also advocate action learning as a tool for coaching supervision; Campone's (2011) three-step reflective coaching practitioner model consists of the same elements as the learning cycle:

1   act: document one's experiences so as to make them serve as opportunities for learning and meaning making (this is research in action, reflection in action or thinking in action);
2   reflect: evaluate critically the underlying mental models, reframe and review lessons learnt (this is a process of naming and reconfiguring mental models);
3   plan: formulate a plan of action (this step leads to experimentation in action or active experimentation).

This three-step process enables the coach to translate knowledge into action as a reflective practitioner and to articulate and become aware of his or her own underlying ideologies and theoretical assumptions.

The benefits of supervision include continuous learning (Brookfield, 1991) and application (Basseches, 1984). Supervision

- adapts services to new situations;
- improves relationships;
- coordinates activities.

In practice, supervision, like coaching, is more of an art than a science, as it involves personal judgement and artistry (Patterson, Wilcox and Higgs, 2006).

Appreciation of Cultural Environment

Our cultural environment can be envisaged at two levels:

1 at micro-level: in a narrow local context (organization, family, local communities);
2 at macro-level: in a large context (global environment, environmental change and the planet).

Or, to translate these spatial levels into the dimension of time, our cultural environment can be looked at

- in the short term: this suits when the change we are dealing with is rapid (recent changes in the market shares, or day-to-day changes in the weather conditions can be approached from a short-term angle);
- in the long term (which is suitable in dealing with climate change or gradual cultural shift).

The two dimensions are summarized in Table 6.1, but keep in mind that they may or may not be interrelated; for example, there may be a long-term development in a local community or a rapid change in the global financial market system.

The culture or the environment in which we are engaging as learners is identified by the appreciation of the distinguishing features present in it, and these include features stemming from the physical environment – buildings, heat, light, sound; features that impact on health and safety; the shared vision and purpose, motivations, functional and professional status, social distinctions and characteristics of groups; ways (both tacit and overt) of ritualized being or doing in that localized environment; criteria of success and the understanding of stakeholder benefits; communication rituals and contextual protocols that smooth understanding among individuals and

Table 6.1 Appreciation of the cultural environment

Macro	Micro
Long-term	Short-term

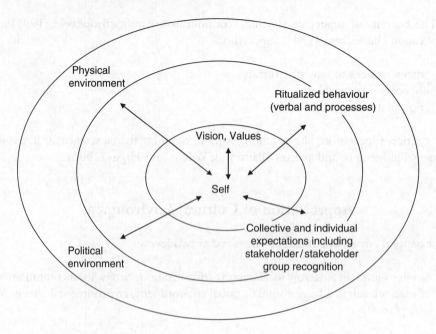

Figure 6.4   Appreciation of the cultural environment

elements unique to them (motivations, teamwork style, experience of tension and conflict, learning style and risk strategy). All these have to be appreciated if they are to work harmoniously (Figure 6.4).

The culture or context of operation might be the environment we occupy or the attributes we extend to it – and such factors include the players who are part of our networks. The interplay between our own values and our perception and assessment of what we observe and experience is key to our appreciation of this context. Our values are influenced by our upbringing and by the family culture we were exposed to, within the wider context of the community. Our understanding of success and happiness, our sense of self and our aspirations developed as we grew up. In this process we may have come to have different priorities from those of other people around us; and we were imbued with values for life that ultimately derive from the behaviour of family members and from popular phrases of advice heard at home, which we adopted in our own life. You might want to take a moment to reflect on some of those phrases that have stuck with you. For example:

- Keep your own counsel.
- You've made your bed, now lie in it.
- Waste not, want not.
- Give people just enough rope to hang themselves.
- Family first.
- People look down on us, but we stand tall.
- The world is your oyster.
- Look after yourself, because no one else will.
- We all make mistakes.

- That is someone's mother (on the topic of women).
- Be kind there, for the grace of God (on the topic of disability).
- Keep them on a short leash (on the topic of men).

Some of these injunctions might form the basis of a false view, or one that leads to a false assumption. It is this family culture and, later, the wider cultural experience that give us our sense of what is right and what is wrong and determine how we assess risk and our preferred way of working or being. When family cultures merge – perhaps through marriage, and particularly when there are children – it is amazing how strongly these early models of being and acting in the world battle to replicate some of the significant and favoured elements of one's background culture.

The greatest perceived differences between people are differences in their background, race, gender, physical and mental abilities, and, in the organizational world, functional and professional categorizations. Yet in theories such as Maslow's hierarchy of needs the universal needs we share are clear and succinct. Shared values and goals are more important in collaborative learning than styles and approaches that distinguish (or pay heed to) individual behaviour (Spreitzer, 1995; see also Chapter 3 here on social learning).

There are some core elements that we all share as learners. Learning needs motivation, support, feedback and review, although its style and content may vary. Some writers have drawn up models of intercultural sensitivity, which attempt to explain individual differences as resulting from cultural associations and propose that these differences should be acknowledged if the potential of relationships is to be actualized and developed (see Bennet, 1991; Rosinski, 2003).

The significance of culture

One of the key themes of the UIF has been that it aims to address the significance of culture. Understanding a culture also opens the general problem of understanding the life experience of others. Learning, relationships and ritualistic behaviours are illusory because they are located at the boundary between the 'internal life' of an individual and the 'external world' of relationships, customs and organizations. Cultural themes are consciously and unconsciously reproduced in conformity with the previous pattern (Krause, 1998).

So what is culture? How is it defined and reproduced? Can culture be treated as a variable and separated from other things? What does it look like? 'Culture' is multi-layered, like an onion – a system that can be peeled layer by layer and made to reveal its content (Hofstede, 1991). Using Geertz's (1986) analogy, culture is 'the icing on the cake'. But, if culture is like a cake, is it a layered cake or a marble cake? One can argue that culture is the process that bakes the cake (Strawson, 1996).

Hall (1976) divides culture along two dimensions: high context and low context. He argues that, in the low context or outer layer, individuals would not understand much about the meaning and context of communications within the group. When they are in the high context (inner layer), individuals have already become familiar with their context ('contextualized'). Thus, when coachees are not familiar with the organization's culture or with the context of a situation, the coach should be more directive and provide them with contextual information (this is the low-context communication that occurs in coaching). When coachees are familiar with their environment, the coach can use a more facilitative style (this is the high-context communication).

Hofstede (1991) regards culture as a kind of 'human mental programming' (a product of the 'collective programming of the mind'), which is specific to a group and is learned. It is a system of meanings, values and beliefs, expectations, and goals. These characteristics are acquired from and shared by members of a particular group of people, and they enable them to distinguish themselves from members of other groups (they contribute to the difference between in-group and out-group). In other words, culture makes us who we are. Hofstede's model has five dimensions:

1 power distance: the degree of equality–inequality due to individuals' different positions in a society;
2 individualism–collectivism: the degree to which a society values individual or collective achievement (which governs interpersonal relationships);
3 masculinity–femininity: the degree to which a society reinforces the traditional masculine work role model;
4 uncertainty avoidance: the level of tolerance of uncertainty and ambiguity;
5 long-term orientation: the degree to which the society embraces (or not) long-term devotion to traditional forward-thinking values.

Trompenaars and Hampden-Turner's (1997) model of culture is also multi-layered but has seven dimensions:

1 universalism versus particularism: rules versus relationships;
2 individualism versus communitarianism: self-centred versus society centred;
3 specific cultures versus diffuse cultures;
4 affective cultures versus neutral cultures: emotion versus cognition;
5 achievement versus ascription: active status seeking versus passive status seeking;
6 sequential cultures versus synchronic cultures: single-tasking versus multi-tasking;
7 internal control versus external control: self-determinant versus cooperative.

From all this we can see that culture is a complex property. It is interwoven with individuals' self-identity, professional and organizational values, and beliefs. It governs one's behaviour and social interactions (Hall, 1963; Hofstede, 1980; Kondo, 1990; Levi-Strauss, 1966; Schwartz, 1994a).

On the basis of the work of socio-cultural anthropologists Hofstede (1980) and Schwartz (1994b), Rosinski (2003, 2006) proposed that leveraging cultural differences may take the following stages and steps:

1 recognition and acceptance: acknowledge and accept differences of culture; understand that to accept means to respect – which does not mean to agree; appreciate the positive aspects that differences may bring;
2 adaptation (not assimilation or adoption): empathize with the cultural differences even though this may cause some discomfort;

3 integration: evaluate situations from different cultural perspectives, yet stay focused on the reality, without being distracted by having too many options (this is useful in the GROW coaching process in cross-cultural applications);
4 leverage: make the most of differences, strive for synergy, proactively look for gems in different cultures, achieve unity through diversity.

Rosinski's (2003) cultural orientations framework deals with the following aspects (each consists of a number of elements or dimensions):

1 *Sense of power and responsibility* (control, harmony, humility) People from different cultures have different beliefs about their power and responsibility to determine control, harmony, and humility.
2 *Time management approaches* (scarce–plentiful; monochronic–polychronic; past–present–future) People from different cultures have different views about the value and the flow of time and different emphases on the past, the present or the future.
3 *Definitions of identity and purpose* (being–doing; individualistic–collectivistic) People from different cultures may have different values and different points of emphasis about their identity and purpose.
4 *Organizational arrangements* (hierarchy–equality; universalist–particularist; stability–change; competitive–collaborative) Different cultures have different traditions in organizational arrangements and place different values on the way things are done within an organization or favour different ways of doing things.
5 *Notions of territory and boundaries* (protective; sharing) People from different cultures have different preferences in terms of the extent to which they share information.
6 *Communication patterns* (high–low context; direct–indirect; affective–neutral; formal–informal) People from different cultures have different communication patterns. Some assume a high context while others assume a low one; some prefer indirectness while others communicate directly; some observe formal protocols while others like informal communication.
7 *Modes of thinking* (deductive–inductive) People from different cultures have different patterns of thinking. Some tend to perform logical reasoning while others are grounded in their experiences.

Rosinski (2003) emphasizes that, 'by integrating the cultural dimension, coaching will unleash more human potential to achieve meaningful objectives' and, thereby 'enriched with coaching, intercultural professionals will be better equipped to fulfil their commitment to extend people's worldviews, bridge cultural gaps, and enable successful work across cultures' (p. xviii). Appreciating and understanding cultures is important not only in coaching, but also in counselling and supervision (Sue and Sue, 1990; Ryde, 2000).

So how useful are these typological approaches to the cultural classification of difference for leveraging individual learning in diverse settings? There are many problems with such approaches, not least that we live in a hybrid world, an eclectic mix. In terms of ethnicity, we find individuals who display many of the cultural and ritualistic behaviours and attitudes of their country of origin, even though they may be of different ethnicity. For instance, there are Chinese businesspeople operating out of China who have been educated in Europe or America (Law et al., 2009). We live in a world where an increasing number of people are of mixed parentage or of dual heritage. Therefore, faiths and beliefs may also derive from the cultural heritage. These are observed in a great variety of ways, and the commonality of beliefs and behaviours may be greater at the boundaries between different faiths than within each one.

Professional cultures are identified through traditional functionality, which is usually ring-fenced by professional governing bodies. However, professionals have been forced to merge and disseminate their skill sets – for example, doctors to nurses, professionals to technicians – in order to compete effectively and to add value for money to their services. So people with professional knowledge and skills may not be members of the profession. This is why typological approaches produce a false sense of absolute categorization and only serve to give us another boundary to cross. They are attractive because they offer 'fixed' knowledge and expertise (albeit a pseudo-knowledge set) as a way to advance interpersonal development – rather than offering a process designed to engage individuals in the identification of their emergent self and context of operation. Although such approaches have some value as general background information, many find their usefulness to consist in a literal application and endorsement of fixed knowledge or stereotypes.

Environmental pressure to make sense of what we see immediately on the basis of retrospective choices – playing safe, being aware of the here and now, taking action and moving to closure (to 'tick the box') – takes precedence over a more reflective process, which explores new modes of vertical categorization, distinguished by the maturity of the process. Our tendency to draw a closure in our engagement can be understood from the perspective of the gestalt theories (developed in Europe); but such theories cannot explain the personal and collective history, or any variation in meaning and significance within the wider environment (until they embody the holistic philosophy from the East). The application of mindfulness in the West is a good example of such a *half-baked cake*: it utilizes the meditation techniques from the Eastern tradition (Buddhism) very well, but it offers neither an understanding of nor acknowledgement of the essence of its philosophy (such as the value of compassion) that underpins its practice (Law, 2011, 2012). Thus we may have a model that encourages individual understanding of the past through the urgency of the present and the processing of a structured framework that is intertwined with Western acculturated behavioural processes; it may gloss over the deeper principle that provides a foundation.

It seems to me that there is a tension between similarities and differences in cultures, even within an organization. In addressing the diversity of the organization (which has been discussed at some length in Chapter 5), many more questions may be asked: 'Can people transform the workplace by expressing their cultural values rather than giving them up?' 'Can cultural differences be regarded as if they reflected fundamentally the same thing at some deeper level?' Resolving the tension and addressing some of these questions is important for our development of a universal framework, if such a framework is to be applicable across cultures. If we can find something that is cross-culturally the same, we may also be able to discover the human condition we all share. The human condition may serve as an anchor for us working across cultures.

Like many of the cultural models that have been reviewed, the UIF accepts that culture is multi-layered. However, it emphasizes the unique aspects of every intervention, as all behaviour changes and value shifts are contextualized but not automatically transferable. One solution does not fit all; and the person who knows most about their environment is the person who experiences it constructively, being supported and challenged by his or her coach and mentor. Working with individuals to identify differences and celebrate the uniqueness of all situations and circumstances reflects real universality and encourages best-fit solutions.

Coach/Mentor/Mentee Fluidity

Coaching and mentoring training sessions have traditionally focused on the development of coaches and mentors. In the UIF model, coachees and mentees are also trained as coaches and mentors, so they are better able to drive the coaching or mentoring process. Having the experience of being a coachee or mentee, one would know the whole process – and what elements in it need to be optimized if the benefits are to be realized. Individuals are encouraged to be both coachees (or mentees) and coaches (or mentors) so that they may recognize the learning opportunities involved in both roles and identify both as transitory – as an aid to learning rather than set and 'boxed-in' positions. It is essential to learning that leaders experience both roles. This is also consistent with the so-called 'double-loop learning' in organizations (Argyris, 1977).

Language may impose psychological barriers around these roles. The role of coach or mentor suggests that this might be a driving role, linked with an action-centred approach; but in reality the coachee's or mentee's role is the one that drives. Hence coachees' and mentees' training is important in helping individuals maximize their opportunities for learning; and there is some evidence that simply having to find a coach or mentor is useful for development and for developing the coaching contract that follows.

Integrative Continuum

As discussed in Chapter 4, some schools of thought encourage the separation of mentoring from coaching, stressing the distinction between the personal and the performative. However, a rigid distinction might cause mentoring to be marginalized in the organization's business agenda and distanced from personal development.

Despite some differences between coaching and mentoring, within the UIF coaching and mentoring are regarded as an *integrative continuum*. Both coaching and mentoring are underpinned by the same set of skills. For example, when coachees and mentees are driving a goal-centred process in an exploratory way, the outcome of both mentoring and coaching is 'action' (which is also the outcome of the learning process, as described in Chapter 3).

It is also in the interest of sustainability and of embedding mentoring and coaching as a holistic approach that the connections with the core business and central systems and processes are emphasized. Linking personal development with a performance improvement underpinned by the same set of skills enables users to develop a more coherent integrated framework of their own. This ensures that coaching and mentoring remain, by association, at the core of the business agenda and that coaching addresses leadership development as well as organizational improvement. The emphasis on the connections between coaching, mentoring and core business processes ensures that coaching and mentoring remain at the heart of the business agenda. Embedding them within the organization also guarantees the latter's sustainability. If coaching were just a scheme or an initiative, one would expect it to be a strand of work outside the main agenda; that way it would be vulnerable in a world of changing priorities. Organizations are more likely to discontinue add-on schemes or programmes that are not well embedded within core processes. Sustainability is achieved through an integrated approach, which ensures that mentoring and coaching are part of the way the organization supports reform and develops leaders. The link between coaching, mentoring, personal development and performance improvement has to be established in an integrated framework for a sustainable leadership improvement process that ensures short-term and longer term gains.

Cross-Cultural Emotional Intelligence

Although the idea of emotional intelligence (EI) was made popular by Goleman (1995), the concept was not new; it goes back to the 1920s through Thorndike's (1920) work on social intelligence. Gardner (1983) argued for intrapersonal and interpersonal intelligence as alternative attributes of individual achievement. A formal definition of EI was developed by Salovey and Mayer (1990) and later re-elaborated in this form:

> the ability to perceive emotions, to access and generate emotions so as to assist thought, to understand emotions and emotional knowledge, and to reflectively regulate emotions so as to promote emotional and intellectual growth. (Mayer and Salovey, 1997: 197)

Petrides and Furnham (2001: 64) define EI as

> a constellation of emotion-related dispositions and self-perceived abilities representing a distinct composite construct at the lower levels of hierarchical personality structures.

Self-efficacy is also one of the motivation mobilizers at our disposal, which have been shown to impact on our likely success (Bandura, 1977, 1982, 1997). We can get sponsorship and support from others, including stakeholders, who might encourage us, invest their time and energy, and then benefit from our learning achievements. We can also discover the learning methods that will suit us, and we can plan to achieve our goals so as to own them and the methods we employ. We need benchmarks and a clear vision of what success looks and feels like if we are to stay motivated and on track.

'Self-efficacy' is included as one of the elements of the UIF. However, this element needs to be handled with care. A lot of the underlying assumptions are embedded in Western – more specifically, American – culture. The meaning of self-efficacy may not be universally relevant. Some individuals derive their sense of purpose and the power to get things done from a positive and yet passive life force; for others, a sense of destiny may be the driver; for others still, a sense of control is anathema – instead, harmonization and integration provide the route to holistic progress. Yet all produce what counts as a 'can do' attitude. So self-efficacy scales may measure observable or self-assessed outcomes, but their meaning may be far from transferable across different cultures or contexts.

While emotion draws our attention to issues that are important to us, it may not be the best guide for action. Combining feeling and thinking with knowledge of the cultural context enables us to deliver the most effective results in our professional engagement. Thus the UIF was developed to embed Goleman's (1998) approaches to emotional intelligence. However, although Goleman's emotional competence framework was popular, its cultural competence dimension was underdeveloped. The initial UIF expanded Goleman's framework by adding two dimensions, cultural competence and coaching professional competence, with 360-degree feedback built into the system. The next section describes these dimensions in detail.

Integrating Cross-Cultural Coaching and Mentoring Intelligence into the Universal Framework

The initial UIF has four dimensions (see Figure 6.5):

1 personal competence;
2 social competence;
3 cultural competence;
4 professional competence.

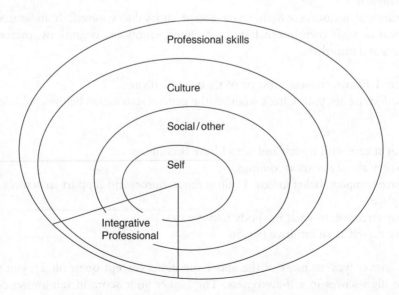

Figure 6.5 Universal integrated framework: a pragmatic model

The framework translates into a practical model all the elements described earlier. The integrative professional seamlessly crosses all the boundaries – personal and social (with emotional intelligence), cultural and contextual. Such a professional aims to help coaches and mentors to develop especially EI, and to do so from a cultural perspective. This process was referred to as the cross-cultural coaching/mentoring and social intelligence (CMSI) in the first edition of the present book. Over the years, I have developed and refined the same tool further, and now I simply call it 'cultural and social competence (CSC)'.

A total of 18 elements of core competence have been identified within these dimensions. Taking into consideration the need to balance the number of statements at each dimension and at each element, a total of 100 statements have been created in a form of self-assessment questionnaire (SAQ). The initial CSC questionnaire was referred to as self-review questionnaire (SRQ), and it was in binary response format – YES/NO. The newer version (second edition) of the questionnaire uses a seven-point Likert scale in response to the users' feedback. The users are invited to choose their response according to whether they agree or disagree with a CSC statement by clicking the appropriate point on the scale; the points range from Never (Point 1) to Always (Point 7).

The updated version of CSC SAQ – in a form of the online tool – is now available. Readers interested in trying out the CSC SAQ can contact the author. The four dimensions together with their elements and related statements are described next.

Dimension I: Personal competence

This competence reflects how you manage yourself. It consists of two parts:

1   awareness of oneself (self-awareness);
2   management of oneself (self-regulation)/self-management.

Self-awareness
Self-awareness measures whether you accept and value yourself. It measures your awareness of your own internal states, feelings, emotions, cognitions, preferences, resources and intuitions.

ELEMENT 1 EMOTION: AWARENESS OF ONE'S OWN EMOTION
How self-aware are you? Check whether the general statements below could describe you:

- I am at ease with myself and who I have become.
- I worry about my shortcomings.
- I have complete belief in how I utilize the resources and support structures I have in place.
- I pay attention to what my body tells me.
- I see myself as an intuitive person.

If you answer 'yes' to most of the above questions (except question 2), you would achieve high scores in self-awareness. The higher your score in self-awareness, the more aware you are of how you feel and of what you know, and the better you recognize the sources of that knowledge.

ELEMENT 2 COGNITION: SELF-REFLECTION AND EVALUATION, KNOWING ONE'S
OWN VALUES, SELF-WORTH, CAPACITIES, STRENGTHS AND WEAKNESSES
This may be achieved by reflecting on one's own experience analytically, critically evaluating the validity of one's assumptions, beliefs, and values, and drawing conclusions.
Indicators:

- an accurate evaluation of one's own strengths and weaknesses;
- intuition;
- confidence.

For example:

- I know my own strengths and weaknesses.
- I can express my view that I believe something to be right even though this view may be unpopular.
- I worry about my shortcomings.
- I have complete confidence in how I utilize the resources or support structures I have in place.
- I see myself as an intuitive person.

Self-management
Self-management is the ability to manage one's emotion and motivation and to control them productively. It measures whether you invite the trust of others by being principled, reliable and consistent. The self-management score has a total of 13 questions and is divided into *resilience*, *flexibility* and *trustworthiness*.

ELEMENT 3 MOTIVATION
Motivation is a positive emotion that drives you towards your goals or aspirations. It gives you the ability to perform consistently in a range of situations under pressure, to stick to your commitments, to take the best course of action to achieve your objective in the face of obstacles, personal challenge or criticism, and to manage your awareness of emotion and control it productively. For example, *resilience* measures whether you are able to bounce back when things go badly. *Realism* measures whether you balance optimism with realism. Indicators:

- ambition;
- achievement;
- commitment to oneself, the team, the organization's objectives;
- standard of excellence;
- optimism (emotional resilience) – persistence in achieving goals in spite of obstacles.

For example:

1 I actively take opportunities to set challenging tasks in order to fulfil the organization's mission.
2 I get despondent or depressed fairly easily.
3 I am a very resilient person in hard times.

4   I always build in contingencies so that I can increase the likelihood of a good
    outcome.
5   I believe that when one door closes another opens.

ELEMENT 4 CONTROL

Control is the ability to deal with disruptive emotions and impulses. It measures
whether you are emotionally balanced, namely whether you are free to express your
feelings but able to decide whether, how and when you do so. For example:

1   I am able to show how I feel as well as to conceal my feelings.
2   When I am upset or cross I have a compulsion to let it our no matter what.
3   I can express my feelings easily, but I choose when and how to do it.
4   I keep calm when others are angry.
5   When I am angry or upset I tend to take it out on others.

ELEMENT 5 TRUSTWORTHINESS

Trustworthiness also means honesty or integrity. It measures whether you invite the
trust of others by being principled, reliable and consistent. For example:

1   I confront unethical actions in others.
2   My beliefs and attitudes shift depending on whom I am with.
3   I know what my inner principles are.
4   If I make a mistake I might try to blame it on others.
5   I am true to myself even if I risk disapproval from others.

ELEMENT 6 CONSCIENTIOUSNESS

Conscientiousness takes care of personal improvement and performance. For example:

1   I do not always make commitments.
2   I do not always keep my promises.
3   I hold myself accountable for getting the job done.
4   I am well organized in my work.
5   I pay attention to detail in my work.

ELEMENT 7 FLEXIBILITY

Flexibility measures whether you are able to adapt your thinking and behaviour to
match changing situations. Key questions include:

• Do you inquire into and respond openly to others' ideas?
• Could you address your own fear of losing what is familiar and try something new,
  rather than playing safe?

Self-assessed statements include:

1   I can perform multi-tasking well.
2   Once I've made my decision I stick to it no matter what.
3   I particularly like to learn new ways of doing things.

4   I find unexpected changes unsettling.
5   It's easy for me to adjust my responses to changing conditions.

ELEMENT 8 CREATIVITY

Creativity consists in being innovative, comfortable with new ideas and novel applications. Self-assessed statements include:

1   I am creative.
2   I am open to new ideas.
3   I enjoy doing new things.
4   I like novel solutions to problems.
5   I can generate a lot of new ideas easily.

Dimension II: Social competence

Social competence reflects how you manage relationships. It is a didactic process, as individuals gain insight through social interaction and awareness of others. This social process simply could not exist individually (Senge, 1990). It consists of the following elements:

*   awareness of others (empathy);
*   management of others (social skills).

Awareness of others (empathy)

Awareness of others' feelings, needs and concerns measures whether you empathize with others. There are 20 questions.

ELEMENT 9 UNDERSTANDING AND TRUST

This is an ability to see things from the perspective of others, to understand key issues, to see the whole picture and to draw a clear conclusion when presented with incomplete or ambiguous information. This ability measures whether you trust others, but it also protects you from being exploited. Self-assessed statements include:

1   I find it difficult to understand people who have opposite feelings or beliefs to my own.
2   I aim to accept people rather than judge them.
3   I feel empathy with others easily.
4   I tend to be suspicious of other peoples' motives.
5   I incline to trust others in a way that allows me to be aware of the risks.

ELEMENT 10 EMPOWERING

To empower others is to help them develop to the point where they can satisfy their needs and achieve their aspirations. Indicators:

*   customer-centredness;
*   service orientation.

Self-assessed statements include:

1   I help others to achieve their aspirations.
2   I help foster others' skills.

3   I provide my subordinates with assignments that are challenging.
4   I reward others' accomplishments.
5   I provide constructive feedback.

Management of others (social skills)

Social skills cover the ability to influence others, collaborate and cooperate with them by identifying a common ground and shared objectives, by taking a leadership role, by managing team spirit, by resolving any conflicts and by communicating clearly, with a display of interpersonal sensitivity.

Element 11 Communication

Communication is about listening to others' points of view and providing clear and convincing messages about one's position and rationale. Self-assessed statements include:

1   I listen well.
2   I am receptive to good news, but not to bad news.
3   I find giving clear, precise and concise messages difficult.
4   I welcome the sharing of information appropriately.
5   I like to create an open communicative environment.

Element 12 Facilitating conflict resolution

This element measures how well you can balance the requirement to be assertive – to stand up for what you want – with staying calm and respecting others while you do it. It helps mentees and coachees to handle conflict. The coaches and mentors engage the emotional and social aspects when confronting conflicts. These include:

- an ability to persuade others to change their viewpoints;
- negotiating;
- resolving disagreements;
- relationship management – building bonds, nurturing relationships;
- collaboration and cooperation – identifying a common ground; working with others to achieve common objectives.

Self-assessed statements include:

1   I can disagree with people regularly without falling out with them.
2   I prefer to use indirect influence to build consensus.
3   I prefer win–win solutions to conflicts.
4   I seek agreement from all stakeholders in conflict situations.
5   I readily collaborate or cooperate with others to work towards shared goals.

Element 13 Leadership facilitation

This consists of providing guidance and inspiration to individuals and groups. Self-assessed statements include:

1   I coach by example.
2   I articulate coaching objectives well.
3   I generate enthusiasm for a shared vision.
4   I guide others to perform according to their abilities.
5   I would hold others accountable for their duties.

ELEMENT 14 COACHING THE TEAM

This activity consists of creating synergy in team or group coaching in order to achieve collective objectives. Self-assessed statements include:

1 I create synergy in order to work towards group goals.
2 I create a model of team qualities.
3 I generate enthusiasm within a team.
4 I engage all members of a team in active participation.
5 I readily gain credit among the team members.

ELEMENT 15 COACHING FOR CHANGE

To coach for change is to champion change and modernization. Self-assessed statements include:

1 I encourage coaches to take action to champion change.
2 I help coaches to identify the need for change in their organization.
3 I help coaches to take action to remove barriers to change.
4 I engage others in the process of changing.
5 I create a model of change according to others' expectations.

Dimension III: Cultural competence

This competence reflects how we manage organizational change. It consists of the following elements:

- awareness of other cultures (being enlightened);
- management of organizational cultures (being a diversity champion).

Cultural competence measures the extent to which coachees and mentees inquire into or respond openly to others' culture, ideas and values, and their willingness to challenge and question their own assumptions as well as those of others. Coaches and mentors have the ability to mediate boundaries between cultures, connect to others' and their own culture. In doing so one experiences oneself as part of a larger, collective consciousness, both culturally and spiritually. One recognizes that collective awareness and morality transform the organization and society as a whole.

Awareness of other cultures (enlightenment)
This includes:

- cultural awareness: understanding the organization's and group's culture and politics and the power relationships across culture;
- cultural sensitivity: assesses whether you are culturally comfortable with yourself and with others from different backgrounds;
- cultural flexibility: measures whether you align yourself with Euro-centric or African/Eastern values.

ELEMENT 16 APPRECIATION

Appreciation in this context relates to other cultures and religions. Self-assessed statements include:

1 We all have to struggle. I wonder why it is so different for people from other cultures.

2   I make an effort to learn some of the languages of those in my community who speak something other than Standard English.
3   I have interest in different types of ethnic cultures.
4   I have interest in different types of organizational cultures.
5   I can articulate aspects of my own culture and background.
6   I cannot articulate distinguishing aspects of organizational cultures.
7   I can identify goodness and badness accurately across cultures.
8   I do not have an appreciation of the role of education, money, values and status across cultures.
9   I have an understanding of how my own background and culture is seen by others.

ELEMENT 17 RESPECT

Similarly, showing respect relates in this context to what is different in others cultures. Statements include:

1   I respect people from other cultures.
2   I relate well to people from various backgrounds and cultures.
3   I recognize that most black minority and individuals from ethnic backgrounds want to be treated just as those in the majority culture.
4   I believe that the majority culture should help staff of different backgrounds be assimilated into it.
5   I believe there is one unitary model of coaching and mentoring that suits all.
6   I believe there are many different options for different people.
7   I accept that individuals outside the majority culture may face disadvantage.
8   I recognize that individuals are more likely to choose leaders from groups of people who most resemble themselves.
9   I believe that individuals from minority backgrounds are less likely to have negative views about other minority groups than individuals from the majority culture.
10 I feel insecure when I speak to people from a different background to mine.

Management of organizational cultures (champion)
ELEMENT 18 CHAMPIONING EQUALITY AND DIVERSITY

This element elicits high performance from people from different cultures and backgrounds. One contributes one's voice to a collective endeavour. Statements include:

1   I see diversity as an opportunity to increase the performance of my organization and of society at large.
2   I create an environment where people from diverse cultural backgrounds can excel and achieve their potential.
3   I am not personally responsible for the policies of racist institutions.
4   When the chance occurs, I take a positive stand against racism, even possibly at some risk.
5   I take positive steps to implement discussions in coaching and mentoring that aim at understanding and at the elimination of racism, sexism, and ageism.

The elements and dimensions presented above are summarized in Tables 6.2 and 6.3.

The 18 elements are comparable with Petrides and Furnham's (2001) 15 components of trait EI, which is summarized in Table 6.4:

Table 6.2 Dimensions of UIF pragmatic model

Competence	I. Personal (Self)	II. Social (Other)	III. Cultural (Culture)	IV. Professional (Competence)
Awareness	Self-awareness	Empathy	Enlightenment	Reflective practice
Management	Self-regulation	Social skills	Champion	Continued professional development

Table 6.3 Elements of cross-cultural EI

Dimensions	Elements	Qs
I. Personal competence	1. Emotion	5
	2. Cognition	5
	3. Motivation	5
	4. Control	5
	5. Trustworthiness	5
	6. Conscientiousness	5
	7. Flexibility	5
	8. Creativity	5
II. Social competence	9. Understanding	5
	10. Empowering	5
	11. Communication	5
	12. Facilitating conflict resolution	5
	13. Leadership facilitation	5
	14. Coaching the team	5
	15. Coaching for change	5
III. Cultural Competence	16. Appreciation	10
	17. Respect	10
	18. Champion cultural diversity	5
Total		100

Table 6.4 Petrides and Furnham's (2001) 15 components of trait EI

Facets	Perception
Adaptability	flexible to adapt to new conditions
Assertiveness	willing to stand up for one's rights
Emotion expression	able to communicate one's feeling to others
Emotion management	able to influence others' feelings
Emotion perception	clear about one's own and others' feelings
Emotion regulation	able to control one's emotions
Impulsiveness (low)	able to hold back one's urges
Relationship skills	able to have fulfilling personal relationships
Self-esteem	successful and confident
Self-motivation	able to drive on in the face of adversity
Social competence	able to network with excellent social skills
Stress management	able to regulate stress and withstand pressure
Trait empathy	able to take others' perspectives
Trait happiness	cheerful and satisfied with one's life
Trait optimism	able to 'look on the bright side' of life

Petrides and Furnham's framework consists of overlapping elements, which are not logically distinct. Furthermore, like other EI tools, their framework left the cultural component undeveloped. The EI elements are better organized in a hierarchical structure, as exemplified by the pragmatic UIF.

Dimension IV: Professional competence

The final section reviews some of your knowledge and approaches as a coach or mentor. This professional dimension has an impact on coaching and mentoring outcomes. It requires coaches and mentors to adopt professional approaches, giving and seeking authentic feedback to and from others. Statements include:

1   I believe people have their own solutions and they just have to find them.
2   I believe a coach or mentor can also be a coachee or mentee.
3   I recognize the importance of goals and expectations in checking to help a coach to progress.
4   I am comfortable with silence.
5   I listen more and say less.
6   I keep most of my interventions for challenging questioning.
7   I often find myself interrupting the mentor or coach.
8   I always offer advice to coachees and mentees on how to improve their situation.
9   I stick to the rules of my chosen coaching approach at all times.
10 I can summarize accurately what the coachee or mentee is saying.
11 I tell people if they are not fit for the coaching process.
12 I rely on my own judgement about whether the relationship is working well.
13 I need to have knowledge of the individual/organizational culture before I begin a mentoring relationship.
14 I need to be aware of the expectations of other stakeholders when questioning/ exploring the perspective of an individual mentee or coachee.
15 I facilitate the process for mentees or coachees by reviewing their learning.
16 I do not question coachees or mentees on their understanding of the process of change they are experiencing.
17 I encourage mentees or coachees to experiment with their learning.
18 I hook mentees or coachees into useful networks.
19 I do not encourage individuals to review their expectations.
20 I initiate discussions on how the mentoring or coaching relationship will work.

The pragmatic model described above embeds the psychology of learning. It is consistent with other meta-frameworks in learning and development; but the model grows wider, extending social aspects to cultural competence – for example, compare Taylor, Marienau and Fiddler's (2000) development intention framework (see Table 6.5).

The statements provide indicators for respondents to assess their own intention to develop and thereby to improve their future performance. By completing the test, the participants become more aware of how they feel and construct knowledge.

Table 6.5   Comparison of UIF with the development intention model

UIF	Development intention model
Personal competence (self-awareness)	Towards knowing as dialogical process
Personal competence (self-awareness: cognition)	Towards a dialogical relationship to oneself
Professional competence	Towards being a continuous learner
Personal competence (self-management)	Towards self-agency and self-authorship
Social/cultural competence	Towards connection with others

Feedback Mechanism: Peer Rating 360-Degree Feedback

To complete the learning cycle within the dynamic coaching and mentoring model (Figure 6.1), the process needs to embed a feedback mechanism. Feedback from others can have an impact on one's learning and understanding. This is traditionally illustrated by means of the Johari window (Figure 6.6). Coaches and mentors aim to provide feedback to coachees and mentees and to help them to discover their own blindspots and transfer their awareness from the known to the unknown (Luft, 1970; Jones and Pfeiffer, 1973).

In the initial UIF, a 360-degree feedback mechanism was developed online, which tested the perspectives of participants in a coaching and mentoring programme against those of their peers and line managers. This was a 'systematic collection and feedback of performance data on an individual or group derived from a number of stakeholders in their performance' (Ward, 1997). The mechanism provided a powerful opportunity for the participants to gain insight into and self-awareness of their own competence and to shape their behaviour accordingly.

The online UIF has a 'welcome to the peer review' section. Coaching and mentoring colleagues can name peers to give an opinion about them on the basis of their behaviour. The peers can complete a scoring of the statements as follows:

1   They seem at ease with themselves.
2   They seem to accept people rather than judge them.
3   They seem able to read accurately how people are feeling.

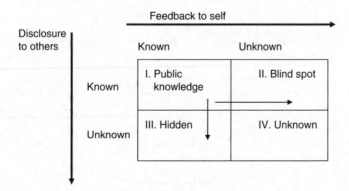

Figure 6.6   Giving feedback: the Johari window

4   They seem to be in tune with their own feelings.
5   They seem able to manage their stress.
6   They seem unperturbed by changing conditions.
7   They seem to be consistently themselves with different people and in different situations.
8   They express their feelings easily but choose when and how they do it.
9   They seem to keep calm when others are angry.
10 They tend to trust others, but in a way that allows them to be aware of the risks.
11 They tend to have contingencies in place to be sure of a good outcome.
12 They seem sensitive to the needs of people from a different ethnic and cultural background.
13 They seem to have an understanding of other cultural differences.
14 They seem comfortable with people from different backgrounds.
15 They seem to be able to motivate others to set inspirational goals for themselves.
16 They check how the mentoring and coaching relationship is working from the mentees' and coachees' perspective.
17 They check the resources at the coaches' and mentees' disposal.
18 They seem to defend their own approach when they hear a different view.
19 They use body language effectively to support their communication.

The 360-degree feedback mechanism can map onto the UIF, as shown in Figure 6.7.

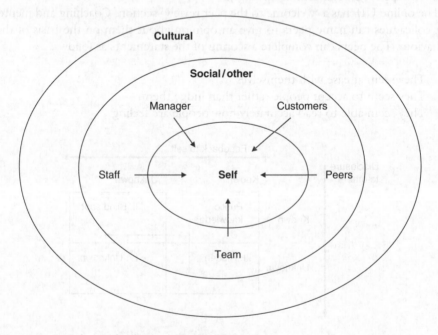

Figure 6.7 360-degree feedback within the UIF

UIF Revisited

Over the years, I continued consulting, teaching and presenting the UIF across cultures wherever I went – at conferences, workshops, master classes, and so on. I have always invited participants' feedback and reflected upon my work as part of my learning and continuous development. A number of critiques and feedback I have collected are summarized below:

- While it may be very well to advocate that the UIF is designed to be applicable across cultures and that it stimulates criticism of the established European frameworks as Euro-centric, the structure of the UIF itself (the onion-shaped model) places the concept of self at the centre of the framework. Is this rather Euro-centric (self-centred) also?
- The four dimensions need not be arranged in the order of the layers, as presented in Figure 6.5. In fact they can be presented as a table (like Table 6.2), or even as a list (as they are described in the text). In other words, the model is free to be reshaped and restructured. Furthermore, the interrelationships of these dimensions and elements (variables) change from culture to culture.
- While it seems a very novel project to develop a framework that is 'universal' and applicable across cultures, how would it work in practice? In fact in practice (as I observe from my students and many participants at workshops), in comparison with other models (like the GROW model, which is linear and easy to follow), such a framework is not easy to use in coaching conversation.

In response to the feedback and reflection described above, I often invite the students and the participants, as an individual or group exercise, to redesign the structure of the UIF in such a way as to find it useful in their own context. A number of different models emerge. Three of the alternative configurations of the UIF are shown in Figures 6.8, 6.9 and 6.10 as examples.

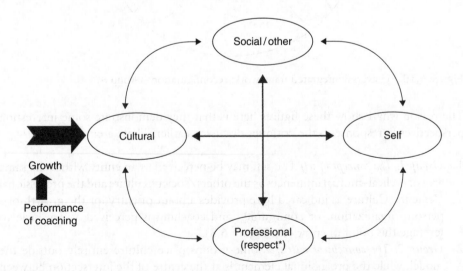

Figure 6.8 Universal integrated framework: reconfiguration (Group 1). *Respect is perceived as part of the professional component.

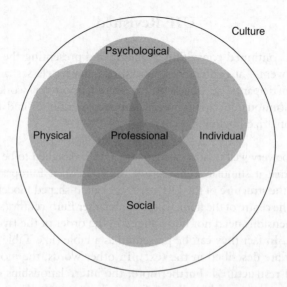

Figure 6.9   Universal integrated framework: reconfiguration (Group 2)

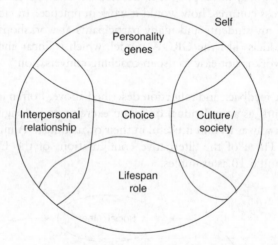

Figure 6.10   Universal integrated framework: reconfiguration (Group 3)

The reason why I show these figures here is that they demonstrate some interesting perspectives in response to the critiques discussed earlier. These are:

1   *Group 1: The concept of self* The self may be perceived as an entity within the same area of cyclical–mutual influences as the others/society, culture and the professional elements. Culture as indicated here provides a point of entry for the growth of a person, organization, or community; and coaching is perceived as a vehicle to leverage this point of entry (see Figure 6.8).

2   *Group 2: The concept of culture* Some groups place culture entirely outside the model, while the professional element is at the centre of the intersection between self and others, psychological and physical factors. Culture is viewed as a part of the space and environment that has no boundaries (see Figure 6.9).

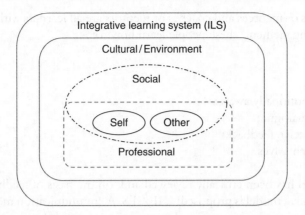

Figure 6.11   Revised UIF: an integrative learning system

3   *Group 3: The notion of free choice in relation to self and others* The other group
    views the concept of self as falling entirely outside the model, the socio-cultural
    relationship, and so on (see Figure 6.10). Interestingly, this group places the
    notion of 'choice' at the centre of the model – indicating that it is the choice (or
    the fact that one is free to choose) that makes all the difference in the world!

It may be a good idea for you (the reader) to try this exercise yourself and see if you
would come up with a different model of the UIF – this would then become your
own coaching model.

   Here, by way of offering another example, I'm making an attempt to rearrange
the shape and components of the framework according to the learning culture that
we have reviewed (in Chapter 3) and to apply a systems approach in a logical way,
Figure 6.11 shows such an integrative system. From this figure we can see that the
system in question is an integrative learning system (ILS), which is regarded as the
updated version of the UIF (UIF/ILS).

   In response to the problem of the difficulties of applying UIF in practice, I have
restructured the tools and exercises according to the four dimensions presented in
the next two chapters. You are invited to practise these techniques and exercises as
often as you can, so that you apply them seamlessly, without worrying about following manuals or procedures. Remember that UIF/ILS is a flexible framework: it is a
spatial model like a compass, which you can 'hold in your head' and use to guide your
practice, rather than following rigidly a procedural model like GROW.

Chapter Summary and Reflection

In this chapter the initial version of the universal integrated framework (UIF) was
described in full. The UIF embeds international cultural dimensions and emotional
intelligence. The framework looks like an onion, with many layers: self, social, cultural
and professional. Its core – self- and social development – is grounded in the learning
theories described in Chapter 3. It is consistent with the psychology of learning,

where coachees or mentees and coaches or mentors are all learners within the process. During their engagement, these people learn how to:

- learn;
- reflect;
- become emotionally aware;
- engage in dialogue;
- give and receive feedback;
- evaluate themselves.

The UIF model has been critically reviewed and, on the basis of feedback and reflection, an alternative model is proposed: UIF/ILS. A communication method of implementing the framework online using Internet technology is also described. The UIF questionnaire, with its 360-degree feedback, can be viewed as a snapshot – or a knife slicing through an onion. It enables participants to review their learning across all four dimensions.

The impact assessment of individuals' performance and satisfaction is a key to realizing the benefits of coaching and mentoring. It ensures that coaching and mentoring offer value to the business. Its implementation will be described in a case study in Chapter 9, and its impact assessment forms part of the evaluation strategy discussed in Chapter 10.

The next two chapters describe some of the technical know-how in terms of tools and exercises, so that you can continue to develop yourself as a competent coach, mentor, learner or supervisor.

7

Techniques and Tools

Introduction

This chapter provides you with a set of tools and techniques that are appropriate for the psychology of learning and the universal integrated framework elaborated in the previous chapters. Some of the practical exercises related to these techniques are described in Chapter 8; they can be used as an aid in coaching, mentoring and self-learning.

Different practitioners would have different approach orientations depending on their background, experience, perspectives and training. Broadly speaking, there are two types of technique. Techniques that emphasize outcome are task-focused or goal-oriented; the others emphasize psychological intervention and transpersonal quality. The two types are culturally bound. Western cultures tend to be goal-oriented, while Eastern cultures tend to adopt transpersonal approaches (e.g. gestalt psychology and storytelling). So, apart from the fact that the two criteria of being general and cross-cultural are met, specific techniques have been selected in the search for the appropriate approaches for inclusion. These techniques are designed to help you

- identify the sources of barriers along the coaching journey;
- build your own meta-model;
- combine multiple techniques and apply them in appropriate situations;
- structure a coaching conversation;
- conduct coaching in one-to-one as well as one-to-many group situations.

I shall structure these techniques according to the components of the integrative learning system (ILS) described in Chapter 6. These are:

- related to self: developing your self-awareness, emotion and cognition;
- social or related to the interaction between self and others: the social context in coaching or mentoring;

The Psychology of Coaching, Mentoring and Learning, Second Edition. Ho Law.
© 2013 John Wiley & Sons, Ltd. Published 2013 by John Wiley & Sons, Ltd.

- cultural: techniques that are sensitive to one's own and the others' culture;
- professional: techniques that are useful for continuous professional development (this component continues in the next chapter).

Let's look at these in turn.

Tools for Developing the System of the Self

In order to identify tools and techniques that can help coachees to develop the dimension related to their self, we need first to understand the structure of the self. Applying the systems approach as discussed in Chapter 6, we can expand the self, which is a component, and treat it as a system in its own right. Figure 7.1 provides a map for the self regarded as a system and its subsystems or components. These are:

- the head, which contains the five sensory receptors and the brain, where our thoughts and emotions are processed;
- the body, which is the seat of physical action and reaction (movements, behaviours and so on).

Perception, cognition, emotion and physical reactions are the four basic components that influence our behaviour in response to the environment. All these components (including behaviour and the environment) interact with and affect each other. Small changes in any one area can lead to changes in other areas. For example, thoughts and beliefs:

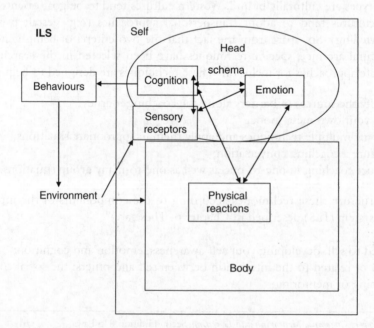

Figure 7.1   Head and body: five aspects of your life experience

- can help define the emotion we experience;
- can affect our physiological responses;
- can influence how we behave, what we choose to do and not to do, and the quality of our performance.

Environmental influences help determine the attitudes, beliefs, and thoughts that develop in childhood and often persist into adulthood. To overcome a challenge that the environment presents to us and to find a solution to a problem, one must first perceive the situation (which can be described as a group of stimuli) and then become aware of that perception and of the sensation associated with it. Thus self-awareness is the first step in any intervention in the world.

Tools for developing your self-awareness and for managing your emotion: gestalt approaches

Gestalt practitioners regard 'self-awareness' as a key to self-regulation and personal growth (Perls, 1969). There are many ways (gestalt techniques) in which, if one practices often, one can increase one's self-awareness (Perls, 1973). Active experimentation has that effect. Gestalt approaches provide some simple, yet powerful tools for the coaching process. This is evidenced by the fact that numerous articles on gestalt coaching have been published since this book's first edition (Gillie, 2009; Simon, 2009; Magerman and Leahy, 2009). In this section I shall describe some of the classical techniques, but first let's examine some background information about gestalt psychology.

Gestalt theory initially came from our understanding of how the brain operates, processes information and determines structural groupings. The idea was first put forward by Max Wertheimer in 1912 (Hergenhan and Olson, 1997). The need to categorize and organize our perceptual information – for example, in terms of proximity, similarity, closure, simplicity, or separation of the 'figure' from its 'ground' – is well known (Koffka, 1935). The focus of the theory is the idea of 'grouping': the characteristics of certain stimuli cause us to structure or interpret a visual field or problem in a particular way. The primary factors that determine grouping or its laws of organization are:

- proximity: elements tend to group together according to their nearness;
- similarity: items similar in some respect tend to group together;
- closure: items are grouped together if they tend to complete some entity;
- simplicity: items will be organized into simple figures according to symmetry, regularity, and smoothness.

However, there have been some recent developments that suggest that there are other ways in which we categorize, in addition to the laws of gestalt. It seems that, rather than having a central storage area in the brain, we have a gateway to storage, and thereafter memory, emotion and facts about an event, where circumstances may be stored. This means that we are less restricted by gestalt categories of structural representation than we first thought: there are more processes working to fill the gaps in our perception.

More recently a deeper structural view has been developed. This view involves changes in the functional meaning, the grouping and other characteristics of the items. Directed by what the structure of a situation requires for a crucial region of the brain to be activated, one is led to a reasonable prediction, which, like other parts of the structure, calls for verification, whether direct or indirect. Two directions are involved: getting a whole, consistent picture (top-down processing, driven by the internal cognition) and seeing what the structure of the whole requires for the parts (bottom-up processing, data-driven). In general, the theory offers some useful explanations about the interaction between individuals and the environment.

The humanistic–transpersonal revolution in psychology (for instance, the human potential movement) has provided gestalt psychology with a 'quantum leap' onto the platforms of philosophy and practice. Like with many other useful approaches in Western culture – such as cognitive behavioural therapy (CBT) and narrative approaches – its earlier applications were found in therapeutic settings, for instance those pioneered by Fritz Perls. However, Perls was also influenced by Zen Buddhism, which is a form of meditation that aims to achieve a state of mind characterized by purposelessness (*wu hsin*). In this state, one retains consciousness and at the same time lets go of it all. The practitioner watches the ebbs and flows of his or her consciousness without being carried away. Gestalt techniques resonate with meditation exercises that can be practised in everyday life. This creates an opportunity to make every waking moment an occasion for personal growth (see the gestalt exercises in Chapter 8). As a result, the gestalt approach is firmly grounded in its attitude and practice. This resonates with Eastern philosophy rather than with the familiar pair of theory and practice, which have been dominant in Western societies. In this sense, the gestalt approach is both transpersonal and cross-cultural. This combination makes it unique among many techniques, since it is built to a large extent on intuitive understanding rather than on theory.

The transpersonal aspect of gestalt approach

Unlike other transpersonal frameworks, which emphasize the collective unconscious, gestalt approaches focus on the primacy of awareness. For gestalt practitioners, awareness itself associates the transpersonal with the visionary realm. Awareness is transpersonal and spiritual; it awakes as a result of the transpersonal impinging on the personal beyond the 'spiritual state' (the environment). It is thus conceptually more accurate to describe gestalt techniques as 'transpersonal' rather than 'humanistic', as they are commonly known (Naranjo, 1993).

A gestalt approach has the following characteristics:

- an act of expression that stretches one's awareness;
- the presence of a witness, which enhances attention (in the narrative approach, it enhances resonance);
- the presence of interpersonal relationships: it should be at least a one-to-one interaction, which is what defines the coaching and mentoring processes (in this sense the coach and coachee are co-creating the present);
- organicity: like in a dance, coaches and coachees freely move their attention from one issue to another rather than according to a set of procedures or formulae (compare CBT approaches).

The gestalt approach is relevant in the twenty-first century not so much for its therapeutic application, but rather in coaching. In the previous chapters you have learnt that it is the personal relationship between coaches and coachees that is important in the coaching process.

Translating gestalt psychology into coaching can be summarized in the formula:

Gestalt coaching = (awareness + coaching support) coach–coachee relationship

The primacy of present-centred attitudes

Coaching is an interactive process. In this process, gestalt coaching can be defined as the transmission of experience from coaches to coachees. It is based on the assumption that experience can be passed on. This depends on an implicit attitude: the *Weltanschauung* (world-view) or philosophical posture of the coaches, who transmit the quality of the coaching experience to their coachees. This is communicated by means of a set of exercises, without any need to explain them. Thus gestalt psychologists talk about using oneself as an instrument. Coaches are like artists who transform through their art. In this context, the content of the transformation transcends the instruments (coaches) through other instruments (coachees), in a form of expression (in coaching, this usually takes a form of conversation, but in gestalt coaching it may take the form of mindfulness exercises). In other words, gestalt psychologists value action more than words and experience more than thought during the coach–coachee interaction: action speaks louder than words. Gestalt coaches also share some of the qualities of counsellors: for instance, they are non-judgemental. This entails the positive acceptance of a person: there are no good or bad people, only their behaviour, response or performance in the context of executive coaching.

Thus gestalt practitioners make the following distinctions:

- being versus knowledge;
- action versus utterance;
- experience versus understanding;
- effectiveness and acquisition.

However, in their practice, they attempt to blur the following boundaries:

- feeling versus thinking;
- intuition versus judgement;
- awareness versus morality;
- spontaneity versus intention.

All this is consistent with our learning wheel described in Chapter 3. Gestalt psychologists regard experience as their source. Attitude is formed through reflection and expressed in action/style. Experience is self-replicating. The ebbs and flows of experience ensure the continuous movement of the learning wheel.

Gestalt coaches regard themselves as 'naked' in the sense that they see their practice as an art form, which, like music, is communicated from heart to heart. The meaning

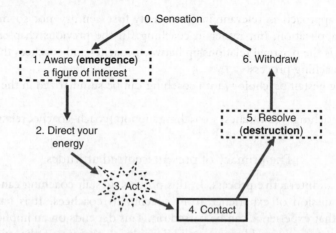

Figure 7.2   Gestalt cycle of continuous flow of experience: a complete cycle

of gestalt techniques is an artistic expression, an embodiment of a living understanding. Gestalt coaches are grounded in their living experience, from which they communicate their understanding through action.

Gestalt psychology gives primacy to the present. Both the coaches and the coachees practise living in the moment. All the issues are reflected in present-centredness. Gestalt practitioners regard 'present-centredness' as a technique. Framed within the coaching process, present-centredness is the goal itself.

The paradoxical theory of change

The paradox of change is central to gestalt thinking. Change occurs naturally, and one becomes what one is (Beisser, 1970). One therefore should not (and usually one cannot) resist the change that takes place naturally. According to gestalt theory, change is a continuous learning process. The gestalt approach to change is to focus on the here and now – on who or what you are now. Change occurs as a natural phenomenon. This is illustrated in Figure 7.2 and is known as the gestalt cycle of the continuous flow of experience (Melnick and Nevis, 2005).

According to the cycle, we become aware of our perception from our sensory input. A figure of interest emerges from the background within our consciousness. We direct our energy and effort to acting on the area of interest or concern – the point of contact. We concentrate our effort and attention on the contact point until we lose interest or the issue is resolved. Then we withdraw our effort and redirect our energy to the next area of interest, and so on, as the cycle repeats itself. (Can you see the similarities/differences between the gestalt cycle of continuous flow of experience and the learning wheel?)

To repeat, in the gestalt cycle of the continuous flow of experience, change happens naturally; however, it can only happen in the here and now. Paying attention to what is in the here and now (e.g. thought, emotions, behaviour; conflicts and contradictions within oneself and between people) helps us to find meaning and direction and to make choices. Change emerges and unfolds organically.

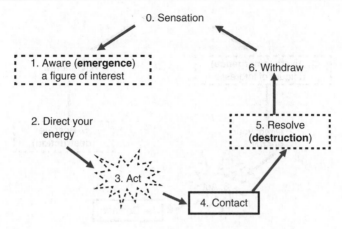

Figure 7.3 The nature of resistance: interruption at the awareness stage

The nature of resistance

When one attempts to resist change and tries to become what one is not, interruption or resistance occurs, which hinders development. Sometimes resistance is a form of defence mechanism, which appears when an interruption to the gestalt cycle of experience has already occurred. If there is an interruption, resistance to an emerging process, and destruction of figures of interest, one gets 'stuck' and cannot learn or change. For instance, in a state of emergence, in response to fear (e.g. of being hurt), one may get stuck in the area of interest and fail to direct one's energy so as to act accordingly. The classic example of the fear/freeze response occurs in life-threatening situations such as being caught in a fire. One may then experience resistance to contact or to the engagement with action (see Figure 7.3).

Sometimes resistance is healthy: for example, a child needs to resist the urge to have a tantrum, as this may incur the parents' disapproval. Short-term resistance may even be desirable, such as one's resistance to hunger until a meeting is concluded. However, prolonged interruption may cause a conditioned response whereby one fails to act appropriately: for example, one becomes reluctant to let go for fear of the withdrawal of love or support from another person. In cases of this sort the person gets stuck at the point of contact (Stage 4) and fails to allow the issue to resolve (see Figure 7.4).

Resistance or interruption causes concerns when it is unconscious and leaves unfinished business (a lack of equilibrium: an incomplete gestalt). This may restrict contact and growth in new situations. Negative experience may stand in the way of change and may create a blockage or interference (e.g. fear, lack of confidence, stress) due to cross-cultural experience. The gestalt techniques described next may be helpful in cross-cultural coaching.

Tackling resistance

Paradoxically, when the resistance or blockage happens during a coaching session, if the coach can help the coachee stay with it, this allows the coachee to experience the issue fully. The blockage will then dissolve naturally, after which the coachee can move forward. The role of the coach is to help coachees to focus on the here and now and see what they are doing that might be causing the psychological blockage.

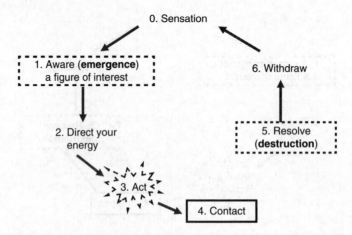

Figure 7.4   The nature of resistance: interruption at the point of contact

The gestalt coach advises coachees to stay with the 'resistance' until its nature is experienced, understood and accepted. Change can then take place. In the form of self-acceptance facilitated by coach, this leads to personal growth.

Gestalt techniques

In gestalt psychology there are a number of techniques and exercises intended to help practitioners develop a present-centred attitude and to ensure that the cycle of experience continues to flow. Techniques include:

- suppression;
- expression;
- integration.

The principle of these techniques is discussed in the next section; the practical exercises related to them are described in the next chapter.

Suppressive techniques
Suppressive techniques are based on the principle that, if one can stop blocking/resisting the nature of change, change will happen. In other words, suppressive techniques aim to undo what one has done wrong – to unlearn the bad habit.

The starting point of suppressive techniques is surprisingly simple: *do nothing – give yourself an experience of nothingness.*

Once we accept nothingness, everything is added unto us. Nothingness becomes a 'ground' (background) against which every 'figure' (foreground) freely emerges. It also provides a foundation for self-awareness and resilience to develop.

Expressive techniques
As the name suggests, expressive techniques are the opposite of suppressive techniques. While suppressive techniques aim to prevent coachees from doing something, expressive techniques attempt to encourage them to initiate or complete an action. In this sense, the coach acts as 'midwife', helping to bring the hidden voice into expression.

Furthermore, the gestalt coach invites coachees to maximize their expression. This can be achieved by providing prompts during the coaching session. For example:

- What do you experience now?
- Take an open posture (when the posture is closed).
- Breathe deeply (when breathing is shallow).
- Use the left hand to draw instead of using the right hand (or vice versa).

Expressions can be intensified through:

- simple repetition;
- exaggeration and development;
- explication and translation;
- identification and acting.

The effect of asking coachees to repeat an exercise or to exaggerate their behaviour, voice or movement is obvious. The practice of explication, translation, identification and acting can be quite complex, and we shall expand on them next.

Explication and translation
There is a big difference between 'thinking about' a certain behaviour and empathizing with it. Explication and translation techniques aim to help practitioners make an implicit expression explicit by translating non-verbal expression into words. For example:

- Give words to your action.
- If your tears could speak, what would they say?
- What would your left hand say to your right hand?
- Give a voice to your loneliness.
- If your business were a cereal, what would it be?
- Give your story (or the system) a name.

The process of explication leads to the desired end: interpretation. It is not the role of a coach to tell the coachee the meaning of his or her action. Coachees are guided to contact their message themselves.

Identification and acting
The techniques of identification and acting are based on the assumption that we can understand other people or things better by being them rather than by analysing them. In gestalt coaching, acting functions as a form of role play. The unique difference from the usual acting in this exercise is that the only 'actor' is the coachee her- or himself. Acting or taking on a different role forces one to experience oneself as another person. Coachees are encouraged to imagine themselves as possessing the attributes and actions of other beings in the here and now.

Having identified psychological barriers such as anxiety, guilt, shame or lack of confidence, CBT practitioners attempt to devise a strategy to overcome them. Gestalt coaches help coachees overcome these barriers through role play – which is like a rehearsal designed to overcome stage fright. Unlike psychoanalysis, the gestalt approach emphasizes recovery of awareness of the blockage, the feeling that one is doing it and the feeling of how one is doing it. Self-awareness, not introspected, can continue to exist after the role play. One of the functions of identification and acting is to undo retroflection (that is, the defensive substitution of self for environment): from being 'done to', one becomes a 'doer'.

Techniques of integration

An interesting twist of a gestalt coaching exercise occurs when coachees are asked to imagine themselves in the future. The future self is brought back to the here and now. Acting in this special case is a way of completing one's own (future) expression. In gestalt terms, the past, present and future are all 'sub-selves'. The exercise of acting in and acting out brings the coachees' 'sub-selves' into contact with each other by instructing them to play their parts and to have their characters talk to each another.

The actor identifies with the character being played. The 'present self' becomes one with the 'future self' that one is acting and recognizes the future attributes as present. The same role play can apply to any other characters. For example, in a three-chair exercise, the coach instructs the coachees by making the following suggestions:

- Image your future self sitting in the other chair [= empty: the 'hot seat'].
- When you move and sit in that chair, be her.
- When you are ready, move and sit in that chair.
- With some visualization exercise, the coachee moves to the other chair and sits down.
- Now you start speaking like her.
- Be your future voice.

The acting out of the two selves is known as an intrapersonal encounter. Coachees are encouraged to switch from one chair to the other to reinforce the reality of their identification with alternating sub-selves. These tend to have a dialectic quality, which develops between 'I should' and 'I want'. Perls calls these internal selves 'top dog' and 'underdog' respectively – the 'I should' critic versus the hopeless 'I want'. The 'top dog' may reflect the attitude of an influential adult or educator from the past – an attitude that one may not have come to terms with until the present.

The top dog/underdog dichotomy

The 'top dog' has the following characteristics. It is:

- authoritarian;
- bullying;
- persisting;
- primitive;
- righteous.

The top dog tells us:

- how we 'should be';
- how inadequate we are;
- to try harder to change.

The 'underdog' has the following characteristics:

- complies half-heartedly;
- feels guilty;
- finds excuses;
- passively resists;
- says 'yes, but…'

'Top dog' and 'underdog' are two clowns performing inefficiently and ineffectively on the stage of the 'tolerant and mute self'. The top dog–underdog dialogue is like an internal mediation service. One needs to invest oneself fully in each role, with all the uncomfortable feelings that go with it, before one can really hear the points put forward by the other. If one can overcome the 'top dog–underdog' conflict, integration can be achieved. The two selves come to their senses and listen to each other.

Dos and don'ts in gestalt coaching.
There are some dos and don'ts in the gestalt rules themselves. Dos:

- Do nothing – experience nothingness.
- Focus on the here and now.
- Focus on what is – on who or what you are now.
- Focus on your senses – smell, taste and so on.
- Focus on how something is experienced.
- Experience the real.
- Pay attention to the moment.
- Be aware of what is going on around yourself in the present and all the time.
- Redevelop the innate awareness of yourself and the environment.
- Be aware of the ebb and flow of your own awareness of various sensations.
- Stay with (or work with) any 'resistance'. ('Resistance' is regarded as healthy and positive.)
- Encourage the externalization of the internal debate.
- Open yourself up to your environment.
- Be receptive.
- Trust your own nature and intuition.
- Accept the positive experience as well as the negative (pain, imperfection and the like).
- Accept who you are – 'surrender to being'.
- Express yourself.
- Take responsibility for your actions, feelings and thinking.
- Insist on the rule of engagement.
- Initiate action.
- Maximize expression.
- Choose between doing nothing (emptiness) and doing something (expression).
- Be direct.

Don'ts:

- Don't focus on past or future.
- Don't deal with what is absent.
- Don't imagine.
- Don't question why it is.
- Don't preoccupy yourself with what it should be.
- Don't theorize about events.
- Don't 'try' to change.
- Don't lock into one of the clients' roles – for example, by supporting the 'trying' to change.
- Don't work with what should be, could be or must be.
- Don't work against 'resistance'. (The more force one applies in order to resist, the harder the resistance becomes. Going with the flow may create new mindsets, e.g. it could take account of everyone's needs.)
- Don't manipulate (e.g. explain, judge, justify).
- Don't talk 'about…'
- Don't emphasize 'should'.

Managing yourself, your cognition and emotion: cognitive behavioural therapy (CBT)

According to the Special Group in Coaching Psychology (SGCP) 2004 survey, carried out by Palmer and Whybrow (2004), cognitive and behavioural techniques constitute the most common approach adopted by coaching psychologists – with a majority well over 60 per cent. While neuro-linguistic programming (NLP) has gained popularity in life coaching, it is the least used technique among professional psychologists. The theoretical underpinnings and techniques of NLP will not be covered here, as they are covered elsewhere and in the companion *Practitioner's Manual* (Law, 2013).

CBT was developed by Aaron Temkin Beck, a psychiatrist working in the United States in the 1960s and 1970s (for examples of its clinical application, see Beck, Rush, Shaw and Emery, 1979). The link established in CBT between emotion, cognition and behavioural intervention (whence the name of this technique) is based on Beck's observation that individuals preoccupied with their emotional thoughts tend to talk to themselves – they have an 'internal dialogue'. They may not be aware of the origin of their thoughts, but they usually find them disturbing, as these thoughts pop up in their mind without any conscious control (Beck and his team called this phenomenon 'automatic thought'). If individuals can become more aware of their emotions – say, by reporting them to a counsellor or psychologist, or by writing them down in diary form – they can overcome them by working out strategies, usually developed in collaboration with their counsellor or psychologist. Greenberger and Padesky (1995) call this process 'mind over mood' (which is different from 'mind over matter').

CBT belongs to the facilitative style of coaching in that coaches do not provide coachees with direct solutions to their problems. It is also congruent with the psychology of learning approaches advocated in this book. Here too, coaching is regarded as a 'collaborative process' that corresponds, in CBT terminology, to the so-called 'guided recovery'. Coaches build scaffolding to guide and support coachees to rediscover their signature strengths or to devise a strategy for the future – for example, in the form of a narrative theme or CBT structure.

In common with many coaching techniques, CBT is goal-driven and solution-focused; it emphasizes the present and future. A typical CBT programme is limited in time, which partly explains its popularity with the National Health Service (NHS). More importantly, its explicit nature makes its outcome amenable to evidence-based evaluation (see Chapter 10), which is recommended as good practice in both the public and the private sectors in the Western world. CBT is regarded by the National Institute for Health and Clinical Excellence (NICE) as the treatment of choice, and it is probably one of the best treatments available (Chambless, 1988: 12; Rothbaum, Mesdows, Resick and Foy, 2000). Thus it has become the most popular technique and is widely practised in the NHS. CBT is consistent both with the philosophy of Socrates and with modern positive psychology. In this section it is presented as one of the coaching techniques that are relevant for managing cognition and emotion.

Although CBT offers evidence-based enquiry and economic constraint, its use in coaching and mentoring is relatively new. Cognitive behavioural coaching enables clients to identify and subsequently modify the cognitive, behavioural and emotive blocks that impede the execution of their goal-directed activities (Neenan and Palmer, 2001; Law, 2003).

CBT is based on the assumption that cognition has the power to influence one's emotion and behaviour – 'mind over matter'. Although, like many coaching interventions, CBT focuses on the future, it does take past experience as its starting point and uses the present as an opportunity for planning to change. It consists of three parts, each one dealing with a temporal dimension:

1 the part concerned with the past reviews past achievements, experience and values;
2 the part concerned with the present assesses current thinking and feeling and mobilize the cognitive capacity and resources to plan for change;
3 the part concerned with the future works towards the future.

There are seven steps in applying CBT in coaching. These are:

1 setting a goal;
2 assessing the value of the goal;
3 setting SMARTER objectives;
4 assessing the emotion of coachees;
5 identifying possible barriers or problems;
6 developing strategies to overcome barriers or problems;
7 reviewing progress.

Step 1: setting a goal
This step is consistent with the coaching process. Usually setting the goal takes place in the first session, when coaches and coachees meet. To identify the coachees' goal, the coach attempts to establish the coachees' aspirations, hopes and dreams. The goal should be ambitious, inspirational and for the long term, and it should have a sense of purpose whether it relates to life or to career. In executive coaching, the goal may be related to organizational objectives or to the coachees' personal performance. In life

coaching, the goal may be one's sense of purpose, work–life balance or personal relationships. There should be considerable overlap between personal and organizational goals, executive and life coaching. If not, coaches should draw the coachees' attention to the tension that may arise as a result of the gap between personal fulfilment and the work performance demanded by employers. In such cases some intervention may be required to achieve a work–life realignment through programmes of change.

Step 2: assessing the value of the goal
Coachees are asked to rate the attractiveness of the goal on a scale of 1 to 10. This resembles project appraisal in an organizational context. However, the rating is based on the coachees' perception and subjective judgement. In executive coaching, the line manager may also be asked to provide a rating. The values of the coaches may need to be negotiated with the coachees and their line managers.

Step 3: seting SMARTER objectives
Coaches will help coachees to formulate a set of SMARTER objectives from the goal. Objectives should be:

- *Specific* Coaches should describe specifically what is to be achieved.
- *Measurable* Coaches should describe how one could measure the output and successful outcomes when the obejctive has been achieved.
- *Agreed* The objectives should be agreed upon by all the stakeholders. The obvious ones are the coachees and the coaches. In executive coaching, stakehoders may include the line manager of the coachees. In life coaching, the coachees may like to discuss these objectives with their family. Coachees and coaches may discuss them with their supervisors.
- *Realistic* The objectives need to be realsitic: in other words, achievable. This is important, as coachees may feel frustrated if they fail to achieve the agreed objectives. Failure may result in coachees giving up their programme prematurely.
- *Time-bound* It is important for coaches and coachees to agree on a deadline by which the latter would acheive the set target. Coaches also need to ask coachees to agree on a starting date: the period of work towards achieving the set objectives should be well defined.
- *Evaluate and review* At the end of the implementation period, coaches and coachees should evaluate how successfully the obejctives have been achieved and what impact the action has had. They should also hold a meeting to review progress and possibly to set future plans.

Step 4: assessing the emotion of coachees
Coaches would then ask coachees to rate their degree of confidence in achieving the agreed objectives; again, the rating should be on a scale of 1 to 10. This is the equivalent of a feasibility study of a task, but it's done from a psychological perspective.

Step 5: identifying possible barriers or problems
Coaches should encourage coachees to look to the future and identify any possible barriers, problems and risks that might prevent them from achieving their objectives. To do this, coaches need to describe potential problems before the coachees encounter them. Some of the barriers may be psychological – for example, lack of self-esteem or

Table 7.1 Action plan adopted from cognitive behavioural techniques

Objective	Start time	When by	Possible problems	Strategies to overcome barriers or problems	Progress
Recall your main or primary goal – make it SMARTER Purpose Value Rate attractiveness of goal 1–10 scale Rate confidence of success 1–10 scale			Describe the problem, e.g. performance-interfering thinking (PIT)	Describe solution, e.g. performance-enhancing thinking (PET)	Describe output Describe outcome Rate progress 1–10 scale Rate confidence of success 1–10 scale

confidence to do the job. Neenan and Palmer (2001) refer to cognitive barriers as performance-interfering thinking (PIT).

Step 6: developing strategies to overcome barriers or problems
Having identified barriers or problems, coachees should be encouraged to think about possible solutions. Coaches may work with them to devise an action plan or strategies to overcome certain problems or to reduce certain risks. The coach can help the coachee to develop performance-enhancing thinking (PET) instead of PIT (Neenan and Palmer, 2001).

Step 7: reviewing progress
Coaches should have regular review meetings with their coachees, to ensure that they are on target. Coachees should describe the outputs and the outcome of the action plan. They should ask coaches to rate their progress on confidence or cognitive scales (as described in Step 1) on a regular basis.

The seven steps are summarized in Table 7.1.

CBT is similar to a personal development plan in the workplace. This makes it an ideal candidate for adoption in organizations. The major difference between CBT and a personal development plan is that the former focuses on emotions – such as coachees' perception of their competence and confidence. Coachees need to rate their mood on a 1 to 10 scale. Coachees working in a technical environment may prefer to use a 1–100% scale. This is fine, provided that the scales are used consistently throughout the coaching or mentoring programme. Another important feature of CBT is that coachees need to identify possible barriers and how to overcome them. If coachees are prepared for the challenge, they are more likely to succeed.

CBT can also be used to increase the coachees' aspirations. To achieve this, coachees are usually guided by a coach to set a goal – for example, a coachee may wish to increase his or her self-confidence. In a self-esteem building session, the coachee is encouraged to think about how someone with high self-esteem behaves and achieves results, and to set as a goal being this type of person. One of my coachees described her experience of this process as 'capturing the moment of aspiration', and it opened up an opportunity to take positive action.

Practical experience suggests that, for some people, CBT works better with mindfulness exercises embedded as part of the process – that is, by using the gestalt approach suggested earlier. The mindfulness exercises serve as a vehicle to heighten the coachees' awareness of their own self-limited belief and thereby to identify novel solutions to overcoming barriers.

Techniques that Are Sensitive to the Self and the Others' Culture: Narrative Approaches

Narrative therapy has been systematically developed by Michael White at the Dulwich Centre (White, 1995a, 1995b, 2006). Following a similar historical–cultural trend, the narrative approach has been applied in therapeutic practice and advocated by White as narrative therapy (White, 1995a, 1997, 2000, 2006, 2007). Its clinical application has been widespread, like that of CBT; this is especially true of its principle of respecting people's stories as a route to recovery from psychotic episodes (Hartley, Whomsley and Clarke, 2006). However, narrative therapy was originally grounded in cultural anthropology (Turner and Brunner, 1986) – in particular in the work of Myerhoff (1980, 1982, 1986) and in the psychology of learning (Vygotsky's proximal development), which are concerned with non-clinical populations with specific sensitivity to cross-cultural issues. I feel that it is appropriate to relocate narrative applications within the mainstream area of coaching.

In Chapter 3 you learnt about constructive–developmental theories and how they link developmental growth to the construction of meaning. In particular, Vygotsky's idea of proximal development was outlined as a possible candidate for scaffolding the coaching practice. This section expands on that concept and shows how it fits into narrative coaching.

Applying Vygotsky's levels of learning (or distancing tasks) to coaching practice, we devise the following steps:

1   description: encourage coachees to characterize specific objects/events of their world (characterization of initiative);
2   relation and initiative in relationship: develop chains of association by establishing relations between these objects and events (analyses/pattern matching);
3   evaluation: reflect, draw upon your realization and learning about specific phenomena from the chains of association;
4   justification: judge above the level of evaluating; abstract your realization and learning from their concrete and specific circumstances, to form concepts about life and identity;
5   conclusion/recommendation: formulate the planning for and the initiation of actions; predict the outcome of specific actions that are founded upon this concept development.

According to Michael White (2006), the narrative approach is based on the following assumptions:

1   Meaning shapes our lives. (See Chapter 3 for a detailed theoretical discussion of this principle.)
2   Life is multi-storied; it is not one single story. However, some stories become more prominent in a coachee's life while other stories may be neglected, which might be important for that person's development,
3   The primary meaning-making frame is the storylines. Narrative practitioners regard the storyline given by the storyteller as a primary meaning-making frame, which enables her or him to construe meaning from it. In turn, this primary meaning derived from the storyline gives meaning that shapes our lives (as stated here at point 1).
4   Individuals and communities have strengths, knowledge and skills that we come in contact with, although these features may not be noticeable to the individuals and communities possessing them.

Following on from the last point, the forgotten/hidden strengths that individuals have may appear as thin traces in their stories. The role of the coaches (and mentors) is therefore to develop these strengths, skills and knowledge. Their task is therefore to locate the significant moments in their clients' life journeys and to help them take stock of their living experience, which they tended to neglect up until now (this is why it left only thin traces). Viewed from the narrative perspective, coaches and mentors can be regarded as 'meaning-makers'.

Narrative approaches in coaching and mentoring enable clients to become aware that they have more knowledge and skills to cope with the situation than they previously realized. Through the coach–coachee engagement, the coachees redevelop, from the story they have told, an account of what they give value to in their lives. This account may embody concepts about their life and identity, hopes and dreams, and so on. The new story, developed through narrative practice, provides a foundation from which they can proceed. The coaching task is to contribute to the scaffolding of the proximal zone of development. According to White (2006, 2007), the structure of scaffolding the proximal zone of development can be designed by mapping it onto the distancing tasks (which White called 'landscape of action' and the 'landscape of conscious' respectively). In developing this scaffold, one takes a conceptual journey, travelling through the 'landscape of action' and the 'landscape of identity' (which links to one's consciousness via effective questioning) to help coachees develop the stories of their lives and personal identity. As Michael White used to say to me during his teaching, 'it is through scaffolding questions that these alternative landscapes of the mind are richly described'.

The landscape of action

Landscapes of action are composed of events described by the storyteller. These events are likely to be interwoven or linked in sequence through time, which makes an auto-biographical/historical journey out of the storyteller's life. Like in any story, the sequence of events told by coachees is likely to develop a theme or a plot that reflects their coping strategy, success or failure. In other words, the landscape of action consists of the following elements:

- time line: the time of the events in terms of recent, distant or remote history;
- events: a number of singular events;
- circumstance: the circumstances under which each event takes place;
- sequence: the interrelating of events into clusters or sequences;
- plot/theme: the consequences of events (for instance, strategy, success, loss or failure).

Looking at the landscape of action through the lens of a Johari window (Figure 6.6), the stories that coachees choose to disclose during the coaching session represent what is known and familiar to them about themselves; but some of the themes could remain hidden from the coach (quadrants I and III).

The landscape of consciousness

Landscapes of consciousness are composed of the storytellers' identities, conclusions about their actions, and events that are shaped by their identity and contemporary culture. The landscape of consciousness represents the understanding that the listener has gained from the story. These understandings may be intentional or internal:

- intentional understandings: value, purpose, aspiration, personal agency and restoration;
- internal understandings: realizations (self-awareness) and learning.

In a Johari window, the landscape of consciousness may highlight a storyteller's blind spots, which usually appear as thin traces in the plot, and which the coach needs to understand and develop further. I shall describe how this can be tackled through the narrative process.

Broadly speaking, the narrative process can be divided into two parts:

1   externalizing conversation;
2   re-authoring.

However, strictly speaking, one could regard re-authoring as a form of externalization.

Externalizing conversation

Part 1 – externalizing conversation – consists of two stages: description and relation mapping. Part 2 – re-authoring – consists of three stages: evaluation/re-evaluation, justification and conclusion/recommendation. I shall describe all these stages in greater detail next.

STAGE 1: DESCRIPTION

The coach invites the coachee to tell a story about life or work (depending on the topic of the session, which could be business or work issues, relationships, work–life balance, and so on). Note that the story may have many themes or plots (Elsbree, 1982), and these may be dialectic in nature. How the story is told is as important as what it contains. The themes could be intertwined, isolated, frozen, incomplete, unspoken or evolving (Roberts, 1994). Listening to the coachee's story, the coach tries to identify the key themes and plots indicating any 'internalized problem' that might have affected the coachee's sense of self and identity. For instance a 'frozen' theme may have become a dominant plot in the story and may be rigid and difficult to change. The known and familiar themes may be repeatedly told. Such elements present the coach with the challenge of re-authoring (to be discussed later). The coach encourages the coachee to externalize the problem – for example, by giving it a name.

STAGE 2: RELATION MAPPING

In the coachee's story, the coach attempts to identify the aspirations, values, hopes and dreams that give the coachee a sense of purpose more consistent with his or her desirable self-identity. However, the evidence for all these elements that appeared in the story as told might very often be in thin traces. This is because life experience is richer than discourse. Although the narrative provides one with structures and meaning to describe one's experience, there are always 'feeling and lived experiences' that 'are not fully encompassed by the dominant story' (Brunner, 1986: 143). Borrowing from the anthropological theories of Brunner (1986) and Geertz (1973), Michael White (1997) spoke about a 'thin description', in contrast to the foreground dominant storyline – the 'thick description'. The coach needs to identify any unique outcomes that might have been neglected by the coachee, because these neglected events may help them both to co-construct the alternative storylines. The coachee may give many examples of failure to support his or her predominantly negative storyline – his or her negative thick description. The coach may ask the coachee to think about any exceptions that may constitute a successful outcome – a counterplot – in his or her own experience. This counterplot provides 'a point of entry' (rite of passage) to the alternative storyline, which may prompt the coachee to see new possibilities. The coach helps the coachee to create a map for the zone between the latter's positive self-identity and the negative description of his or her actions, as the sequence of events unfolds – in other words, the zone between the thin and the thick descriptions. This would enable the coachee to identify the 'learning gap' or – to use Vygotsky's term – the 'zone of proximal development' that the two need to bridge.

The dynamics of the externalizing conversation can be illustrated in Figure 7.5, where Michael White described narrative development as the mapping of the landscape of action upon the landscape of consciousness.

Re-authoring

Like everything else in coaching, re-authoring is future-oriented or focused on the future. In this process the coachee's story is regarded as a 'script', and the coachee as the 'author'. In this capacity, coachees should have the power and freedom to re-author the story of their own lives. Here one can regard re-authoring as another form of externalization, whereby the coachees are taking an external(ized) position in order to look at their own 'life story' as an author. Here I shall describe the narrative approach as a general process and integrate the re-authoring technique within the practice of externalizing conversation.

As described in the previous section, re-authoring, as part of externalizing conversation/narrative practice, is a co-construction or co-authorship between the

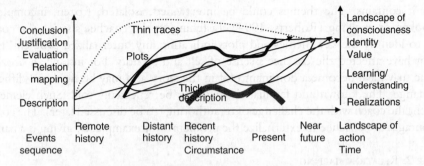

Figure 7.5   Development of storylines illustrating thin and thick descriptions

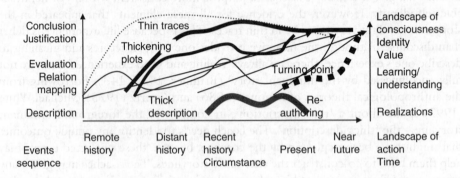

Figure 7.6   Revisiting the development of storylines, which shows many possibilities

coachee and the coach, the two working in equal partnership, whereby an alternative story emerges. This new story is filled with possibilities, unlike the 'problem-full' old story (Bor and Legg, 2003). Here the role of the coach is to facilitate the conversation. This facilitation privileges certain alternative accounts of the coachee's lived experience, which are judged to be more desirable (e.g. more positive: for further references, see also Gale, 1992; Gale and Newfield, 1992; Kogan, 1998; and Kogan and Gale, 1997).

In re-authoring, the narrative discourse of the coachee's beliefs and values is regarded as a 'restraint' when a particular storyline has been chosen 'instead of' many possible alternatives. This concept of 'restraint', with its use of 'instead of' rather than 'because of', is fundamental to re-authoring (see Figure 7.6; see also Bateson, 1972: 399; Bor and Legg, 2003: 270). So the re-authoring process consists of the following stages.

STAGE 3: EVALUATION/RE-EVALUATION
To bridge the learning gaps that have been identified at Stage 2, the coach continues to focus on those thin storylines that could strengthen the coachees' sense of identity, try-ing to gather more evidence to support the alternative storyline or thicken the plot. This stage provides 'scaffolding' to bridge the coachees' learning gaps by recruiting their lived experience. The coach asks coachees to re-evaluate the impact of their actions upon their own sense of self-identity, values and beliefs, to stretch their imagination and to exercise their meaning-making resources. The coach also encourages coachees to map their aspirations, values and self-identity upon their actions in terms of new future possibilities on the life's horizon. This stage is very often referred to as 'the turning

point' where a coachee begins to change: he or she moves from reiterating the old storyline to start discovering new possibilities and actions.

STAGE 4: JUSTIFICATION

The coach makes the plot thicken still further and consolidates coachees' commitment to change. The aim of the narrative approach is to develop a 'thick description' of an alternative storyline 'that is inscribed with [...] meanings' and finds linkages between 'the stories of people's lives and their cherished values, beliefs, purposes, desires, commitments, and so on' (White, 1997: 15–16). At this stage, coachees are asked to justify this evaluation of the alternative storyline in terms of their aspirations, beliefs, values, self-identity and strengths.

STAGE 5: CONCLUSION AND RECOMMENDATION

The coach guides coachees towards drawing conclusions by making value statements about their self-identity; these statements are based on their beliefs, values, hopes, and dreams. The coach may ask the coachees to write down these statements: put them simply on a piece of paper or cast them in the form of a letter or some other device. Finally, the coach invites coachees to make a commitment to action by putting together an action plan for change and for the achievement of their hopes and dreams (the 'bridging tasks').

Remembering conversations

When the externalizing conversation involves significant people in the story (for example, important family members, or friends who have made a significant impact upon the coachee's life), the coach may use these figures as a vehicle to leverage the re-authoring process. This specific form of narrative technique is called 'remembering'. Conversations of 'remembering' (or 'remembering conversations') are not about a fragmentary and passive recollection of people that one has met. The figures to be remembered and retold in a story are significant others from one's history or from one's present life. Using 'remembering' as a metaphor from the work of Myerhoff (1980, 1986), White (2006) describes remembering conversations as conversations that:

- evoke 'life' as a 'membered' club, 'identity' as an 'association' of life;
- contribute to a multi-voiced sense of identity, rather than the single-voiced sense of identity, which is a feature of the encapsulated self that is the vogue of contemporary Western culture;
- open possibilities for the revision of one's membership of life: for the upgrading of some memberships and the downgrading of others; for the honouring of some memberships and for the revoking of others; for the granting of authority to some voices in regard to matters of one's personal identity, and for the disqualification of other voices in regard to this matter;
- describe rich accounts of preferred identity and knowledge of life and skills of living that have been co-generated in the significant memberships of people's lives.

In reviewing memberships, the coach can further explore the accounts of the storyteller's own identities, knowledge and skills. From the rich description, many significant outcomes, conclusions, learning and problem-solving practices may be discovered. They can make a significant contribution to the storyteller's sense of identity, knowledge and skills. This awareness provides a foundation for the coachee's personal development. As a result, it enables coaches and coachees to draw up specific proposals about how they might go forward.

Outsider witness retelling

Externalized conversations can also be applied in group or team situations, where one or more members are asked to act as a witness to the story. Participants are offered the option of telling the story of their life before an audience. The selected outsider witnesses can also act as assistants to the narrative coach, as they can provide extra support for the coachees, beyond the tradition of acknowledgement. After they have listened to the story, the outsider witnesses are asked to retell it. In particular, they are guided by the coach's questions to those aspects of the story that resonate with their own experience. The retellings by outsider witnesses do not necessarily constitute a complete account of the original story, but they focus on aspects that have most significantly engaged their imagination.

The outsider witnesses respond to the stories by retelling certain aspects of what they heard. Depending on the culture of the place where the outsider witness retellings take place, these activities may be shaped by certain traditions of acknowledgement. According to White (1995a, 1997, 2000, 2006), there are four categories of reflective responses from outsider witnesses. Narrative practitioners can ask or guide the outsider witnesses to:

- identify the expression of the storyteller;
- describe the image that the story has evoked;
- demonstrate the embodiment of their responses to the coachee's story by articulating their understanding of the meaning that story and how it resonates with their own life experiences;
- acknowledge any 'transport' of knowledge from the story to their own life by thanking the coachee for sharing his or her story.

One may argue that, even in a one-to-one coaching conversation, the coach acts as a first outsider witness by listening to the coachee's story – which is a form of acknowledgement.

Definitional ceremony (community): retellings of retellings

The practice of outsider witness retellings can be expanded to a larger group, organization or community. A large group can be subdivided into smaller ones. The process of retelling the coachee's story in a definitional ceremony is reiterative and sequential. It is multi-layered and has the following structures or steps:

1 storytelling, undertaken by the coachee (storyteller), who is at the centre of the ceremony;
2 retellings of the story (first retelling), undertaken by outsider witnesses;

3 retellings of retellings (second retelling), undertaken by the coachee (initial storyteller);
4 retellings of retellings of retellings (third retelling), undertaken by outsider witnesses of the initial group to the secondary one, and so on.

Within the context of narrative practice (and within the broader context of poststructuralism), a person's self-identity is not governed by private and individual achievement but by the following forces – which are social, historical and cultural:

- one's own history;
- one's own sense of authenticity;
- public and social achievements;
- acknowledgement of one's preferred claims about one's own identity.

Theoretically speaking, the process of retelling could continue indefinitely. In practice, the layers of retelling depend on physical and temporal constraints.

The definitional ceremony is the 'moving' of all the participants, and therefore it is ideal for group or community work in conference-style or community gatherings. It provides an opportunity for storytellers to become who they want to be rather than who they were in the past. Metaphorically speaking, both the storyteller and the participants are 'being moved' (they are in an emotional state) and 'transported' from one place to another in their life as a direct consequence of participating in the ceremony.

From this we can see that the definitional ceremony is a powerful way to confer social acknowledgement upon the storyteller's self-identity, which may have been previously denied as a result of his or her social condition, especially at the intersection of cross-cultural factors. In narrative terms, a definitional ceremony thickens many alternative themes or counterplots and amplifies the empowerment the storytellers received, which would not be available to them otherwise.

The narrative coach's attitude and posture

In response to specific developments in coachees' stories, it can be very tempting for coaches to construe a unique positive outcome prematurely. Coaches should guard themselves against committing the error of 'false positive' identification (type 1 error) by observing the following rules. Do:

- Let coachees discover the unique positive outcome by themselves.

Don'ts:

- Convince coachees that they could take more notice of certain developments.
- Point out the consequences or potential implications of, or possibilities associated with, the developments of certain storylines.
- Take a strongly positive position on these consequences, implications, and possibilities – you yourself, as a coach.
- Justify your position on the recommendations you make by voicing a range of positive conclusions about the coachees' lives and identities.

Table 7.2   Narrative coaching attitude (adopted from Michael White's 2006 therapeutic posture)

Attitude/effect	De-centred	Centred
Influential	De-centred and influential (potentially invigorating coach/coachee)	Centred and influential (potentially burdening coach)
Non-influential	De-centred and non-influential (potentially invalidating coach)	Centred and non-influential (potentially exhausting coach)

White advocates maintaining a 'de-centred posture' for narrative practitioners; this can contribute to the scaffolding of externalizing conversations. We can transport this posture to the training of the coach's attitude, which may give coaches the opportunity to attribute significance to various personal developments that might otherwise be neglected in their stories (see Table 7.2).

Coaches in narrative practice should adopt a 'de-centred and influential' posture when they are in conversation with coachees (the top-left quadrant in Table 7.2). The notion of 'de-centred' does not refer to the intensity of the coach–coachee engagement, but to the coachees' achievement of according priority to their personal stories and to their knowledge and skills. By taking a de-centred but influential stand, coaches allow coachees to have a 'primary authorship' status with regard to the stories of their lives. The knowledge and skills that have been generated in the course of retelling the history of the coachees' lives are the principal considerations in narrative coaching.

Coaches are influential, but not in the sense that they impose their own agenda. Their role in this process is to build a scaffold by means of questions and reflections. This makes it possible for coachees to construe their own problematic stories as well as to discover solutions. The aim of narrative coaching is to help coachees to:

- describe the alternative stories of their lives (hopefully more richly);
- explore some of the neglected areas of their lives by following up and developing some of the thin traces in their storylines;
- become more significantly acquainted with their own knowledge and skills, as reflected throughout their lives, as well as with their aspirations, hopes and dreams. All these will be relevant to addressing their past or present concerns, predicaments and problems.

Putting It All Together: Developing Your Own Authentic Coaching Process

In this chapter you have been introduced a range of approaches. Each has its own school of thought and different attitudes and styles that it expects from coaches and mentors. If you are a coach or a mentor with a specific orientation, you may be familiar with some of the techniques described here, such as CBT or gestalt psychology; others may find the techniques to be entirely new and overwhelming in their diversity. This section aims to bring readers from the unknown to the known and on familiar territory, while at the same time gathering together all the different strands.

The GROW model revisited

The GROW model is one of the best-known and most practised models in the coaching industry. Although the GROW model was made popular by Sir John Whitmore through the publication of his book *Coaching for Performance* (which is regarded by many coaches as a core text), the psychological theories and principles that underpin it are relatively elementary. For example, Maslow's model of a hierarchy of needs is well known among undergraduate psychology students, though its application to coaching may be new to many business coaches (Whitmore, 2002). Nevertheless, the GROW model provides a useful description of the different stages of the process. It helps you and your coachees to clarify the expected outcomes (e.g. improved performance in relation to the coachees' GOAL, or specific behaviour change according to an action plan in the WILL stage). GROW is a useful tool for structuring a coaching session. It offers a framework for discussing and exploring goals, reality (the current situation), options, and the way forward or willingness. The natural starting point is the goal; however, the goal is not always clear until later in the session, so it may need revisiting. Although the structure seems linear, the process is a reiterative or circular one, such that the goal set can be reviewed in future sessions. After discussing the way forward it may be necessary to revisit the options or realign the goal.

I hope that, by reading this book, you are learning and developing further the rich and diverse psychological principles that are relevant to your practice. So a key question is: 'How do different techniques fit into the GROW model in your own practice?'

For example, one could map the major coaching approaches onto a time line with the present – the here and now – as the pivot (Figure 7.7). The learning wheel of transformation turns on the pivot in the centre of the timeline. Here I have loosely indicated different approaches that may associate with each stage of the GROW model, as follows:

1   Topic: Initial understanding (psychodynamic → gestalt)
2   Goal: What do you want? (CBT)
3   Reality: What happens now? (gestalt)
4   Options: What could you do? (gestalt → CBT)
5   Will: What will you do? (CBT)

An exercise for the reader: Where would you locate the narrative approach on the map?
   I shall expand on how the mapping may be implemented at each stage.

Goal setting

The primary objective of this model is goal setting. Coachees should set a long-term goal, a short-term goal, a goal for the session, a goal for their issues, and so on. For instance, coaches may ask: 'What would you like to get out of this coaching session?'

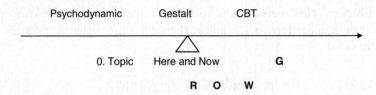

Figure 7.7   Mapping different coaching techniques along the time line

The goal should be optimal and challenging. Coaches also need to facilitate the process by which coachees take ownership of the goal by asking: 'Whose goal is this?' One may like to break down the goal into a set of manageable SMARTER objectives. Initially, as part of the CBT scheme, the coach may like to check a coachee's emotion and cognition in relation to those objectives.

In practice, some coachees may find that it is not that easy to identify the goals without setting the context (topic) or reviewing the current situation (Megginson and Clutterbuck, 1995). Hence the GROW model may sometimes be referred to as TGROW. One needs to be guided by the aspirations, knowledge and skills that are brought to the interaction by the coachees. Here the externalizing conversation may be useful in that it enables coach and coachee alike to understand the narrative that underpins those hopes and aspirations.

Reality
The goal needs to be realistic and objective so that coachees do not suffer from early failure as a result of unrealistic expectations. Coaches need to get feedback from coachees about their performance: 'What worked? What didn't?'

For example, during a session, a coach may set out a CBT framework for a coachee and find she or he is stuck in a past worry and cannot move forward. In this case, the coach may apply a gestalt mindfulness exercise within the CBT session, to bring the coachee back to the here and now and to focus on the solution in the present.

Options
The coaching task involves guiding the coachees towards writing an action plan and making a list of specific tasks designed to help them to achieve their goal. Generating a list of options enables coachees to maximize their choices. To avoid negative assumptions and an undesired limitation of possible options, the exercise should be non-critical and non-judgemental. Questions include: 'What options would help you move towards your goal?' A useful question at the end of the session is: 'Can you come up with one more option?' After a list of options has been compiled, coaches and coachees work together to sort them according to priority and feasability. In CBT terms, coaches may sometime need to help the coachees to identify the problems associated with the options, which very often are emotionally charged. The coachees need to work through their thinking patterns (PITs and PETs) and develop possible strategies to overcome these problems. Coaches may ask: 'What barriers might you encounter? What will you do about them? Who will be able to help you overcome those barriers?'

Will
As a typical coaching practice, the GROW model is future-oriented. At the end of the session, coaches may ask coachees: 'What will you do now?' A list of questions may

include: 'What is the action plan?' 'How will this action meet your goal?' 'When by?' In conclusion, the narrative coach may ask how the action plan resonates with the coachee's sense of identity, values, beliefs, hopes and aspirations and may invite the coachee to indicate the commitment required to take the plan forward.

I hope that learners, coaches or mentors who are reading this book will find the map a useful pointer towards the application of different techniques in different contexts. In practice, one needs to be flexible about ordering the stages of the process – ready to move to and fro between them, as needs be.

Coaching off-piste

In the first edition, Sarah Ireland emphasized that, as coaches and mentors, we need to enhance our focused exploration of the multiple contexts of experience and optimize the scope for creativity and learning at the intersection between boundaries. She suggested including 'coaching off-piste' as an example of coaching and mentoring beyond boundaries that readers may find useful. This idea is fully dealt with here, as part of putting together a concept of coaching off-piste. Where appropriate, I have added further questions, comments, information and references. I hope you too will find it useful in developing your own coaching process.

Coaching off-piste can be described as meaning:

- creating momentum and change, a passion for learning that goes beyond goals and targets;
- establishing an evolving purpose and sense of the longer journey, where conscious and unconscious strands of life can be considered in new ways;
- involving new explorations, new means and new collaborations.

In the universal integrative framework / integrative learning system (UIF/ILS), the simple ability to use our existing set of skills with a different emphasis goes a long way. We have addressed these areas for emphasis at the exploration stage as questions. You can encourage people to use pictures, tell stories or use challenges in order to extend their thinking.

The UIF (ILS) can help you to develop in the following areas:

- cultural agility/individual differences among universal concepts;
- bridging the collective and individual purpose;
- learning to live with temporary states and with delay in gratification (emotional intelligence);
- beyond goals;
- beyond language to meaning;
- life stages/universality in the system and framework;
- prophecy and spirituality for creativity (transpersonal).

We provide below some questions as tools for each area.

Developing cultural agility
On the concept of time, different contexts gauge time and timeliness differently. Questions include:

- How does time work for you?
- What does it mean?
- What does it mean in this context?
- How much value do you put on time?
- How much value do others put on time?
- How does business work generally?
- What specific elements are important to you? What are the differences in this setting?
- How do you know?

The above questions resonate with Rosinski's (2003) cultural orientations framework and time management approaches. Depending on the individual culture, time may be perceived as a 'scarce' resource or as a 'plentiful' one. Individuals manage it differently. One may concentrate on one activity and/or relationship at a time, or be monochronic; another may concentrate simultaneously on several tasks and relationships, or be polychronic.

From the perspective of ILS, questions can be used in a funnelled and probing approach, moving across personal, social and cultural domains. For example, from your personal perspective:

- What skills and knowledge do you have in your situation?
- What role do you take in this situation?
- Why do you take on that role?
- What beliefs do you have that inform what you do in this situation?
- What beliefs do you have about yourself in this situation?
- What issues do you have with time?
- How does time affect the way you work and live?
- What impact do the seasons have on you?

You may want to separate some of these questions from an environmentalist perspective:

- What are the significant features of the environment that impact on the scope of your knowledge and skills and on your use of them?
- How do beliefs and rules impact on you?
- What are the bigger picture issues – history, threats, opportunities, impetus for change?
- What are the majority beliefs about the environment that impact on your beliefs and the way you work?
- What are the minority beliefs about the environment that impact on your beliefs and on the way you work?
- How aligned are you with the context in which you operate? Or how happy are you here?

To be culturally agile, we need to be able to recognize an opportunity for movement and learning and to make the shift to get there. The questions below can increase that momentum by stimulating adaptability and agility from one's own perspective:

- How effective are you in monitoring what is going on in your environment?
- What do you use to keep abreast of fine changes in your environment?
- What indicators do you use to track changes and movements?
- How 'in tune' do you feel you are with adjustments in your environment?
- How adaptable have you been in the past to changing situations?
- What has gone less well?
- What example can you give of adapting to change in a timely way?
- When have you successfully instigated a change?
- How do you decide when to respond quickly?

The questions below can stimulate adaptability and agility from an environmentalist perspective:

- What are the features and characteristics in the environment that make it slow to react to change? (Beliefs, policies, systems, rituals, ways of working etc.)
- What are the features and behaviours of the players that make the environment less receptive to change?
- What are the features and behaviours of marginalized or minority groups that are slow to react to change? And what are those that are receptive to change?
- What are the features and characteristics of the collective players that make the environment quick to change?
- What are the features and characteristics that make minority or marginalized groups receptive to change?
- What prevents the environment from responding in a timely way?
- What enables the environment to respond quickly?

Bridging the collective and the individual purpose
Parents and other family members can use their vision or faculty of imagination to consider the kind of family life they want, and from there they can work out the frameworks, roles, responsibilities and behaviours that support their vision. For example:

- How do you visualize your family?
- What distinguishes your family from others?
- What values does it have?
- Whom do you relate to in the wider community?
- What traditions and behaviours are important in your family?
- How realistic is the model they create?
- Where are the challenges to achieving such an ideal?
- What knowledge, skills and resources will you need to enable that to happen?

For people who take the longer view of life, visioning can embody eternal life as well as earthly life.

Learning to live with temporary states
One of the challenges to mental agility arises within our own mind. Many of us struggle with temporary states – in ourselves and in our contexts of operation.

Typically, such states are boredom, frustration, fear, loss of self- control. We may have to struggle or cope with temporary destabilization, uncertainty and chaos in the external world. We may feel that we want to give up when there is a long delay before we can reap the benefits of our actions. What is certain about temporary states is that you know you are on the cusp of something new. For example:

- Can you think of a time when you had to work for a long period before seeing the benefits?
- What were the particular challenges?
- How did you get through?
- What kept you going?
- How did the benefits manifest themselves?
- How does this help you to prepare for discomfort now?
- Why are you so dissatisfied with how you are thinking?
- Why do you feel so uncomfortable?
- How could you make a small but significant impact or shift the situation?
- Where do you see yourself in the bigger picture?

Beyond goals

Apart from the goal and the objectives designed to establish a longer term direction, we can also consider alternatives. The notion of hypothesis setting and opportunity spotting may be more congruent with us as learners, and inherently with our total context. Unlike the goal, which limits the outcome to success or failure, the hypothesis encourages us to be explorers of learning. Here are some examples of questioning that takes individuals beyond goals and focuses on the exploration itself:

- What are you enjoying learning at the moment?
- How can you transfer that learning to other areas?
- What kind of thinking interests you?
- What unexpected connections have you made between different elements in your experience?
- What ideas excite you?

Beyond language to meaning

When we are working with people in business, we often ask them to use metaphors and language from their work world to describe themselves, and then we help them to translate it all into language that relates to their personal selves. They often find they are more able to express themselves in the language of work and have become more separated from their 'personal selves'. To do this, you can use the following questions:

- What are the demands upon you?
- Where have you positioned yourself on this?
- Who are the stakeholders in this?

We can also find metaphors from family and community life – for instance, we create the analogy with a football team and ask people to say who they are in that team.

Life stages

We can help people get in touch with their universality by focusing on the common elements. For example:

- Where do you feel you are in your life – at what stage?
- How would you describe it?
- How does this life stage impact on how you see the world?
- What are you expecting to learn in this life stage?

We can use life roles (spouse or lover, child, parent, adult) to explore wider issues from different perspectives. How would you perceive this team issue as a parent?

Prophecy and spirituality for creativity

By its very nature, prophecy has roots into a whole range of faiths and cross-cultural traditions. Using prophecy and understanding the element of spirituality in people's stories – finding signs of spirituality and fulfilment of vision – is a way to motivate ourselves as well as to ensure that we are on track. It enables individuals to cross time zones and consider the bigger picture, and it draws both new perspectives and old learning into the exploration of current issues. Useful questions might include:

- How does this experience add to your sense of how the world works?
- What patterns and themes can you see in your experience that now have meaning?
- Where does this fit in with your action plan?
- Where is this taking you?
- How much do you feel driven to do this? (to check commitment)

With each of these questions, we hope you extend your exploratory emphasis on the integration of cultural factors into personal, social and epistemic areas relevant to your coachee or mentee. Coaches and mentors might also want to challenge themselves to remember their own latest creative thought or intervention.

- How did that thought change the situation?
- How did that thought change the relationship with the coachee or mentee?
- What did you learn about yourself?
- What did you learn about the bigger picture?
- How did it change the world?

This is an eclectic set of questions; in a way they resonate with Megginson and Clutterbuck's (1995) approach, which is known as the British eclectic model and in which they listed 107 coaching and mentoring questions as a reference. This section has proposed a new set of questions, which resonate with the UIF/ILS value; and instead of simply making a long list of them, we have organized them according to the structure the UIF/ILS. We hope that you can easily utilize them in your coaching or mentoring conversation.

Chapter Summary and Reflection

This chapter has shown how the integrative learning system is used in practice by showing a range of possible techniques that may be applied at each system level.

Gestalt focuses on the present but acknowledges the past. The coach draws attention to the client's posture, voice, gestures and so on, to build awareness and to work through emotional blocks. This approach addresses contact boundaries and uses three main techniques to facilitate learning, namely supression, expression and integration. Gestaltism recognizes our connectedness with our environmental field, where the whole is greater than the sum of its parts. The aim of gestaltism is to accept our complete 'true selves'. For example, gestalt approaches systematically support genuine self-expression by means of a negative reinforcement of insincerity. In positive psychology terms, these are the signature strengths of the gestalt coach and mentor.

While CBT is regarded as a powerful tool in executive coaching, it needs to be refined to adapt to the context of the organization and culture of individual coachees. To make it effective, coaches and mentors need to pay attention to other factors, such as interpersonal relationships (Safran, 1990). Common ground exists among different coaching approaches; they are a collaborative intervention between coaches and coachees. In this journey, participants attempt to explore meaningful interpretations and modify them in order to reach their destiny, the end game, the goal – which may be for example to improve performance, or to achieve a better work–life balance.

From a cultural perspective, tolerance of difference does not equate with cultural agility, and learning is likely to be minimal when only homogenous relationships in familiar contexts prevail. At the edge of the boundary of our own experience lies the opportunity for learning, and if several of these boundaries are crossed concurrently – which is a situation of maximum complexity – then we demonstrate cultural agility. As coaches, we can help coachees to tell their stories in new ways, explore new thinking and acquire a new sense of self. There are many techniques to the narrative approach that can help one to cross personal and cultural boundaries. To summarize, the combined narrative approach that has been discussed in this chapter consists of the following techniques or stages:

1   externalizing conversations (1:1);
2   remembering/re-authoring (1:1);
3   outsider witness retelling (1:1:n);
4   definitional ceremony (community) – retellings of retellings.

In conclusion, the ILS advocates:

- flexibility of design and transparency of process;
- contextualizing the person in her or his story;
- aspects of positive psychology in identifying history, strengths and track records or strategies of successful transitional boundary crossing and management of complexity;
- the importance of a systemic consideration of the cultural and contextual landscapes from a variety of perspectives;
- in-depth planning for the application of strategy to specific contexts;
- flexibility of learning;
- the importance of reviews and paying attention to the system boundaries of coaching);
- basic training and supervision for coachees and for coaches.

Within the ILS coaches and mentors are encouraged to share frameworks, techniques and insights with coachees and mentees, so that the process is transparent and positions in the relationship are not fixed. While coaches tend to use probing questions, you might, as a gestalt practitioner, focus on expanding the coachee's own awareness instead. For practitioners of the three-step or five-step coaching process and GROW, there are ideas to extend your exploration. Chapter 8 includes exercises that give you the opportunity to practise such ideas.

8

Continuing Professional Development, Learning Resources and Practical Exercises

Introduction

Following on from Chapter 7, this chapter provides you with some of the particular aspects of the integrative learning system (ILS) that need to feature in coaching or mentoring training and with some of the resources and exercises to support those main areas. The chapter does not attempt to cover a training course, not least because every programme needs to be different. As a starting point, it describes a supervision approach that fits in with the ILS; this is followed by a consideration of the 'receptiveness' approach to coaching and mentoring as a precursor to selection for training. We then go on to consider exercises from cognitive behavioural therapy (CBT) and gestalt that can strengthen your practice whether you are using a simple, three-step approach to coaching and mentoring or the GROW model. The chapter then discusses storytelling exercises, which can also inform generic coach or mentor practice and one aspect of the narrative psychodrama – for those who want to experiment. We go into specific techniques and questioning areas, which readers can readily adapt to their exercises. Similarly, the other techniques discussed in Chapter 7 are easily adapted for triad work in which one participant in training observes the dialogue between the others and gives feedback.

ILS Training and Continuous Professional Development

ILS can be mapped onto your own training provision for coaching and mentoring. On the whole it advocates that all participants in the process receive basic training in coaching and mentoring (ideally for at least one to two days), so that coachees and mentees have enough information on the process to know how to steer it. This process should also be transparent, so that all players may be able to access information

The Psychology of Coaching, Mentoring and Learning, Second Edition. Ho Law.
© 2013 John Wiley & Sons, Ltd. Published 2013 by John Wiley & Sons, Ltd.

and techniques that allow them to coach both themselves and others. The training should be a partnership where the roles of helper and helped are fluid. Sometimes the same person is being mentored and coached by the same person, other times by different people. All participants can attend basic training together and learn together.

In general, coaching and mentoring offer the clients some degree of social support. Thus both coaching and mentoring require empathy and share some of the features of counselling. So, training programmes might have some core elements in common; but they differ in their contextualization. For instance, there is usually a need for those who feel they can offer more as mentors to do more training in a specific domain; but that specification will vary depending on the type and level of mentoring required. Often training is differentiated by the proficiency level into introductory, intermediate and advanced. Executive coaching might require higher level skills and greater knowledge of how organizations work and of the nature of management in a complex environment. Advisory coaching might be a short-term intervention with coaching elements infused into information giving – as for example in coaching for career change or re-employment.

Supervision is an important part of continuous professional development (CPD), and it is designed to ensure accountability, collective practice, shared learning and personal development. It eases the flow of information between individual and the collective entity so as to shape policies, steer priorities and assure levels of practice. In addition to supervision, one should have appropriate individually based CPD, in line with the individual caseload, complexity, professional and organization requirements. Having inclusion, options and flexibility is the name of the game.

In the ILS the process is transparent, and in consequence all participants to it can potentially develop to perform any one of the required roles: coach, mentor, coachee, mentee, supervisor, coordinator, trainer. In ILS coaching, the emphasis moves away from the hierarchical structure of supervision to CPD; coaches and mentors may train to become supervisors as part of their CPD. Working with colleagues in this role, in a range of settings, improves their competency and extends their learning. In organizations that employ external and internal coaches, CPD provides an opportunity for everyone to get together, review and learn.

The ILS proposes that CPD should be open to all stakeholders, in group or individual settings, to help them consolidate their learning. These sessions can look at experiences of learning in coaching and mentoring and help those with problems in their transition from one context or stage in the process to another. Where there is mystery, participants can share learning and insights. They may be offered a range of opportunities via e-chat rooms – a virtual forum designed to facilitate their learning and develop a community of practice. This learning process can be backed by email or Skype supervision, or both – a model of teaching that I use in the distance-learning programmes in coaching and coaching psychology. In addition to e-coaching and mentoring, workshops can be provided to demonstrate further coaching techniques and practice – for instance, classroom-based teaching on the campus. Depending on one's aptitude and experience, each of these modes of training has much to offer.

CPD also serves as a forum for sharing personal learning – understood as learning about the coaching process. Individuals can arrange completion of the cultural social competence, self-assessment questionnaire (CSC SAQ) tool (described in Chapter 6) to derive their own learning needs within a whole ILS approach to evaluation. Participants in training, or the wider CPD community, can use these lists as areas of discussion to start reviewing their learning. They can identify the areas of development that they need to work on and reflect on the ebbs and flows of learning over sessions, on outcomes for distinctive phases in the process and on whether the learning areas are synchronous between the coach and the coachee. In summary, the ILS enables the learning partners separately, together, or in the wider community of learners to explore their journey into development. Much learning comes after sessions, between sessions, and at points of change in the stages of exploration.

Writing and Keeping a Reflective Log

Writing and keeping a log to reflect on one's practice is another important component of learning. I often require my coaches, students, or supervisees to keep a reflective log as a component of their assignments. Many coaches (especially those who have not been academically trained) often find this exercise difficult. Here I offer the following structure to help.

To embed the learning cycle and CBT framework, a reflective log should include the following components:

1 Description: briefly describe the session, including the context, background of the coaches, contracting, etc., stating what happened and/or you did.
2 Cognition and emotion: reflect on your thoughts and feelings. What were you thinking/feeling during the engagement? What do you think about the coachee's thoughts and feelings?
3 Analysis: try to understand what happened and draw meaning from the experience.
4 Evaluation: assess the intended and unintended consequences of the experience. What have you learnt? If a similar situation arose again, what would you do? What are you going to do to further improve and develop yourself and your performance?
5 Conclusion: summarize the meaning and the lessons learned; look for improvement.
6 Action plan: recommend a future plan of action for further learning and improvement.

When you evaluate your learning and develop an action plan (Steps 4–6), you may like to use the components of ILS to structure your learning and identify the areas for further developments as follows:

personal: self-awareness:

• self-belief;
• confidence;

- motivation and passion;
- self-management;

social: awareness of others:

- empathy with others;
- assessment of difference and universality;

cultural: increase in the knowledge of how systems work:

- application of new knowledge and thinking to familiar situations;
- application of new knowledge and thinking to new situations;

professional: skills and techniques for the coach or mentor:

- skills and techniques that I can use as a leader;
- skills, knowledge and techniques that I can use in new situations;
- knowledge and skills that I can use as a universal learner.

Exercises in Learning

The following exercises will help you to focus on the nature of learning as a foundation for coaching and mentoring. The exercises can be carried out individually or in groups, in a training session. If conducted in a group, the coach may like to instruct each group to nominate a facilitator or spokesperson to summarize the common key points and feedback to the larger group.

Identifying sources of negative learning

Exercise 1

List any negative experiences you have had in the past that may stand in the way of your change.

If you have difficulty recalling any such experiences, think about a significant person associated with the time when you had difficulties learning something new. This person and the experience may be recent or from the distant past. For example, the person might be your schoolteacher or a difficult colleague.

Identifying psychological factors

Exercise 2

List the attributes of the poor coach or mentor. If you do not have any coaching or mentoring experience, think about a trainer or a teacher.

Exercise 3

List the attributes of the good coach or mentor.

Identifying intervention

Exercise 4

Describe how you overcame the barriers/difficult situation that you described in exercise 1.

You may find it helpful to consider the following questions:

- After you have experienced this, what would your next goal be?
- What are the expected outcomes?
- Did your intervention consist of some kind of strategy?
- What form does the strategy take?
- If you were a coach, what coaching techniques would you use?
- What are the resources required?

Practising Cognitive Behavioural Coaching

I always ask my clients to keep a diary in a CBT format, so that we may analyse them together in the session, together with reviewing progress. Some clients did have difficulty in writing down their thoughts and feelings. It took practice. Over time, they could think, feel and analyse events that happened in their lives in a way they had not experienced before.

A similarly useful tool I have found in applying cognitive behavioural coaching is to ask the coachees to keep a personal diary, journal or logbook to record the details of activities that are related to their goals according to the structure described in Table 7.1 and the six-step reflective log described earlier. Writing a log is an important part of reflection, and hence of learning.

Cognitive behavioural diary: writing it down

In writing a reflective diary, coachees arrive at an understanding of events that would not have been possible before. Some may even find profound meaning when they discuss this diary with their coaches and mentors. The cognitive behavioural diary (CBD) has three components:

- the past;
- the present;
- the present working towards the future.

All this fits naturally into the six-step reflective log. In CBD this process of fitting the six steps into the three parts can be summarized thus:

- Part 1: Describe your lived experience – Description (Steps 1 and 2 in the log);
- Part 2: Interpret the meaning – Analysis and evaluation (Steps 3 and 4);
- Part 3: Plan your strategy and action – Conclusion and action plan (Steps 5 and 6).

Here I shall describe these parts in detail.

Part 1: describe your lived experience
In your diary, write down:

- when: date and time of a significant event;
- where: location where a significant event happened;
- what: what happened (the significant event);
- who: who was involved (the significant 'actors', who of course include you);
- how: how did you feel? (your emotion).

For example, a negative emotion may be referred to through one of these words: angry, annoyed, anxious, apprehensive, ashamed, bad, concerned, depressed, disappointed, disgusted, dissatisfied, embarrassed, enraged, exhausted, excluded, frightened, guilty, horrified, humiliated, hurt, insecure, irritated, afraid, frustrated, jealous, lonely, mad, nervous, overwhelmed, panicky, poor, sad, scared, sick, tired, worried.

Positive emotion may encompass words like: aspired, better, cheerful, confident, delighted, eager, empowered, energetic, enthusiastic, excited, fulfilled, good, happy, included, inspired, loved, loving, joyful, peaceful, pleased, proud, relaxed, satisfied, secured, well, zestful.

Part 2: interpret the meaning
Write down your reflection:

- Why did the 'actors' behave in a particular way?
- Why did you feel that way?
- What have you learnt from the experience?
- How did the experience help you to achieve your future goal?

Part 3: plan of action (your strategy)
When writing your action plan, ask the following questions:

- What are you going to do about it?
- What is the purpose?
- What do you want to achieve?
- When by?
- Who can help you to achieve this?
- Who needs to be involved?
- What would be the likely obstacles?
- How would you overcome them?
- How do you feel about the task (your emotion)?
- Describe your experience now (the turning point).
- How do you feel now?
- Sign off.

Gestalt Exercises

Gestalt techniques can be practised as a series of exercises to increase awareness and as a continuum of awareness. Gestalt exercises aim to help practitioners to be fully aware in the present – in the here and now. This 'living in the moment' practice is also known as the mindfulness practice, which is increasingly well known in the West. The task of the coach in the mindfulness exercise is to bring coachees back to the present if they are distracted from it. Coachees are coached in persistent attention to their ongoing experience. They are reminded when they are failing at the task of expressing their awareness.

Remember, in the previous chapter we talked about using the self as an instrument. In the following exercises you will find that your presence, the way in which you use your 'self', is an essential part in the process of change. These exercises aim to help you to increase your awareness of the continuum and of asceticism. In other words, the exercises directly access the realm of your personhood and presence, beyond any biological input and output. The demand for directness increases clarity and reduces the message-to-noise ratio.

There are three levels in gestalt exercises. These levels progressively increase participants' self- and social awareness and engagements. Classified by level, the exercises are:

- I/you exercises;
- awareness of continuum exercises;
- top dog/underdog exercises.

Level 1: I/You exercises

These exercises help you to develop awareness that is implicit in Gestalt psychology.

Exercise 5: Presence

This exercise focuses on the sense of presence. It can be performed alone, in pairs or in a group. If you work with pairs, ask each member of a pair to sit face to face and to close his or her eyes. Then each participant should follow these instructions:

1 Be as you want to be.
2 Pay attention to your body sensations, posture and facial expression.
3 Make any necessary adjustment in your posture on the basis of your awareness, moment by moment.
4 When you feel comfortable and ready, open your eyes while remaining still.
5 Relax your eyes.
6 Relax your body.
7 Focus on the sense of being in the present – the 'I sense'.
8 I sense that 'I am here'.
9 Relax.
10 Focus on this 'I sense' for a moment.
11 Be aware of your breathing.
12 Silently, speak to yourself: 'I am here'.
13 Synchronize this inner speech, 'I am here', with your breathing. For example:
    a. Breathe in and focus on 'I'.
    b. Pause and think of 'am'.
    c. Breathe out and focus on 'here'.
14 Continue the breathing exercise until you fully achieve a sense of presence or it feels appropriate to end.

Exercise 6: You-ness

This exercise helps you to become aware of the presence of others and to develop a sense of the personhood of others – the sense of 'you' instead of an experience of 'it'. Working in pairs, follow these instructions:

1   Sit face to face with your partner and close your eyes.
2   Be as you want to be.
3   Pay attention to your body sensations, posture and facial expression.
4   Make any necessary adjustments to your posture on the basis of your awareness, moment by moment.
5   When you feel comfortable and ready, open your eyes while remaining still.
6   Focus on the person sitting opposite you without making a conversation.
7   Be conscious of the fact that you are seeing this person as a person who truly exists.

Exercise 7: I/You

This effectively is an extension of exercises 5 and 6 (the first two in this section). The procedures include:

1   Practise exercise 5.
2   Practise exercise 6.
3   Now focus on both 'I' and 'you', and at the same time evoke a sense of infinity around 'I' and 'you'.
4   Speak silently: 'I – you – infinity'.

Exercise 8: I – You – I

Work with a different partner and write down three traits of a person you admire and three traits of a person you do not admire. Then, in turn, say, 'I am...' followed by the traits you have listed.

You may find it hard to identify with the traits for either person – for different reasons. For example, it is hard to say 'I am brave', as it feels like boasting; but it is also hard to say 'I am rude', as it feels very critical of oneself. Saying the negative traits helps you to realize that maybe you are also some of those things.

Level 2: Awareness of the continuum

These exercises help to heighten your awareness of actual needs, so they can be acted on. They help to bring to your attention things that you might otherwise not have noticed, such as the way you are sitting. In group exercises, pay particular attention to the moment of silence. A deeper silence may attract to it a deeper communication.

Exercise 9: Perception

This exercise takes a few minutes, so it is advisable to choose a time when you will not be disturbed. Have a piece of paper and a pen at hand and try to focus on the following sensations:

- sight;
- sound;
- texture;
- taste;
- smell;
- bodily sensation.

Jot down each item (or draw a figure if it is an image) as you become aware of it. Stay with it until the next one develops and comes to the fore. For example:

- the colour of the wallpaper;
- the paintings on the wall;
- the voices of other people;
- the pressure of clothes against the skin on the back of the thighs;
- a jagged tooth against your mouth;
- a sour taste in the back of your mouth;
- slight discomfort of your ankle;
- moving your leg and relief of the discomfort.

You need to empty your mind of preoccupations and be as receptive as possible. You do not have to do all the senses. You may find that your receptivity and reverie incline you to be aware of certain senses (e.g. sight) rather than others (e.g. smell).

Note that you become aware of one thing (the figure) and then it fades into the background (ground) and another figure takes its place. You become increasingly aware of the boundary between yourself and the outside.

Try not to think of what the noise, smell or sensation is, or why it is. Just be aware of the ebb and flow of your consciousness of the sensations. Open yourself up to your environment. Be receptive.

Exercise 10: Living in the Moment

Repeat exercise 9 without writing anything down. You can do it anywhere where you can concentrate for a few minutes – for instance, when lying in the bath or sitting quietly outside.

Exercise 11: Monologue: Self-Reports

This is a group exercise. Working in a group of three, each person switches roles after 10 minutes. There are three roles:

- coachee/reporter/actor;
- coach/listener/witness;
- coach supervisor.

The actor and witness sit face to face with the coach sitting next to them. Repeat exercise 9 in a group. The actors recite in turn what they are aware of externally and internally.

Instructions for the coachee (actor)
There are three basic realms of awareness: perception, feeling and action. In this exercise you emphasize, out of all your feelings about the occasion, the one that is grounded in perception; and in order to do this you use an action that mirrors your feeling. In other words, feel what you perceive and express your feeling through action. Report to the 'listener' your perception – what you see, hear, smell and so on – but emphasize how you feel about those perceptions. For example, you may say:

- I could hear my own breathing and I feel relaxed.
- As I speak, I could hear my own voice and I feel self-conscious.
- Now I'm aware of my heart beating.
- Now I'm aware of the sound of the air-conditioning unit.
- Now I feel distracted by the sound of traffic outside.

Instructions for the coach (listener)

- Listen to what is being said.
- Observe the body language.
- Act as a witness.
- Don't give cues.
- Don't respond to the speaker.
- Don't approve or disapprove. For example, don't smile or shrug your shoulders.
- Keep still.
- Be non-judgemental.
- Adopt a meditative stance.
- Do nothing.
- Be present.
- Relax your face.
- Relax your tongue.
- Don't try to understand what the reporter says. You will notice that, by not trying, you will understand better.
- Put your effort into attending, both inside and outside.
- Focus on your perception: what you see, what you hear – the voice and words of the speaker.
- Focus also on how you yourself feel, moment to moment.

Instructions for the coach supervisor
The coach supervisor performs the supervision using a gestalt approach. The role is to ensure that the coachee (actor) and the coach (witness) observe the rules. Point out any infringement of rules. For example:

- Point out that what is being said is not an expression of experience (e.g. in case someone was telling a story).
- Point out the posture of the witness (e.g. if he or she did not appear to be relaxed).
- Draw the witnesses' attention to what they should not do within the exercise (e.g. nod, smile, etc.).

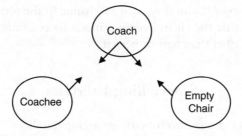

Figure 8.1   Three-chair exercise

Level 3: Top dog/underdog

Exercise 12

This exercise is also known as the 'empty chair' technique or 'three chair' exercise. It takes at least 20 to 30 minutes and consists of four stages:

1   *Self-accusation as a top dog* Let the words, voice and gesture of emotion flow.
2   *Underdog reversal* Ask the actor to impersonate his or her underdog, its personality, its attitude and so on. The underdog tells the top dog off in a full display of words and gesture.
3   *Top dog reversal.*
4   *Working towards an agreement.*

Work in a pair: one acts as a coach (sitting in one chair) and the other as a client (sitting in another chair); the third chair is left empty (see Figure 8.1.) If there are three or more participants, others can act as observers.

   Coach:

- Ask clients to express their concerns, objections, and doubts directly rather than in an abstract and generalized way.
- Ask questions beginning with 'How do you experience that now...?' or 'Tell me directly how you feel about this...'.
- Get the clients to act out an unfinished situation, either by making them imagine the others to be in the room or by using actors. This helps clients to experience the psychological block and then to complete it in the present.

The coach's assessment of what is happening, followed by active involvement, is essential. For example, client B describes his or her relationship with another person P and how B felt about P. The coach then asks the client to move to the empty chair and become P. Client B describes P's personality and life in the first person, using expressions such as 'how "I" felt about P'. B then moves back to his or her chair and describes his or her feelings towards P. Throughout this, the coach should pick up on aspects of how the clients change in their attitude and behaviours. For example, the coach may say to B: 'The way you're sitting as P, you're almost looking down at people.' This kind of feedback helps clients to see how they portray themselves and others. The exercise helps clients understand differently both the relationships and why other people act in certain ways.

When a client becomes P, you may notice a change in the tone of his or her voice; you may also notice that the client becomes much more aware of the environment when she or he is P rather than him-or herself.

Storytelling Exercises

Narrative approaches typically involve coaches asking coachees to tell a story in order to recount an experience, and then prompting them, through follow-up questions, to connect the story with a concept they would like to explore. The story development may consist of the following plots:

- re-authoring: story development rich in skills and knowledge;
- re-authoring and remembering conversation: story development rich in skills and knowledge;
- outsider witness (group exercise): retelling of the story;
- definitional ceremony (community): retellings of retellings.

The re-authoring conversation

The goal of a re-authoring conversation is to redevelop coachees' skills and knowledge by re-authoring the stories of their life experience. Re-authoring conversations provide a platform for participants to step into the near future of the landscapes of action of their lives. Questions are introduced that encourage the storytellers to generate proposals for action, accounts of the circumstances likely to be favourable to these proposals for action, and predictions about the outcome of these proposals. Note that the narrative coach first needs to scaffold the rich story development in the landscape of consciousness before proceeding with the re-authoring questions. This exercise helps you to develop some of these questioning skills.

At first, participants are likely to respond to landscapes of consciousness questions by talking about various categories of their self-identity – such as attributes, characteristics, deficits, drives, motives, needs, resources, strengths, traits, and so on. However, these responses may provide an inadequate basis for the coachees to proceed. In other words, the coachees get stuck. Narrative coaches need to guide the storytellers with the help of alternative identities that are more positive and relevant to the empowerment of their lives. Try to discover the storytellers' beliefs, commitments, intentions, purposes, values, visions, hopes and dreams.

Exercise 13: Developing Your Skills and Knowledge through a Re-Authoring Conversation Technique

Note for coaches and mentors
Use the following questions as a guide only. Remember, this is an informal conversation, not a formal interview. So talk as naturally as possible and develop your own questions as necessary. Pay particular attention to the answers and follow their lead.

1   Thank you for volunteering to talk to me. Can you remember a recent skill that you have acquired – or something that you have learnt? If you are happy with it, we shall explore it a bit further.

2   Please tell me what happened.

3   If I were there, what would I see?

4   Was it easy or difficult to learn?

5   Can you remember, was there a significant moment or a 'turning point' at which you felt that you had overcome the difficulty?

6   When you accomplished this, what did you wish to have seen happening as a result?

7   Can you help me to understand your intentions or purposes in learning this skill? Does this stem from any particular values or beliefs you hold in high regard? If so, what are they?

8   Looking back now, can you still say that those values/intentions/purposes are important to you?

9   Why is it important to you to have these sorts of intentions or purposes for what you do now?

10   So if you think about these values/beliefs, what hopes and dreams might they be connected to in your life?

11   When these values/beliefs are present, what would you be hoping for now, at this stage?

12   Can you give a name to the story you told me?

If you have time, ask the following questions:

1   Are there other things you've done recently that fit with what we're discussing now, or are on the same theme?

2   Were there other times in your life when these themes/intentions/values/hopes/dreams stood out?

3   What would I have seen you doing in the past that would indicate these themes/intentions/values/hopes/dreams?

4   Can you give me an example from your earlier life that would reflect these themes/intentions/values/hopes/dreams you hold dear?

5   What's it like to be looking at your recent experience in light of this past event?

Finally:

1   What has it been like for you to have this conversation?

2   What does it make you think about in your own work?

3   What would you be able to do?

4   Are these themes/intentions/values/hopes/dreams sustainable? If so, what would be your next step, and would it support your themes/intentions/values/hopes/dreams?

The remembering conversation

The remembering conversation, as a type of inquiry, is initiated in two stages. Each stage consists of two steps. During the first stage, the coach invites the storyteller to

•   recount what a significant figure contributed to the storyteller's life (figure's contribution to person's life);

- enter the consciousness of this figure on matters of the storyteller's identity, initiating a rich description of the ways in which this connection shaped, or had the potential to shape, the storyteller's sense of who she or he is and what his or her life is about (person's identity through the eyes of the figure).

In the second stage, the coach invites the storyteller to

- recount what the storyteller contributed to the life of this figure (person's contribution to the figure's life);
- enter the consciousness of this figure on matters of this figure's identity, initiating a rich description of the ways in which this connection shaped, or had the potential to shape, the figure's sense of who she or he was and of what his or her life was about (implications of this contribution for the figure's sense of identity).

Exercise 14: Developing Clients' Skills and Knowledge through a Remembering Conversation Technique

Choose a theme around which the conversation will take place. Ask the clients to think about a person in their life who would not be surprised to see them reflecting on their work in the way they have been when they were telling you their stories.

Note for coaches

Use the following questions as a guide only. This is an informal conversation, not a formal interview. So try to talk as naturally as possible and develop your own questions as necessary. Pay particular attention to the answers and follow their lead.

Establish a theme of intentions, commitments, principles, values, beliefs, hopes or dreams, and so on.

Remember: the identities of the significant figures whom the participants describe do not have to be directly known, as long as they have been important to the storyteller (e.g. film stars, authors of books, or characters in movies or comics). These figures need not be people; they may be, for instance, favourite pets or stuffed toys from their childhood memory.

1 Thank you for volunteering to talk to me. Could you please take some time to name one thing that is important to you and and talk about it? This could be part of the way you approach your work or your life, your intentions or your commitments.
2 Please tell me a little story that might help me understand your everyday experience of this approach/intention/commitment.
3 What beliefs/values about this way of working are important to you?
4 Can you think of someone in your life who would be least surprised to hear you talking about what is important to you, someone who would recognize and appreciate these things? (If the clients have difficulties in thinking of someone, tell them that it might be someone from their early life, an aunt or an uncle, a grandparent or a parent, a teacher or a friend. This figure may not be alive any longer. Nor does it need to be someone they have actually known, if they can't think of one – it may

be a character from a favourite book, or a movie they remember. It may be a figure from history. They can choose a pet or a favourite toy that accompanied them through childhood. Any of these would be suitable for this remembering conversation.)

5 Can you tell me a bit about this person (let's say X) as if you were introducing X to me–for example, X's name, when and where you met, and suchlike?

6 Can you tell me something about what X may have brought to your life, or in what ways your life was influenced by X?

7 What do you think X invited you to be a part of, or to share?

8 How did X go about that?

9 Is there an example that comes to mind of the sorts of things you and X did together that captures something of what you both shared?

10 What might X have recognized/appreciated in you that others had perhaps failed to notice?

11 Thinking back, what might you have done to receive X's appreciation?

12 Were you responsive to X's appreciation?

13 Were you honouring X's contribution to your life?

14 Did it bounce off you, or did it resonate with what is important to you?

15 What do you think it might have been like for X to have you join him or her in what was important to him or her?

16 What do you think it contributed to X's life that you, in particular, were available to his or her interest and appreciation?

17 What effect do you think your contribution has had on X's sense of purpose or sense of what life is about?

18 Did it reinforce X's purpose or did it take away from it?

19 Could you imagine how X would have felt if he or she were here now and hearing this conversation?

Finally:

20 What has it been like for you to have this conversation about you and X?

21 What do you think might become more possible for you in your work or life as a result of remembering your connection with X?

22 What in your own work or life does this remembering make you think about?

23 What will you be able to do now?

24 Are these themes/intentions/values/hopes/dreams sustainable? If so, what will the next step be that supports your themes/intentions/values/hopes/dreams?

Exercise 15: Group Exercise – Outsider Witness Retelling

This exercise can be carried out when you have three or more participants in your group. Repeat exercises 13 and 14, but this time invite one or more participants from the group to act as outsider witnesses. After the storyteller has told his or her story, invite the outsider witnesses to ask the questions, but give them the following instructions in advance, then ask them to organize their questions under the headings given below:

Instructions for outsider witnesses during retelling
Don'ts:

- Don't give opinions about the storyteller.
- Don't make declarations about the storyteller's self-identity.
- Don't hold up your own lives and actions as examples to the storyteller.
- Don't introduce moral tales.

Dos:

- Listen.
- Talk about what was heard.

Remember: the initial storyteller should always be at the centre of the definitional ceremony. If the outsider witnesses were carried away and began to talk about themselves and their own stories predominantly, remind them to re-focus on the primary storyteller (T). For example, 'can I interrupt you there, do you think that is relevant to T's life?' or 'how do you think T would feel about that?'

Identifying the expression
As you listen to the story of T, which expressions caught your attention or captured your imagination? Which one's struck a chord for you?

Describing the image
What images did T's expressions of his or her life, identity, and his or her world evoke in your mind? What did these expressions suggest to you about T's beliefs, commitments purposes, values, hopes, and dreams?

Embodying responses
What is it about your own life or work that the story has accounted for? Why did these expressions catch your attention or strike a chord in you? Do you have a sense of the images evoked by these expressions in your own life experiences? Which aspects of your own life experiences resonated with these expressions?

Acknowledging transport
How have you been moved as a result of being present to witness this story? Where has this experience taken you – to what place that you would not have reached if you hadn't been present in the audience to this conversation? In what way have you become who you are on account of responding to these stories as you have?

Exercise 16: The Definitional Ceremony (Community): Retellings of Retellings

This exercise is applicable to large groups like conference and community gatherings. A definitional ceremony may have the following stages:

1   At the outset, the participants meet and sit in a large circle. Some of them introduce and address the chosen themes. These may relate to personal stories or to community folklore.

2   The participants who have introduced the theme invite those in the large circle to break into smaller groups, for the purpose of having conversations that will contribute to linking the stories of other participants to these themes. One or two team members join each of the small groups, as outsider witnesses to their conversations. The participants from each small group negotiate what aspects of the story should be reported by the outsider witnesses.

3   The large circle reconvenes. Now these team members sit together, with the outsider witnesses, either at the centre or at the periphery of the circle. The outsider witnesses of each group retell what they heard and experienced in the small group conversations. (This may take up to 30 minutes per group.)

4   Having retold the story, each outsider witness rejoins the large circle. The storyteller then reflects on what he or she has heard.

Narrative Psychodrama: Physical Exercises

As mentioned in Chapter 7, narrative coaching relies heavily on the articulation of stories by the clients, but the approach may be limited if coaches or mentors rely on verbal communication only. Narrative psychodrama offers a powerful alternative, through which unspoken stories may find physical expression. The exercises described in this section would be of particular interest for those readers who are interested in alternative coaching approaches, especially in dancing and other creative methods.

Narrative psychodrama has a transpersonal psychological dimension too. Through authentic movements, coaches may develop certain attitudes and postures. The exercises described below are based on the experience of performance coaching. The concept has been adopted from the philosophy of paratheatre (Alli, 1977). The approach is invaluable for coaches and coachees, as it focuses on both mind and body. It offers a novel way of preparing one's readiness for change, both psychologically and physically.

The exercises can be performed on one's own as well as in groups. If the group exercises are conducted with a coach or a facilitator, that person should take responsibility for health and safety aspects and ensure that they are observed. The following sequence of exercises is outlined in the next sections:

1   Stage 1: preparation/initiation;
2   Stage 2: the physical warm-up cycle;
3   Stage 3: breathing and balancing exercises;
4   Stage 4: the flow movement;
5   Stage 5: acting out.

In paratheatre, Antero Alli (2003) called the last three stages of the above sequence 'no-form' (towards intimacy with void), 'the contact point' (the concept-free zone of direct intuitive engagement), and 'polarizations' (towards emotional flexibility and strength) respectively. This initial sequence (Stage 1) is explored in an asocial, non-performance environment. According to the paratheatre concept, an 'asocial' attitude relates to the vertical sources of energy, which has a spiritual and transpersonal quality. An assumption here is that each person has inner energy and a hidden agenda. These vertical sources of energy are above, within and below the body itself and can be felt as a stream of inner impulses. From the perspective of the 'asocial' attitude, these inner forces can be witnessed, experienced and made to serve to discover one's innate intentions. The quality of these intentions may be symbolically characterized by certain elements. For example, one's innate agenda to generate heat or to illuminate may be expressed as an element of 'fire'. With practice, this preparatory 'asocial' stage becomes invaluable for increasing awareness of our social conditioning and of the underlying forces that govern our existence (the so-called archetypes). This stage also helps one to assess one's vertical sources of energy and be authentic. Alli (2003) regards this process as 'building [one's] vertical integrity'.

The next stage involves a cycle of physical warm-up exercises. The overall objective is to feel one's body deeply. The quality of your performance depends on the level of personal commitment to the exercises. The breathing and balancing exercises help one to achieve a state of psychological emptiness by consciously directing attention to exhalation in a standing position.

The flow

The concept of flow has an affinity with Csikszentmihalyi's (1991) idea of flow. Indeed this may be a physical way of allowing one direct access to an optimal experience. The concept also reminds one of the saying 'go with the flow'. The approach is nondirectional and has no social intent. Here you give your body primacy to direct your movement; you allow the energy itself to give the direction. To achieve this, you need to relax. Relaxing creates a space for the expression of your physical energy. You are moved by the energy rather than moving at your will. Alli says: 'Like clay in the hands of a sculptor, we learn to be shaped before we start shaping. Allow yourself to be "created" before you start creating.' This statement relates to gestalt psychology too.

Acting out

The overall objective of a coaching exercise is to enable change to take place. Like gestalt exercises, this final stage effectively secures a 'physical rehearsal' for one to act out fear; and it also provides the agenda for change. Like in cognitive behavioural coaching, before you perform change, you need to identify the barriers and to devise a strategy for overcoming them. Acting out physically, the exercise invites you to make two lists. The first is a 'dirt list', which comprises emotionally charged, embarrassing or difficult experiences and their opposites. Very often people live through their inner embarrassment and psychological barriers helplessly. The exercise allows you to act out these experiences in a physical drama and movement. The acting out of the 'dirt list' is an important prerequisite for change as it clears the space, renders the 'emotional ego' more flexible and allows you to prepare to face up to reality. The exercise also helps you to realize that the 'self' has more than one facet.

What comes after these exercises depends on the direction suggested by the coach or facilitator. Coachees may like to discuss the new list with the coach, as an agenda for change (the 'dirt list' remains private and safe). Other techniques, for instance CBT, may follow, depending on context and preferences. In a group situation such as a team-building exercise, the group may decide collectively on an agenda for change that fits with its members' organizational or social context.

Exercise 17: Preparation/Initiation

The object of the preparation (the term used of it is also 'initiation', as in a ritual) is to help the participants to increase their spatial awareness. (If one carries out preparation by oneself alone, this becomes a self-initiation.) This initial stage provides two sub-stages designed to increase your accountability for your own creative states:

1   Take responsibility.
2   Find your own way.

Instructions for taking responsibility
Take the following unspoken vow:

•   Each individual takes responsibility for his or her own creative states.
•   Take responsibility for your own safety.
•   Take responsibility for raising your own energy level.

The vow ensures your personal commitment to pay attention to your fears, needs and personal limitations as they emerge. If you overlook these, you may become dependent and expect to be looked after by others for your safety and so on. Ensure that you have a 'safe space'. This prepares the ground for creativity: 'When a child feels safe, it can play.' Creativity flourishes in a state of trust. Paradoxically, feeling safe also allows you to take risks.

Now, consciously divert your attention from yourself (and from others, if you are in a group; or from objects such as furniture and the like). Redirect it to the 'space' itself as a 'value'. This literally means relating to the space, that is, to the setting (which may be a conference room, a dance studio and so on).

Find your own way
When you are ready, move through the space of the actual setting in such a way as to continually relate to the space itself, rather than to the people or objects in that space.

Before you begin your physical warm-up, you may need to find your own space. This could include the following steps:

1   Physically move through the space within the setting.
2   Locate a small region of that space to claim as your own personal warm-up area.

When you have discovered your personal space, make a conscious effort to 'own' it. Mark it with your territorial instincts – in Alli's (2003) words, 'like animals stalk and claim turf. Find your own idiosyncratic ways to mark the outer boundaries, the centre and then proceed to take charge of this area.'

Exercise 18: The Physical Warm-Up Cycle

The physical warm-up exercises consist of a cycle of four steps: keep still, flex, stretch and move. Each step lasts between 5 and 10 minutes. Repeat the sequence of steps in a cycle for about 20 to 40 minutes, depending on your time constraints.

1   Keep still – adopt any posture that allows you to be physically still. Engage internal thoughts, then empty them. You may choose to meditate or pray silently, depending on your belief or religion.
2   Flex your spine.
3   Stretch and take a deep breath at the same time – feel your body deeply. Try to locate any 'numb' areas in your body and stretch them. Try to perform the exercise within the limit of your physical comfort.
4   Move – now move freely within your personal area, with an objective of generating enough body heat to work up a sweat. Continue to move to contain the heat and to mark your boundaries through your movements. Stay within your own personal warm-up area. This helps you to accumulate and contain the vital energy, heat and presence within your own space.

Exercise 19: Breathing and Balancing Exercises

In a standing position, do the following:

1   Watch your own breath; emphasize your exhalation.
2   Relax. Do not try to control or direct your body. Adjust your physical stance as necessary for maintaining a balance and supporting the spinal alignment. Allow your body to stand and rest in a state of vertical posture.
3   Stay empty – try to approach a psychological state of emptiness. Bypass any distraction such as 'internal chatter' or 'dissociated imagery'.

Exercise 20: The Flow Movement

This exercise consists of free movements that go with the flow:

1   Remain relaxed.
2   Become aware of your physical energy. Follow it. Do not resist it. When you feel that the force of this energy is strong enough to move your body, follow its direction. Do not allow yourself any desire to control or direct the energy.
3   Move with the flow.

Exercise 21: Acting Out

This stage involves acting out some of one's personal emotional difficulties. The process may take the following steps:

1   Introspectively examine your own most personal experiences.
2   Make a 'dirt list' – in your mind, draw up a list of difficult experiences, especially those that are regarded by you as 'not socially acceptable' or as opposite to your 'normal good nature'. These may be very private and highly charged with emotion.
3   Make an expression (acting out) – select an item on the list, give it an expression in a physical form. Act it all out. Do not take yourself too seriously. Do not be afraid of making a fool out of yourself. If you do feel too afraid to act out, or if you become too self-conscious (this could happen in particular in a group

situation), express this awkwardness by giving it a physical form – in movement or posture, if you feel immobilized by it.

4   Make a 'new list' – repeat Step 3, but this time make a list of items that are directly opposite to those on the dirt list. Some of these items may be based on your experience. If they are not, you may choose to invent it as long as it is directly opposite to the one in Step 3.

5   Make a change – repeat Step 3, but this time select the item from your 'new list' in Step 4 and give it a physical expression.

Chapter Summary and Reflection

If you have attempted to practise all the exercises described in this chapter, you will have noticed that some of the techniques may be mutually exclusive, while others are complementary to each other. For instance, gestalt mentors never ask mentees 'Why?', while narrative coaches question every thin trace of a story. However, it is important to realize that both approaches are transpersonal in nature. Also, both approaches perform the transformation at the moment of being present, although the gestalt approach primarily emphasizes the moment-to-moment continuity or duration of being here and now. Like any skill, be it competence in gestalt expressions or competence in the scaffolding questions of narrative approaches, this one is acquired through practice, more practice and then more practice still.

On the other hand, the narrative psychodrama relates to gestalt psychology very well. It regards the body as an instrument – in this case a vessel – 'for containing, mixing, transforming and refining the ongoing union of opposites' – an instrument through which 'top dog' and 'underdog' are in interplay as the movements unfold. The approach also has an alchemic quality. In gestalt coaching, the transformation – for instance, the perception of time cognitively (mental time) – has to be experienced though one's body, physically (in body time); it cannot be taught. You discover your own way through your experience, through your body, through physical movements, with all your senses.

You can adapt your own coaching or mentoring approach to suit your circumstances and to meet the needs of the learner. While techniques might vary, the ILS may be used as an overarching structure, within which you can select appropriate approaches that would help you scaffold your learning and practice. Whether you are a gestalt, a CBT or a narrative therapist, a coach or a mentor, working with executives or former offenders, I hope there is something here you can take away and put into practice. After all, this is about thinking and doing things in new ways.

I shall illustrate the above exercises in some of the case studies in Chapter 9.

9

Case Studies

Introduction

This chapter provides a number of case studies derived from various mentoring and coaching programmes. They aim to show how theories can be applied in practice. Each case is structured according to the action research and learning process: it consists of planning (aims/objectives); action (the process of implementation); reflection and evaluation of the lessons learnt from the experience. I hope that you will gain insight into what makes for successful coaching and mentoring. To demonstrate how the universal integrated framework (UIF)/integrative learning system (ILS) works, I have taken care to select case studies from applications that have either an international or cross-cultural dimension or a socio-community element. The case studies cover:

- leadership coaching and mentoring programmes for the healthcare system (case studies 1 and 2);
- e-coaching – a transatlantic coaching pilot project (case study 3);
- coaching in communities (case studies 4 and 5).

Under the current economic climate, organizations are under pressure to increase productivity and efficiency and at the same time to reduce cost. This requires leaders to motivate employees rather than using traditional management methods of transformational and inspirational leadership (Alban-Metcalfe and Mead, 2010; Alimo-Metcalfe and Alban Metcalfe, 2005). The pressure to improve effectiveness and efficiency is even more acute in the healthcare sector, with its increased number of patients with acute conditions and the complex challenges of rising costs, continuous organizational change, multiple disciplinary management hierarchies and high staff turnover (Lee et al., 2010; Storey, 2010; Contino, 2004; Hartman and Crow, 2002; Mathena, 2002; McAlearney, 2006).

The Psychology of Coaching, Mentoring and Learning, Second Edition. Ho Law.
© 2013 John Wiley & Sons, Ltd. Published 2013 by John Wiley & Sons, Ltd.

The traditional hierarchical and bureaucratic organizational model is no longer compatible with the new complexities of the healthcare system (McAlearney, 2006). The de-centralization of the healthcare system has also placed pressure on ward managers at the mid-management level to increase performance (Casida, 2007). However, ward managers may not have been prepared to assume leadership roles (Mathena, 2002; Grindel, 2003). Therefore, developing leadership capacity at both senior and middle management levels has become an urgently needed item on the agenda of change in the healthcare system. One way to meet this challenge is to embed learning within the organization through leadership coaching.

Case studies 1 and 2 provide examples of how leadership coaching may be introduced into the healthcare system. Case study 1 is based on the initial UIF development in the healthcare sector in the UK. Case study 2 shows how a leadership coaching programme can be introduced in a general hospital in Malta.

Case study 3 describes a transatlantic coaching pilot project undertaken in 2005, which was coordinated by Frank Bresser as part of his MBA (master of business administration) research (Bresser, 2006a, 2006b). The case study is based on an interesting collaboration between the British Association for Coaching and Rice University, Houston, Texas. It also demonstrates the advantages and difficulties of telephone coaching that uses Internet technology or traditional telephone systems. It includes encouraging feedback from the coordinator, coaches and coachees; this feedback is based on a quantitative questionnaire and a qualitative reflection.

Case studies 4 and 5 describe how we can apply the skills and knowledge of coaching in the community context. Case study 4 shows how I applied the narrative approach and the learning I gained from the International Narrative Therapy workshop and conference in Adelaide, Australia, to a community in Peterborough, England. The case study demonstrates the power of storytelling by using the metaphor of a journey and the definitional ceremony to bring together different communities. It also depicts the challenges and difficulties that coaches and mentors face when transporting ideas across places, spaces and cultures. Such challenges include the correct interpretation of sameness and difference among the opinions, interests and values of the divergent multi-partnerships and stakeholders – as well as socio-geographical factors like the weather.

Case Study 1: Leadership Coaching and Mentoring Programme in the Healthcare Setting: UK

The coaching and mentoring programme was part of an agreed leadership development strategy, which was intended to promote leadership capability in a region. There were two main priorities or targeted streams within the leadership cohort:

1   the black and ethnic minority (BME) leaders, who remained under-represented at senior levels (the BME leadership stream or project);
2   those leaders who were acting as change facilitators, to accelerate the spread of good practice in an ambitious improvement programme (the 'Change' or coaching for change stream or project).

Aims and objectives

The aim was to train delegates from the cohort groups in coaching and mentoring in a way that was relevant to their context.

The process

Each delegate was selected for training over five days and agreed to commit to mentoring and coaching for up to four days over a 12-month period. All of them were introduced to the UIF via a spectrum of coaching and mentoring techniques and practical exercises.

The change facilitators learnt about change theories and approaches and practised their techniques in a relevant context. They focused on the cross-cultural implications of transferring good practice from one environment to another. This concept of transferring practice had been shown to be particularly problematic: there were variations in performance on key health and social deliverables across the region despite knowledge about good healthcare practice being readily available and centres of excellence being well cited locally.

The BME leaders looked at the cross-cultural context for the application of their skills, so that they could work with other minority leaders to support them in their career development. At the same time a national programme trained senior managers to coach and mentor BME leaders in more junior positions. This extended the participating pool of coaches and mentors. In turn, each delegate in both streams was offered a mentor of his or her own. After some months, mentors were offered the chance to undertake supervisor training and then widen their roles by becoming supervisors, too.

Matching
After the training, individuals were matched with mentees who had received training in the coaching process. Despite the use of a criterion-based matching approach, the coordinator noted that much of the process required brokering between the two parties involved. Those individuals who selected a mentor without coaching and mentoring training were least satisfied three months later. Experienced mentees were most able to be independent at this stage, and those who had relied on just the paper-led matching service were less likely to end up in a mentoring pairing after the first session.

Core coaching and mentoring training
Both cohorts received five days of core training. This covered basic coaching and mentoring skills and extended periods of context awareness building, so that the cohorts could appreciate their environment of application and the particular issues and barriers to effective movement across boundaries. In the Change project, this related to the transfer of practice across geographical boundaries, professional boundaries, political boundaries, technological, structural and self-limiting belief boundaries. The training focus was on techniques designed to develop a deep understanding of the environment of operation and the main players; this included recognizing the risks to successful change implementation at each stage and developing mindfulness at each transition.

In the BME leadership stream, the boundaries were considered to mark inclusion (political, structural, policy, communication and knowledge boundaries and self-limiting beliefs). The added training emphasis incorporated the notion of personal acculturation, storytelling, developing wider system knowledge and understanding of others' perspectives, political awareness and personal confidence.

Supporting the process

When individuals started the coaching process they signed contracts with one another and both parties agreed to come to CPD (continuous professional development). The coordinator offered a range of developmental opportunities to suit all tastes – from groups of mentees to mixed groups of mentors and mentees to groups of mentors. As many people performed both roles at different times, their choice of event was interesting. All events were supported and, over the 12 months, everyone undertook supervision in some form or another. The most stimulating events, which blended formal CPD with informal chances to discuss areas of interest or concern, were the mixed role events. Some delegates used their experience of one role to inform another role.

Other individuals talked to mentors other than their own and vice versa and transferred the knowledge back into their own mentoring relationships. Most senior mentors described the CPD sessions as 'unexpectedly insightful and extremely useful' for their leadership and mentoring role.

As CPD was rolled out across settings, different patterns emerged; but probably the most successful type was the one based on action learning. This was probably because action learning was already embedded in the organization, as a development method. Coaching, mentoring and action learning are natural partners and together can bridge the individual and collective learning gap.

Reflection

Early learning

Typically there were some early teething problems. Some participants went into the process looking for a quick fix to problems and, having experienced some 'quick wins' on points of information, they struggled to adjust to the process. They were encouraged to review expectations, redefine goals and be open to learning in unexpected ways. In many cases their blockage mirrored the concept of delay in gratification described earlier, and also a natural resistance to new ways of learning. Coordinator support at these points and a focus on building up mentee knowledge and skills to lead the process ensured that few people quit or changed mentors. Those who experienced problems early on tended to describe the process even more positively, having overcome those difficulties.

The other lesson was that the 'Eureka!' or 'Aha!' moments were very likely to arrive outside coaching and mentoring sessions, in later reflection, and that the time lag before the benefits showed up could run into weeks and months. In the BME leadership stream, we found that those mentees who selected BME mentors often sought a change of mentor or an additional mentor sooner than expected. This emphasized the fact that, for many participants, initial homogenous matching had a significant but limited value.

Evaluation: 12 months later
We can evaluate the impact of the coaching and mentoring programme by using the UIF/ILS framework – that is, by examining success along four dimensions:

1 personal;
2 social;
3 cultural/organizational;
4 professional.

We shall describe these dimensions in turn. There were quite a few surprises at a number of levels.

At the personal level The BME cohort was now well established. Individual mentees described expanded job roles and half of the delegates in the first training programme had been promoted. The learning from the programme emphasized the importance of a flexible understanding of culture in all its forms. All the individuals, be they coaches, mentors or mentees, identified with different parts of the process. Gender perceptions, inter-racial perceptions, issues about how power was perceived, the value of career success in hierarchical terms – all these were experienced differently by them all. This was the result of their unique identities, which in many cases were self-determined in the context of a different experience of socialization. However, for the most part, the shared experience of a standard British education or training system generated a common understanding. Likewise, working for the National Health Service or for social services develops a strong sense of alignment with the community of service users, and with it comes an understanding of majority culture.

At the social level There were far-reaching alliances between people, and some successful pairs managed to find common values and ways that worked, despite proceeding from diverse starting points. Mentors in the BME stream who were drawn from the ranks of senior management and did not have a BME background seemed to benefit enormously. They stated that they had found the mentees challenging, probing and exciting to be with. This impact was, no doubt, enhanced by the empowerment that BME mentors had experienced as a result of their coaching and mentoring training, which helped them to steer the process so as to make it meet their own learning needs.

At the organizational/cultural level The programme of change was followed by a major restructuring of the organization. As result, the formal, funded coaching and mentoring programme for both cohort groups was indefinitely delayed. However, the informal infrastructure that was in place and was based on training, multiple roles and a network of supervisors ensured that, where there was a champion of coaching and mentoring, the programme had a development process embedded in it that supported change. As a result, the coaching and mentoring programme was integrated into the mainstream of leadership and change in some areas, becoming aligned with the core business and inherently sustainable – even without funding. In areas where there were no champions, the programme fizzled out rapidly.

BME leaders got more involved in wider roles and became generic coaches or mentors working in the area of change. They also got involved in coaching and mentoring senior managers on how to make the most of the variegated talent pool in their own organizations. They continued to supervise others from the mixed cohort of coaches and mentors. Directly or indirectly, their involvement in coaching and mentoring ensured a so-called marginalized group got closer to the core and power base of the organization. Those individuals were also better able to work on the change and improvement agenda that the organization valued, and as a result they came more to be valued for their contribution. The BME and Change cohorts exchanged their knowledge, which was further diffused into other areas of healthcare practice.

At the professional level   In the online assessment of competency in leadership, BME leaders scored consistently above their pay scale expectations; they also demonstrated a higher orientation to change than the rest of the sample. This same group also received the highest mentor performance feedback in a bespoke 360-degree feedback tool (this will be discussed in Chapter 10). There may be a link between undertaking the coaching and mentoring training and improving general leadership effectiveness, because coaching is in itself a style of leadership. This notion fits in with the concept of a coaching culture (Clutterbuck and Megginson, 2005).

The scores for mentor performance feedback from both the BME stream and the Change stream were significantly above the scores for those who had received other coaching or mentorong training. This could be put down to factors like the length of training or the UIF emphasis.

Two years on
Where there are champions from the original cohorts, coaching and mentoring still flourish in two years' time, and they are delivering evidence-based improvements to patient care and to the leadership capability of a stretched service. It took the BME leaders some real drive and courage to champion diversity within the organization. A shared commitment went beyond goals, targets, hierarchical structures and ring-fenced budgets. However, in the largest part of the healthcare sector in the region, the general coaching and mentoring programme was uncoordinated and sporadic, as no specific funding had been assigned to it. The BME coaching and mentoring programme expanded beyond the region and was adopted nationally, and funding was assigned for its continuing development.

Seven years on
Despite the funding cut under the current economic climate, the national BME coaching and mentoring programme continues to expand in various regions in the UK. At the time of preparing this second edition, I could still observe pockets of initiatives running in London.

Learning
One thing that this case study demonstrates is the importance of planning for coaching and mentoring and of ensuring that any programme is capable of sustainability beyond the limits of short-time funding. External and internal funding and resourcing entities can work in partnership with coaching and mentoring agencies from the outset, to

emphasize the transitory nature of funding and to work towards the mainstreaming of coaching and mentoring as part of their key service or business delivery. They can:

- help these agencies set up sustainable plans for coaching, which are built around the identification of informed and strategic champions;
- develop strategic alignments on core business or service areas they support;
- encourage flexibility in programme design, which is contextualized in key areas of improvement;
- promote fluidity between roles, so that coaching is able to reproduce capability and capacity organically;
- embed supervision into existing organizational learning practices, so as to work towards the promotion of these organizations as coaching cultures (Clutterbuck and Megginson, 2005), in an extension of the learning organization model discussed in Chapter 5.

Such a strategic alliance between the funder or the funding arm and the agency encourages the latter to focus on the sustainability of the coaching and mentoring process as a condition of receiving funding. As we will see in Chapter 10, there is still a need to evaluate the outcomes of coaching and mentoring for all stakeholders.

Case Study 2: Leadership Coaching Programme in the Healthcare Setting: Malta

This pilot study describes how a leadership coaching programme was being introduced in the healthcare sector in Malta using the action research process. The coaching approaches include a range of eclectic methods. The analytical tools used in the reflective stages include thematic analyses and a systems approach. The study also shows how the UIF/ILS may be used to identify the impact of the programme.

Aims and objectives

The pilot study aims to show how a leadership coaching programme may be implemented for nurse ward managers in a general hospital, with the following objectives:

- to identify the perceived idealized leadership attributes (ILA);
- to identify the skill gap in leadership;
- to inform the management on how to implement a comprehensive coaching program;
- to identify the impact of the programme.

The process

The coaching programme was implemented at Mater Dei Hospital, which is the largest hospital for acute diseases in Malta. The target population was all the nurse ward managers of the hospital. Twelve ward managers were randomly chosen from six departments (two from each department) – seven females and five males, aged between 32 and 46. The programme consisted of four one-to-one coaching sessions. The coaching process of each session followed the GROW model (Whitmore, 2002), with a range of coaching methods embedded as appropriate.

The programme was introduced according to the action research process – in other words it consisted of three steps:

1   planning;
2   action;
3   reflection.

This process was iterated in two cycles or phases.

Phase 1

At this stage planning consists of:

1   arranging the meeting with the director of nursing to discuss organizational objec-
    tives to be met and to agree on the agenda for the focus groups and coaching
    programme;
2   conducting stratified random sampling to select the participants;
3   making decisions about an action plan and scheduling the first focus group;
4   developing the ILA exercise as a pilot.

Action here means:

1   implementing the first pilot focus group by using a nominal group facilitation
    technique;
2   conducting two one-to-one coaching sessions;
3   meeting the group to validate the coaching themes that emerged from the focus
    group discussion and to decide the way forward for the second phase.

Reflection (see next section)

Phase 2

Planning consists of:

1   developing a template for the coaching log;
2   revising the ILA exercise;
3   planning the Phase 2 implementation.

Action consists of:

1   communicating the updated ILA to the participants;
2   implementing the Phase 2 coaching sessions;
3   conducting the final focus group.

Reflection (see next section).

Reflection

The experience gained in Phase 1 suggests that coaching tools need to be made more compact and that integrating the GROW model into the coaching process is helpful to goal attainment. The following four themes emerge from the thematic analysis of the first focus group discussion transcripts:

1 Intrinsic values: honesty, loyalty, fairness, empathy and trustworthiness are regarded as central components of idealized leadership. These values combine to form an ethical foundation for any life situation.
2 Vision: one needs to understand the organizational vision as well as one's own. These visions need to be congruent with one's behaviour.
3 Visibility: being visible and having a presence at work helps to inspire others in the team and makes the leader act as a role model in the promotion of ethical values. It also helps leaders remain in control and better connected to the team. This improves team communication and management.
4 Assertiveness: being assertive gives one a sense of empowerment to realize the vision and competence as a role model.

The thematic analyses of the second focus group discussion in Phase 2 identified 27 idealized leadership attributes of nurse managers. These are:

1 authenticity: honesty, integrity, fairness, equality, transparency, respect, self-awareness, trustworthiness, loyalty, ethical behaviour, role modelling, openness to criticism, acknowledging mistakes;
2 responsibility: accountability, reliability, dependability, dedication, fidelity, constancy, consistency, commitment, self-discipline;
3 collaboration: teamwork, communication, cooperation, partnership, solidarity, support, conflict management, consensus building;
4 caring: empathy, concern, compassion, dignity, kindness, generosity, nurturance, helpfulness, consideration, understanding;
5 excellence: high quality, competence, skills, high standards, aptitude, professionalism, effectiveness, evidence-based practice;
6 safety: security, protection, well-being, risk containment;
7 empowerment; involvement, power sharing, delegation, broad-mindedness, freedom, self-determination, autonomy, non-blame culture;
8 influence: authority, power, decisiveness, assertiveness, command, control, confidence;
9 growth: development, coaching, learning, guidance, counsel, mentoring, supporting, challenging, knowledge sharing;
10 vision: clarity, strategy, purposefulness, direction, future-mindedness, being proactive, having initiative;
11 visibility: support, presence, instruction, supervision, accessibility, role modelling;
12 contribution: serving others, making a difference, leaving a legacy, altruism, generosity, selflessness, abundance mentality;
13 patience: serenity, flexibility, tolerance, endurance, temperance;
14 inspiration: passion, optimism, encouragement, engagement, charisma, motivation, energizing, confidence, stimulation, humour;

15 determination: resolve, certainty, fortitude, hardiness, resilience, persistence, perseverance, steadfastness;

16 courage: daring, boldness, challenge, risk-taking, audaciousness, non-conformity;

17 orderliness: tidiness, neatness, structure, efficiency, organization;

18 appreciation: praising, thanking, gratitude, acknowledging, rewarding, gratefulness, cherishing;

19 creativity: originality, inventiveness, innovativeness, imagination, ingenuity, resourcefulness;

20 humility: serving others, modesty, humbleness, gentleness, reserve;

21 diligence: duty, industry, accountability, conscientiousness, self-discipline;

22 pragmatism: practicality, realism, sensibleness, factuality, expediency, feasibility, convenience;

23 prudence: carefulness, cautiousness, non-risk decisions, discretion;

24 reputation: status, esteem, standing, popularity, admiration, recognition;

25 ambition: achievement, results, success, accomplishment, being the best, competition, superiority, pride, winning spirit, drive, sense of triumph, territorialism;

26 meticulousness: precision, accuracy, perfection, exactness, thoroughness;

27 conformity: stability, constancy, compliance, observance, conventionality.

To show the complex interrelationship between the above leadership attributes and the system environment, a healthcare leadership development system (HLDS) is developed using a general systems mapping approach (Shams and Law, 2012). Figure 9.1 shows such a general HLDS in relation to the coaching intervention.

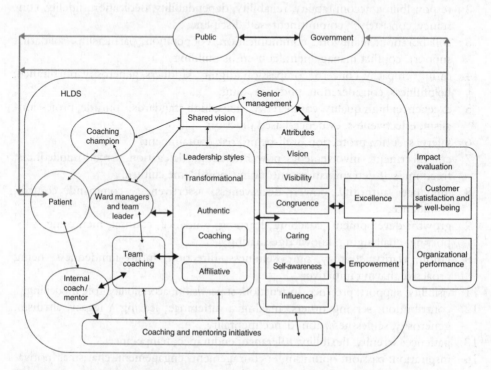

Figure 9.1 A healthcare leadership development system (HLDS) that shows leadership coaching to be embedded as part of it

The ward managers stated that the process helped with identifying both their strengths and their areas of development. It also confirmed the need to provide a 360-degree feedback as part of the developmental process. The managers' knowledge and insights into leadership attributes were increased. It was concluded that coaching should be embedded as part of the organizational culture, such that it becomes available to all ward managers. The following elements should be integrated as part of a leadership culture:

- Formal training: introduces basic coaching and leadership development.
- Individual coaching: facilitates self-awareness and the identification of organizational and personal goals, personal core values, leadership strengths and areas of development.
- Group coaching: stimulates sharing ideas and learning.

The feedback also confirms that four sessions of coaching intervention were effective in terms of achieving a number of tangible organizational goals. These included changes in the medication distribution systems, enhanced interdisciplinary documentation, and the development of training programmes and standard operating procedures.

Learning

The learning could be organized according to the structure of the UIF/ILS:

Personal qualities:

- increase one's self-awareness;
- enhance one's understanding of one's own core values, beliefs and behaviour;
- identify one's personal strengths and areas of development;
- enhance one's expertise;
- achieve one's personal and professional goals;
- develop one's accountability and leadership;
- develop one's insights and multiple perspectives;
- make one learn about creativity, 'out of the box' thinking and flexibility;
- increase one's resilience and self-assurance;
- develop a positive outlook;
- develop authenticity and mindfulness;
- develop openness to discuss concerns;

Social competence:

- develops communication skills;
- develops conflict and anger management;
- makes one appreciate and respect others;
- makes one learn to delegate;
- makes one act as a role model;
- opens one to criticism and feedback from others;

cultural and organizational competence:

- builds cultural bonds to enhance collective consciousness;
- develops new ways to enhance teamwork;
- champions empowerment and supports others;
- supports and integrates those who may seem ineffectual and unable to cope with their responsibilities or situations;
- makes one evaluate the impact of a coaching intervention;
- makes one continue the research on integrating coaching within the healthcare leadership development system;

professional competence:

- develops coaching skills;
- maintains continuous professional development (CPD);
- is an agent of change and helps others to go through the transition process.

Case Study 3: E-Coaching: A Transatlantic Coaching Pilot Project

This was a transatlantic coaching pilot project that was set up to offer one-to-one coaching sessions via email and telephone for the leadership students at Rice University, Houston, Texas, from members of the Association for Coaching (AC) in the UK (Bresser, 2006a and 2006b). The project was monitored and evaluated by four regular questionnaires – both before and after the evaluation.

Aims and objectives

Apart from satisfying the organizational objectives of the hosts, the project aimed to match the goals of both coaches and coachees, so that the students being coached could:

- intensify or support their learning experience at Rice University;
- leverage their maximum potential with regard to personal development and/or leadership issues;
- develop an active, responsible and self-managed role, to facilitate their personal development and their leadership skills;
- be inspired by the international dimension of the coaching programme;
- widen their horizon and become sensitive to their own cultural and individual characteristic features.

As part of an international coaching team, the coaches participating in the programme would also benefit from:

- learning and gaining experience in e-coaching across cultures;
- having the challenge (or pleasure) to work with high potential.

From the organizational perspectives, it was hoped that, through the coaching programme, Rice University would:

- improve its overall organizational performance by optimizing students' learning through coaching;
- become more familiar with coaching as a modern tool for the leveraging of human potential and make use of it in the context of the university.

The Association for Coaching could benefit:

- by getting new perceptions in the area of coaching research;
- as a result of an increase in the popularity of coaching and in the general public's knowledge about it;
- by supporting its members to be part of a leading-edge, highly prestigious international coaching pilot project, and thereby to gain popularity for the organization.

Of course, the coordinator, Frank Bresser, would be able to conduct his coaching research on the basis of the international dimension of the project. His research aimed to:

- analyse the efficiency of external coaches;
- evaluate the impact of culture on coaching;
- analyse an organization's possibilities to increase its overall performance;
- analyse the necessary preconditions to install a successful coaching system;
- evaluate the effectiveness/efficiency of telephone and Internet coaching;
- develop a concept for implementing coaching successfully.

As this was a research project, it was agreed that the pilot was to be conducted free of charge. Only the telephone costs for the coaching sessions were to be paid by Rice University. Rice University and the students agreed in return that the pilot project and the research findings deriving from it could be used in the research and that publications would be accessible to the public. Confidentiality and anonymity were ensured for the students being coached.

The Process

The scope of the coaching content was defined in advance: it was to be related to the personal development and/or leadership issues of the student. The coaching aimed to enhance the learning outcomes of the leadership studies. It was up to the students to take the initiative to contact their allocated coaches by email or phone to arrange the dates of the coaching sessions. Each student was given a coaching 'budget' of 12 hours maximum over a 12-week period. With this time frame, it was up to the coaches and coachees to agree among themselves on the regularity, duration and dates/times of the coaching sessions. Coaches and coachees were also given information on using free Internet phoning software (Skype) for those who preferred Internet access.

Initially it was planned to offer eight places for the students. At the end, owing to the demand, 19 coaches and coachees were paired up. As part of the AC complaints procedure, coachees were informed that any complaints could be made to the AC board via their student coordinator (US) and via the UK coordinator of the programme. The coachees had full control of both the process and the evaluation of coaching at all times. As I remember, Frank Bresser was always saying, 'the coachee is always the "king" of the coaching process'.

Selection

The coaches selected to participate in the programme were members of the AC with appropriate qualifications. At the start of the programme, the coordinator sent a task profile to all the potential candidates (AC members) via the AC email system. The 'best' (the top 20) coaches from the applications were selected. The author was one of the members selected on the list. Before the confirmation, the list of the selected coaches (including their qualification profiles) was sent to the student coordinator (Susan Lieberman) for the students to select their preferred coaches.

Evaluation

RESULTS FROM THE E-QUESTIONNAIRE

The results of the evaluation from the transatlantic coaching pilot project were most encouraging. All the coachees who responded to the questionnaires (84 per cent response rate) said that they would like the pilot to continue and reported that

- the coaching programme had added value to their leadership studies;
- the coaching was different from other experiences available to them.

The majority of coachees indicated increased self-awareness and reflection as value added to their leadership studies (>40 per cent). What made coaching different from other experiences was that

- the coaching was fully personalized and focused;
- it provided an independent, objective setting for developing one's thought;
- it was an interesting way to step out of the box and get wider perspectives;
- coaches were trained professionals with a lot of expertise, experience and knowledge to share.

The coachees especially liked the coaching experience because

- it was tailor-made and personally focused;
- the coaches were great;
- it had diverse viewpoints.

The results also showed that external coaches, especially from other cultures or geographical locations, were highly appreciated by the coachees. The latter said that having external coaches was very beneficial to the whole process, in particular in terms of bringing new perspectives and ensuring confidentiality. It provided a virtual space where the coachees felt 'safer'.

The coaches who participated in the pilot project also reported that they had benefited from the experience in the following ways:

- by coaching internationally and cross-culturally;
- by coaching persons with high potentials;
- by having different viewpoints presented to them.

A significant number of coachees preferred face-to-face coaching. Most coachees found phone cards more difficult to use than Internet phone (80 per cent reported difficulties with the cards, against 20 per cent with the Internet). According to the feedback from the coachees, the e-coaching programme could be improved in the following major aspects:

- by having the coaching sessions run during term time (rather than between two academic years);
- by providing help in scheduling to manage different time zones;
- by offering more guidance at the beginning of the project.

Overall, all the respondents (excluding the 24 per cent 'don't know') rated the coaching programme as 'very good' or 'good'. The majority of coachees (66 per cent) believed that having a permanent coaching programme would increase the attractiveness of the university as a place to study.

ONE YEAR ON

One year after the transatlantic coaching pilot project finished, the coaches on the project formed a network and were still keeping in touch over the Internet, via email and other ways of communicating. We assessed the legacy of the pilot and its impact upon the coachees and upon Rice University. It was a pleasant surprise that we still received very positive feedback from some of our coachees. For example, one of the coaches reported (this comes from the feedback survey):

> Coaching in some form has remained [in Rice University]. A year on and Rice is exploring the possibility of co-coaching for students. My coachee has been inspired to explore training in coaching for himself, as an important aspect of his future work. He told me fellow students were grateful to have had this experience, one they could not have afforded financially otherwise. He stressed how good it was for them to have this opportunity at a young age. His eyes were opened to another way of working with people and he continues to both develop and share his learning. A year on and the impact is still being felt; the young students have taken the gift we gave them and utilized it in their own leadership work.

Case Study 4: Narrative Coaching in Communities

As described in Chapter 3, narrative coaching is adopted from Michael White's therapeutic applications, which were originally drawn from Vygotsky's idea of social learning and from the work of Barbara Myerhoff (1982, 1986) – a cultural anthropologist who developed the definitional ceremony metaphor. The metaphor was applied to develop a community network as part of the coaching and mentoring programme in the UK. Other developments of narrative coaching include Stelter (2007) in Denmark and Drake (2006, 2007) in Australia and the US.

I chose to adopt narrative coaching because I discovered that clients who migrated to live and work in another country find this approach most helpful. The typical problems for clients who suffered from a dislocation of place, and hence of culture, include taking for granted their own signature strength, values and beliefs. The goals of the approach in this case were to develop the coachees' skills and knowledge by re-authoring the stories of their life experience.

Aims and objectives: the vision

The vision was to create

> [a] network of highly inspirational, skilful, talented leaders from diverse communities who come together to empower each other, thereby making each other even more inspirational, skilful, talented; and the communities become sustainable and more vibrant. (Law, Aga and Hill, 2006)

The aim was to create a community network that empowers all the members within the network, who in turn empower the diverse communities.

The objective of the conference was that, by the end of it, delegates would

- understand the nature of the community network and their role in the network and in the communities;
- form a foundation to proceed to the next phase;
- create a list of volunteers (with contact points) to sign up to be champions of the community network;
- consider developing a social contract.

The first step was to develop the skills of the members of the network so that they may become leaders and

- lead the leaders;
- train the trainers;
- coach the coaches;
- mentor the mentors.

It was hoped that all this would create a domino effect. During the initial session in the community network development, the delegates were coached in using facilitation skills. During the second session of the programme, the participants were introduced to the concepts of coaching, mentoring and the psychology that underpins their practice, including key definitions and a wide range of coaching and mentoring techniques.

The process: the definitional ceremony

The conference was held on a Saturday, to ensure that participants from various communities could attend. Over 40 people from the mixed community of Peterborough attended. The conference celebrated the successful completion of the Positive Image project.

Applying narrative coaching to diverse communities is particularly challenging. Snowy Aga described the characteristics of a diverse community as follows:

It sounds like a hundred drummers with different drums, each beating their [*sic*] own rhythm. It sounds like the cacophony of a hundred tribes, each speaking their [*sic*] own tongue. It sounds like a hundred calls for the same purpose.

The campfire

As an introduction to facilitate the definitional ceremony, a story was retold that had been acquired from the International Narrative Therapy Festive Conference, Adelaide, Australia (Combrink, Maree and Mabolo, 2006). The story went:

In Karos and Kambro, drama, dance, stories, mime, creative writing and sharing life stories around the camp fire were all woven into an intricate pattern of hopes and dreams:

> Around the campfire,
> They sang and danced
> It's freedom from all things.
> Because children could talk freely
> About the good moments
> All the good things in life
> They're able to know...

The storyteller then took out a stick, passed it round the group and asked them to try to break it. One man broke it in two with ease. The storyteller then presented a bundle of sticks and asked the group to break it. The bundle was passed round, and some tried to break it with their hands and others across their knees. One by one each member of the group tried and failed. The storyteller pointed out that the bundle of sticks was a metaphor, the point of which was:

> To be alone, we are weak.
> Together we are strong.
> Social collaboration is our strength.

From an outsider witness perspective, this story had a particular resonance for me, as a similar story had been told in China down the centuries. At the conference, a chopstick was passed round and the audience was asked to try to break it. The first participant broke the chopstick without any effort. Then a bundle of chopsticks was brought out, and no one could break it. The story was unchanged – its essence was the same.

A facilitative workshop was then carried out to redevelop the participants' skills and knowledge by using the narrative approach. This was based on the principle of re-authoring the stories of their life experience (as described in the earlier chapters).

Each group was asked to contribute a volunteer storyteller and a volunteer interviewer. The storytellers were asked to recall a skill or a form of knowledge they had recently acquired and to talk to the interviewer about it. The others acted as outsider witnesses. Each outsider witness group was asked to have at least one volunteer to perform the retelling later, at the plenary session.

The theme of the exercise asked the participants to produce:

- a list of skills and knowledge that are relevant for a community network;
- a list of values that are relevant for a social contract;
- a list of actions to proceed to the next phase;
- a list (with contact points) of volunteers for signing up to be champions of the community network, who would take the above actions forward.

The audience in the plenary session became the largest outsider witness group and acted as a community for witnessing and honouring the retelling and the retelling of retelling the various stories. The outcome of the group discussion was both enlightening and empowering.

THE STORY OF LINE DANCING
At the feedback session, Group 1's spokesperson (an outsider witness) retold the story of someone's experience in learning line dancing. Another outsider witness in the group described how listening to that story made her feel like joining the storyteller's line dancing class. When, having listened to the retelling of her own story, she was asked how that retelling resonated with her own values, hopes and dreams, the storyteller reported a sense of reassurance about her own values and the learning of new skills – for example, another language. One participant from another group pointed out the link between food, music and dance. As universal values, they had the potential to engage and communicate across cultures.

THE YOUNGEST LEADER
It was very moving that an 8-year-old girl had the confidence to be the storyteller in Group 2. She told us about her experience of learning to speak English. She reported that when she and her family first arrived in England she could not speak a word of English. Two years later it was very encouraging to hear her addressing the audience in English. Interestingly, once she started, her younger brother joined in, speaking about his experience too. His resonance was transported into the courage to speak.

THE STORY OF THE FUTURE GROUP
The outsider witness in Group 3 introduced the storyteller, who had lived in England for 16 years. This storyteller also spoke about his experience of learning to speak English – in his case, by talking to English people. One of his hopes and dreams for the future was to set up a group to help people from different cultures to learn English. This could act as a means to unify different cultures, he said, and to discover 'the truth to be human'.

'THE RISE AND FALL OF A YORKSHIRE PUDDING'
The Group 4 spokesperson titled the story of their group 'The rise and fall of a Yorkshire Pudding'. (A Yorkshire pudding is made from a flour and milk batter. It used to be popular in England as an accompaniment to roast beef in the traditional Sunday lunch.) The story described how a woman learnt to make Yorkshire puddings as a young wife and mother. Initially it did not work – the Yorkshire

pudding collapsed rather than rising, as it should have. She interpreted this as a failure to perform her role (of mother and wife?). In the end, she learned that it really did not matter whether the Yorkshire pudding was flat or not as long as she had done her best. (This has a resonance with Csikszentmihalyi's (1991) concept of optimal experience – the flow.) The story demonstrated that something as simple as cooking could review one's value, role and identity. When listening to her story being retold by the outsider witness, the storyteller felt that the story confirmed her sense of self and her identity and value. It gave her a sense of pride. She would like to take further action to go out and talk and listen to more people's stories. (I later received the feedback that the story was actually told from a feminist perspective. This threw light on the hidden thread of the storyline. Viewed from the angle of feminist discourse, it might suggest that the original storyteller was trying to express the inequality of gender in society; power relationships operate not just in the workplace, but also at home, as an expression of society's wider cultural expectations.)

THE STORY OF DISILLUSIONMENT
Not all stories were positive. As the conference members came from diverse communities, some of them had suffered discrimination and social alienation. The spokesperson in Group 5 described the storyteller, whose family originally came from the Caribbean: she was a fourth-generation child born in Britain. She (the spokesperson) depicted her story (the storyteller's) as 'a long struggle to mainstream equality and a feeling of disillusionment'. She described many skills and ideas the storyteller had to help people suffering from drug abuse and withdrawal symptoms, such as setting up a drug abuse centre, volunteer groups, and so on. However, she felt that over the last 22 years the storyteller had remained on the margins, received very little or no help and was not in the 'mainstream'. She said that listening to the story from Group 3 about the hopes and dreams to set up a group to help others break down cultural barriers resonated with her own past struggle. She did not want them to experience disillusionment, as she had. The discussion quickly evolved into a political debate about what the government and local authorities should do. This is a good example of the risk of following a negative story line. This requires re-centring by the facilitator, who has to bring it to the central theme. At the same time, the facilitator may highlight the positive strength (such as resilience) that the storyteller showed in the story (22 years of continuous struggle at the margins of society demonstrate a lot of resilience and determination). The art is for a narrative coach to help the person to re-author the story so that it may lead to a more positive conclusion – a new outcome and action. For example, you may ask the coachee to re-imagine how life would be if she could re-direct her positive strength to other avenues.

THE STORY OF ICE SKATING AND ICE HOCKEY
The outsider witness retold how the storyteller learned to skate on ice and as a result injured her back. However, she did not give up. Instead of ice-skating, she learnt a new skill and found a new hobby: ice hockey. The retelling of this story gave the storyteller a sense of pride and self-esteem. It confirmed her value – the courage to take action to 'get out of one's own comfort zone'. This story also resonates with many that I heard during the 2012 Paralympic Games.

LANDSCAPE OF CONSCIOUSNESS MAPPING AND LANDSCAPE OF ACTION

To summarize, the resonance created through listening to the retelling of the participants' own stories generated the following emotions or values (landscape of consciousness) and actions (landscape of actions):

landscape of consciousness:

- a sense of pride;
- respect;
- reassurance;
- the realization of one's self and new skills;
- a sense of self-achievement;
- a realization of past sacrifices;
- self-awareness;
- self-realization;
- moral considerations;
- happy memories;
- a sense of trust;
- a sense of responsibility;
- courage;
- motivation;
- commitment;

landscape of action – an impulse to:

- communicate;
- get involved with others;
- break barriers;
- make decisions;
- make stronger commitments;
- overcome hostility;
- overcome prejudice;
- translate theory into action;
- take positive actions.

ACTION PLAN

From the conference, the groups generated a number of concrete actions:

1   to join the community network;
2   to be part of this community;
3   to be involved (don't just 'talk', but also take 'action');
4   to share and participate at all levels;
5   to create and foster opportunities for the involvement of others, especially the diverse minority groups;
6   to discuss and take forward the ideas of 'campfire' and storytelling in the group members' organizations;

7 to ensure that contact details and interests were shared;
8 to ask the question, 'What can we bring to the party?'
9 to get involved with networking opportunities;
10 to help the community network to regenerate deprived areas.

Evaluation: Follow-Up Feedback

The conference report was published in a form of newsletter called *The Cutting Edge* and was disseminated to all the participants, stakeholders and wider communities in the form of an e-journal (Law, Aga and Hill, 2006). Some of the feedback in emails I received from readers was encouraging:

> I was very inspired to read about how you have ... created ways to share your learning to further community development. Your passion and commitment to your dreams in this area is very evident! It sounds like it worked fantastically well, and was very creative!
>
> What stood out to me, was the expansiveness with which you brought such a diversity of people and projects together, to empower them to be able to use the knowledge you gained from narrative training. [The] story gave me the image of you drawing together many different people – of diverse ages and cultures, ideas and resources to create communities – in a way that involved lots of noise, movement, laughter, and maybe mess! One thing that resonated with me was the care you seemed to have taken to ensure that children and older peoples voices were heard (I leaned this from the retelling and photos), as the inclusion of generations in any community development seems very important to me. Your "telling" has got me thinking how I might include the voices of older and younger people in the lives of the adult women I work with, who have often become very isolated as a result of abuse. So good on you!!

Outcome

It was a pleasant surprise to see the idea of telling stories around the campfire in Karos and Kambro having caught the community's imagination. A participant at the story retelling session asked: 'Where is the campfire in Peterborough?' Many others were inspired to create a campfire in their own communities. As part of the outcome, a new community network was set up.

DIFFICULTIES ENCOUNTERED
Difficulties include:

- The validity, reliability and representation of the primary authors who told the stories. As a narrative practitioner playing the ethnographer's role of retelling, reporting and disseminating the stories of individuals and groups from the diverse communities, we had an ethical dilemma: had we done justice to those people, honouring and respecting them? Some of the stories were very personal and politically sensitive. Questions raised include: Are the retold stories a fair represen-tation of the intention of the storytellers? Are the retold stories valid, and do they represent the meaning of the original stories reliably?
- Acknowledgements to the stakeholders. In order to maintain confidentiality, we kept the names and identities of the storytellers anonymous. As a result,

acknowledgements to those individuals by way of honouring the source of the stories became difficult to make.

- Our responsibility as coaches, consultants and researchers in disseminating those stories. On the one hand, like academic researchers, we felt that we had a professional duty to publish those stories, to share those skills and knowledge among our colleagues. On the other hand, this had to balance with the sensitivities of those individuals who contributed to those stories and knowledge.
- Ownership of the stories. Some of the stories were highly idiosyncratic and personal, yet, once they were told and retold at the conference and published, they were in the public domain; skills and knowledge were shared among communities. While some may be very happy with the dissemination of the stories, which embedded and transported the knowledge, others may feel that the stories were too private to share in a wider circle. This raises the question of ownership and authorship of those stories. Do those who write and report the stories own them, or should the storytellers own their own stories? Who has the power, responsibility and control to disseminate the stories and the knowledge, and for whose benefit?
- Rules and regulations. Owing to the rules and regulations of the organization, setting up a fire at a nature reserve was judged by the management to be highly undesirable. So at the end we had to use a metaphor, lighting up a candle and setting up a marquee instead of creating a real fire.
- The weather. Setting up a campfire and telling stories outdoors in England turned out to be very challenging. Even though the follow-up event was to be held in the summer, during the hottest week of the year, it had to be cancelled at the last minute due to a thunderstorm!

Case Study 5: Coaching in Communities: Community Coaching Café

The final case study addresses the role of the coordinator in leading and supporting the UIF/ILS approach in practice. It considers the experience and reflection of a coordinator and this person's role in working in the local community setting. The project was called Community Coaching Café (CCC). It was situated in St Neots, a satellite market town for London and Cambridge that is outside the high-growth, high-tech purview of Cambridge University. It was part of the activities carried out by Enterprise Pathways (EP), a social enterprise set up in 2010 as a registered community interest company. It had no shareholders and its profits were reinvested for the benefit of the community.

EP developed the CCC as a project in 2010 to provide an accessible, non-stigmatizing and safe environment for the neighbourhood and offered free, independent, confidential, face-to-face peer support, coaching and mentoring services. The need for the project arose from an earlier action research project involving young people, which explored the impact of violence on their lives and the idea that a community drop-in with mentors would be valuable to young people and their parents. CCC was run by local volunteers and aimed to support local people who needed someone to talk to. It provided community coaching for volunteers. It was a standalone community service for people to self-refer to; this service could also evolve into contingency support for users of other organizations, many of whom were experiencing cuts to their services at that time.

Aims and objectives

The project aimed to disseminate the collective experience of the managing staff and volunteers among individuals from local groups by using coaching and mentoring. Many of the participants were community leaders and entrepreneurs of small and medium-sized enterprises. This also created a community resource for the volunteers.

The process

Initially, 12 people trained as the first community coaches. Most of these coaches were already active members of the community, helping in other capacities, including as leader of the town council, mayor, local teachers and health workers. The first participants were community-orientated active residents such as charity workers, town councillors, youth workers, helpline advisers. The later intake divided approximately equally between counselling or social work students seeking placements and unemployed or retired people wishing to share their skills and experience to help others. Seventy-five per cent were females, 60 per cent were aged over 50, 85 per cent were ethnically white UK residents, 5 per cent were South American, 10 percent were black or of a mixed race, and 12 per cent had a disability.

All volunteers were Criminal Records Bureau (CRB) cleared and offered an accredited two-day introductory course (10 hours). This is an intensive coaching and mentoring programme covering a range of techniques in addition to basic coaching and counselling principles:

- confidentiality;
- empathy;
- active listening;
- assumptions;
- barriers;
- boundaries;
- self-disclosure;
- endings.

The training was followed by ongoing group supervisions; these included a number of practical sessions with experienced coaches from the team and reflective journal keeping as part of the coachees' personal development. For instance, each new coachee performed both as a café listener and as a community coachee, in order to gain insights into the coaching experience from opposing perspectives. Although these practical sessions were called rehearsals, they were valuable experiences in their own right, as they provided new coaches with a safe place where they could recognize and respond to any emotions arising from the coaching process. They could also learn to dissociate themselves from their coachees' circumstances; gain personal insights into how they would protect themselves emotionally and practically once they became known in the community as coaches; begin their actual coaching practice; and start honing their own coaching style.

On completion of the course, volunteers were asked if they would like to join the Community Café coaching team and/or be helped to find a placement elsewhere. Each trained volunteer (coach-to-be) completed a volunteer profile outlining what experience she or he would bring to and what she or he wanted to gain from the coaching experience. Coach and coachee were matched for suitability before the coaching commenced. Informal meetings that covered non-confidential matters were arranged in everyday social spaces such as coffee shops, bars or even the local park, where that was appropriate.

Each session took about an hour. All coaching sessions were coachee-led. The session aims and objectives were noted at the outset. The coach began by positioning the coachee and the situation in the present, to achieve a state of mindfulness by focusing on the coachee's cognitive and emotional states and aspirations at that time. The coaches maintained this state through rapport building, exploring boundary setting particularly in relation to any others who might be involved in resolving the situation, and encouraging the coachees to trust their intuition and be aware of their impact on others. They would clarify aims and reframe negative responses in a positive way, by prompting 'what ifs' to discover further options and the names of any obstacles likely to occur. In this way a simple action plan was drawn up. When the session was drawing to a close, coaches checked whether its aims had been properly discussed; if they had not, they would prompt answers about what was lacking. The action plan was then reviewed, the session was summarized and agreed upon, an evaluation form completed, and the session ended. All coaching sessions were recorded, evaluated and stored confidentially, and both coach and coachee received 'debriefings'. Coaches and coachees would reflect on the attitude and helpfulness of the coach, the suitability of the location, how and whether the session helped to achieve the goal and resolve the issues, whether the aim of the session had been met, and whether the coachee would like further sessions. Where appropriate, a referral to other service providers might be offered. Issues arising from the session were discussed in supervision sessions, and they provided feedback for future coaching training.

Each group supervision focused on issues actually or typically arising in interventions: one third focused on elements of professional self-management (session closure, self-disclosure, paraphrasing); one third on emotional intelligence (how to prompt effectively, barriers to rapport building, boundary setting, learning to dissociate); and one third on teaching (note-taking skills, session evaluations, reflective journaling).

In this way more than 20 volunteers were developed as community coaches. They were provided with training, supervision, tools for self-development, and placement opportunities. They formed strong social bonds through training together; these were valuable to all, especially to those who were new to the community.

Evaluation

The CCC project was evaluated in terms of two aspects:

- the community's awareness of the project;
- stakeholder satisfaction (coachees, coachees, directors, funders)

Community awareness

Initial awareness-raising campaigns included posting flyers to doctors' surgeries, hairdressers, cafés and pubs. These attracted no enquiries from the community. A two-pronged, long-term marketing plan was developed to reach healthcare professionals – particularly general practitioners and mental health workers – and the local groups. By getting involved in healthcare forums, participants created opportunities to talk about how their coaching and mentoring services could be both a support to the community and a supplement to their out-of-hours provision. Using the local press – particularly for the launch, the training events and the workshop days, when the local online community newspaper gave the project free listings and the local radio station gave the coordinator airtime to talk about the project – also raised community awareness. These activities increased the number of inquiries.

Stakeholder satisfaction

After six months, the viability of the project was measured by using UIF/ILS to examine the group reflection from the following perspectives:

- self: the participants (directors, volunteer coaches and inquirers, coachees);
- social/culture: the wider community;
- the organization/culture: the company and the funders.

The evaluation drew on users' feedback, publicity outcomes and turnout at events; other comments from other organizations evaluated the strength of the relationships and recommended the creation of a SWOT matrix to highlight strengths and opportunities, weaknesses and threats. The results showed that those people who used the coaching service found it valuable, but the percentage of community members taking up the service remained low. The funders were satisfied with the project aims and its achievements to the extent that further grants and donations were offered.

Reflection

The learning points from this pilot coaching project have been many. The community engagement targets have been met in various ways:

- by strengthening other community services through the provision of volunteers for a local foyer, a young offenders' unit, a helpline service;
- by providing learning opportunities for the wider community by way of workshops, talks and drop-in groups;
- by building mutually beneficial referral relationships with other volunteer-led organizations where coaching skills are valued at a premium, thus increasing the mentoring capacity within the community.

The learning environment for the community coaches

We could see from this case study that the practice of community coaching satisfies different needs of diverse individuals:

- those seeking specific advice, whose issues could be resolved through factual information or by being signposted elsewhere;
- those prepared to talk through their situation and their ideas of how to resolve the issues, and willing to do so with an impartial coach, skilled in prompting reflective thinking;
- dependent people with complicated, multiple, maybe overwhelming, maybe cyclic or recurrent challenges about which they have become paralysed – people likely to require ongoing support;
- isolated and lonely people, for whom the social contact was enough in itself.

Through the process, volunteers were able to gain entry to a social care placement. This improved their skills, built their self-confidence, and enriched the experience of the community.

Reflecting on personal development

On reflection, the coordinator realized how much she enjoyed the experiential learning, the process of converting ideas into actions for herself and others, and particularly the shared learning experience gained from the group supervisions and, more widely, from the coaching psychology peer support group in the region.

Developing and running this project demanded boldness, persistence, effective networking, backroom skills, and a belief in community mentoring. Reflecting on the experience, the coordinator felt that the early days were exhilarating, as she tapped into the energies of local people and the project gathered a momentum of its own, offering interesting options for development. The backroom work was demanding, but it created a satisfying core, which shaped governance and the training resources. The outward-facing aspects – giving talks, talking to the press, the market day launch – were the icing on the cake, creating new energy and new opportunities that became integrated into the practice.

Looking ahead

Given the groundswell of support that the project received from different sections of the community, the stakeholders were encouraged to consolidate their experience, and they plan to do the following:

- share the learning with the professional communities and the wider community;
- source funds to develop the community coaching pilot as an out-of-hours well-being service in support of general healthcare services;
- develop a volunteer management consultancy for the third sector.

Chapter Summary and Reflection

Having read this chapter, I hope you have learnt from it how to take coaching and mentoring beyond the micro-level experience of one-to-one relationships. The case studies have addressed some of the collective and strategic issues that inform the establishment of sustainable coaching and mentoring systems. The process needs to embody the flexibility and informality required to make learning happen at the micro-level of experience, but also to ensure that an infrastructure is in place to support its continuity. At the micro-level of experience, perhaps coaching and mentoring are practised as an art form. At the level of strategy and system development, it has to become more scientific and systematic. Coaching and mentoring cannot stay still. They have to be capable of growing and expanding to take root.

Carl Jung (1875–1961) once said: 'Until you make the unconscious conscious, it will direct your life and you will call it fate' (quoted in Potter, 2012: 108). I hope that, having read the case studies, you will see that the coaching/mentoring process is a transformation from unconscious to conscious – whether through CBT, through story-telling or through self-reflection. In all these cases coaches and mentors performed multiple roles: sometimes as leaders who inspired participants; other times as facilita-tors, or simply as participants who took a back seat (or a de-centred position); and yet other times as thinkers and writers who reflected on the lessons learnt. Throughout these different engagements, coaches and mentors use themselves as a vehicle for change (in terms of gestalt philosophy). We have observed and experienced that coaches and mentors seem to share a common attitude, posture and values, although their forms of expression, terminology, styles and techniques may vary depending on clients, contexts and cultures. A competent coach or mentor seems to be able to bring the process alive by holding on to this core common passion and yet be equipped with a diverse experience, techniques, skills and knowledge for even more diverse applica-tions. That calls for a systematic, scientific approach to learning and to the evaluation of the intervention – as well as practising it creatively.

I shall discuss this matter further in Chapters 10 and 11.

10

Evaluation

Introduction

The literature on coaching tends to illustrate different techniques or psychological approaches. There is a need for an evidence-based evaluation of the effectiveness of coaching. This chapter advocates the impact of assessment as a methodology used in the evaluation of the effectiveness of a coaching programme. The key question is: How will you realize the benefits? The chapter provides a detailed evaluation of the theories, tools and techniques of coaching. It also provides an evaluation framework, its implementation process, and the results in terms of the outcome and impact.

The generic evaluation methodology described in the first section can be used to assist evaluators and managers in the development of plans for evaluating and monitoring coaching and mentoring programmes. It sets out the core elements that should be covered in an evaluation plan. From an organizational perspective, an evaluation plan can be established before the implementation of a coaching and mentoring programme.

Evaluation is an important part of the business process; it is designed to improve the success of coaching and mentoring programmes in achieving organizational objectives, to assist resource allocation and to provide accountability.

Evaluation Methodology

This section offers a detailed description of the evaluation methodology, together with the results of the initial coaching and mentoring programme. It is based on 20 years of experience in research and evaluation. The impact evaluation methodology was developed on the basis of work carried out on a large-scale evaluation of the

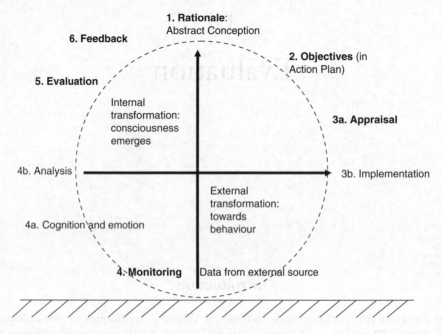

Figure 10.1   Integrated ROAMEF framework (adapted from http://www.hm-treasury.gov.uk/d/green_book_complete.pdf)

Home Office's £30 million Safer Cities Programme (see Ekblom, Law and Sutton, 1996). This is now regarded as the standard for best practice.

The evaluation methodology is also consistent with the ROAMEF framework, in accordance with the Treasury's *Green Book* guidance (HMSO, 1997). As the acronym indicates, the ROAMEF framework has the following components:

1 rationale;
2 objectives;
3 appraisal;
4 monitoring;
5 evaluation;
6 feedback.

The framework can be embedded in the reflective learning wheel (Chapter 3), which yields an integrated ROAMEF framework (Figure 10.1):

Step 1: rationale

The first step is to carry out an overview of the programme in order to ensure that two prerequisites are met:

1 Needs: the needs of individual coaches, as well as the needs of the organization as a whole. These needs must be clearly identified by the person who proposes the programme, be that the coach, the coachee or the project manager.

2   Benefit: the benefit of any proposed coaching initiative is likely to outweigh the cost of the programme itself.

The above overview should include both pros and cons. On the side of the cons, there are two negative perspectives:

1   Negative consequences: List any negative consequences of the coaching programme. Would there be any adverse effect to the organization as a result of the coaching programme? For example, what if the coachees leave the organization after the coaching sessions?
2   The 'do nothing' option: What would be the consequence of not intervening with coaching?

For a coaching programme to take place within an organization, the benefits of the programme must outweigh all the risks that may surface from these negative perspectives. The research involved to answer the above questions would provide scope as well as a rationale for the coaching and mentoring programme.

Step 2: objectives

The second step is to set out clearly the objectives of the proposed coaching programme and its desired outcomes. The objectives should state with precision what the coaching programme is intended to achieve. There may be a hierarchy of outcomes, outputs and targets that will have been identified during the introduction of the programme. The outcomes are the eventual benefits to the organization, coachees or whoever funded the programme. The outputs are the deliverables – for example, the number of coaching activities that can be clearly stated or measured.

Objectives can be expressed in terms of desired outcomes. However, some outcomes may not be quantifiable – for example, increased job satisfaction, motivation, social capital and aspirations. In such cases one can specify outputs as intermediate steps and link them to an indirect outcome – for instance, an increase in productivity and a decrease in absenteeism. It is important to demonstrate how the output and the desired outcomes relate to each other.

In a hypothetical coaching programme assumed to be diverse, the overall objective may be described thus:

> To address the major gap in leadership and equality within in the Region's Health Services by introducing a coaching and mentoring programme so that the senior professional composition reflects the number of diverse employees who have demonstrated their professional competence.

The targets set according to the described outputs and desired outcomes may include:

*   an optimal level of performance;
*   human capital;
*   social capital;
*   the number of coaching places that will be provided by the end of the programme (with a specific date);

- higher productivity for both coachees and mentees;
- proportion of the workforce with the required professional competence;
- reduction in the percentage of the dropout rate.

Step 3a: appraisal

From the executive's perspective, the most significant part of the business process is an appraisal of the coaching proposal. There may be many options (apart from the coaching programme) to be reviewed in order to meet the objectives that have been identified. This review provides the parameters of an appropriate solution for the needs of the organization as well as for the individual stakeholders. A manageable number of proposed options can then be shortlisted. The 'do minimum' option should always be included as a baseline against which to assess alternative interventions, such as coaching or mentoring.

From the outset, executives who own the budget for the coaching and mentoring programme give an appraisal of whether the programme is approved or not. The decision making includes an assessment of whether the proposal is beneficial to the organization as well as to the coachees and mentees. The assessment is done by project managers or by the coaches and mentors who have been recruited for the programme. The conclusions and recommendations are clearly communicated to all stakeholders.

The essential technique of assessment is to evaluate the available options, whereby the coaching programme is validated, objectives are set and options are created and reviewed by analysing their costs and benefits. Within this framework, cost–benefit analysis (CBA) is recommended – as contrasted with cost-effectiveness analysis (CEA) – with supplementary techniques to be used for weighing up any costs and benefits that remain unvalued.

The process of appraising a coaching proposal is iterative – that is, it is repeated a number of times before the best option is selected. This is sometimes referred to as a sensitivity analysis, where the question 'What if...?' is raised in the decision-making process. For example, 'What if option A is £x cheaper, or option B can yield £y of benefit after five years instead of two?' Thus CBA and CEA techniques may also be repeated. The ROAMEF cycle may not always be followed sequentially. It is recommended that the evaluator review the impact of risks, uncertainties and inherent biases more than once. This prevents spurious accuracy and provides a 'good value for money' guarantee despite changing circumstances.

Cost–benefit analysis (CBA)
At the appraisal stage the coaching programme evaluator needs to quantify the benefits that the coaching will bring to the coachees and to the organization, as well as the costs that will be incurred. The former may include increases in productivity, while the latter may include the consultant's fee as well as staff time in participating in the programme. The former may also include items for which the market does not provide a satisfactory measure of economic value – for example, an increase in job satisfaction and in employees' motivation.

Cost–effectiveness analysis (CEA)
CEA compares the costs of alternative ways of producing the same or similar benefits. For example, could an increase in productivity and performance of the staff be brought about through formal training instead of coaching or mentoring?

Step 3b: Implementation

Here I have introduced a substep: implementation that follows appraisal within the ROAMEF framework to complete our learning cycle. After the best option has been selected, it should be translated into action. Implementation should include consultation and involve all the stakeholders; it should also include an impact assessment before procurement takes place.

Step 4: Monitoring

Like any successful project management, a coaching programme should be monitored to ensure that it progresses according to the plan. This usually involves monthly management meetings with key stakeholders – the programme executive, senior suppliers and user representatives. In the coaching programme, it may be useful to ask coachees to keep a journal (a reflective log) to describe their coaching experience. This enables both coaches and coachees to monitor their development as well as to address any barriers or difficulties encountered during the coaching journey.

Step 5: Evaluation

Evaluation examines the outputs as well as the outcomes of the coaching programme against what was expected. It also ensures that the lessons learned are fed back into the decision-making process. This ensures that the future coaching programme is refined so as to reflect what achieves the objectives and promotes the coachees' and the organization's interests in the best possible way. For evaluating the effectiveness of a coaching programme, one may find it useful to refer to the established model by Kirkpatrick (1994). The model examines four levels of impact:

- reaction to the programme and planned action;
- learning;
- behavioural change;
- business results such as return on investment (ROI).

Techniques for evaluation are similar to appraisal techniques in terms of how they link to the programme objectives – its outputs and outcomes. However, owing to the obvious timing of the coaching journey in the learning cycle, at the evaluation stage (that is, after the implementation of the coaching programme) one should be able to use actual (historical) data rather than estimates from forecasts. The purpose of the evaluation is not only to check whether the objectives have been met, but also to learn any lessons that may come up, including analyses of surprise. This process will then be communicated to all stakeholders and contribute to the future interventions or proposals.

The evaluation typically follows a sequence of steps designed to:

1 establish exactly what is to be evaluated and how past outturns can be measured;
2 set new targets, output and desired outcomes, which would be the result of implementing the coaching and mentoring programme;

3   compare the outturn with the target outturn and with the outcomes of the coaching and mentoring programme;
4   present the results and recommendations;
5   disseminate and use these results and recommendations.

Key questions in evaluation include:

- To what extent did the anticipated costs and benefits match the actual outcome? In other words, what was the 'benefits realization'?
- In the light of experience with the target group of coachees, would better results have been achieved if this group had been more tightly defined? For example, if the alternative option of focusing purely on minority workers or on new employees from different cultures had been chosen?
- Has any new information about the impact of the coaching programme come to light since it was implemented?
- How effective is the programme in meeting the organization's objectives?
- Were the assessed risks for completion of the coaching programme justified, or did they understate/exaggerate the true risk?
- About the 'control group': How does the productivity of those individuals who undertook the coaching programme compare with the productivity of workers with similar skills who were not offered the opportunities?

For the case study in the National Health Service, a summative evaluation of the activity was carried out to assess its effectiveness and value in terms of the goals, objectives and scope of the programme as initially defined. This included both process and impact evaluations.

The evaluation aims to provide answers to the following key questions:

1   What has the coaching and mentoring programme achieved by meeting its objectives?
2   What impact has the programme had in the region and what is its contribution to achieving the strategy goals of the health services in the region?

The principal aim of the evaluation is therefore to assess the direct and indirect impact of the coaching and mentoring programme in terms of its remit to health service mentoring across a region (and in several areas identified in the regional strategy and corporate plan).

Impact evaluation requires one to link the input of a project to its output and outcome. It is an effective way to demonstrate value for money and to assess the extent to which the project has met it aims and objectives. In order to understand what works, so that lessons can be learnt for future improvement, one needs to carry out a process evaluation. This requires one to examine the process of the project implementation and to investigate the success and failures of activities involved in the project as a whole.

Impact and process evaluation complement each other. There are two approaches from the evaluation strategy, and they are summarized in Figure 10.2.

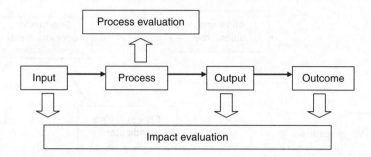

Figure 10.2 Evaluation methodology

Process evaluation

The process evaluation aims at assembling good practice information. In the initial universal integrated framework (UIF) coaching and mentoring programme (2004–5), a process evaluation was carried out by looking for 'success stories' that might show something about good coaching and mentoring practice. Detailed retrospective cases studies of a number of coachees and mentees were collected. An assessment of the successes of the coaching and mentoring activities – and hence of the improved quality of coaching and mentoring – was also conducted. Brief descriptions of each activity and of its impact were collected in order to determine what worked by carrying out semi-structured interviews with coachees and mentees (results are given below).

The views of professional coaches who were not engaged with the UIF coaching and mentoring programme but who used the coaching self-review online tool were also elicited. These professionals provided feedback about the value that the tool might add to their activities and the benefit(s) they gained from it.

The data collected from the process evaluation were mostly qualitative. Data analyses usually involve interpreting the interview transcript and the text. Usually a number of key themes emerge from the qualitative data analyses. A number of qualitative research methods might be used.

Impact evaluation

The overall focus in impact evaluation is on the impact of the project as a whole. In practice, the evaluation requires one to drill down to the aims and objectives of the project and to assess the extent to which they have been met. This is done by mapping the output and outcome of each aim and objective of the project.

Some of the objectives of the UIF coaching and mentoring programme are:

- to support and develop coaching and mentoring;
- to improve the quality of coaching and mentoring;
- to increase the performance of coachees and mentees;
- to build a coaching and mentoring network.

For each of these objectives, some key performance targets for measurement were identified.

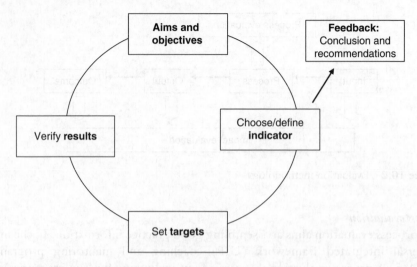

Figure 10.3   Impact evaluation

Measuring outcome
The impact evaluation methodology requires one to link measures of the input–
output (project action) to measures of the outcome. Our first step is to link the programme's coaching and mentoring objectives to its aims. For each aim and objective,
key performance indicators can be identified. These are summarized in Figure 10.3.

Input data
The impact evaluation drew on the following sources of data sets:

- demographic data from the coaching database;
- processed data from lists of participants;
- supportive data (e.g. research reports and pilot activity reports);
- qualitative data from interviews, discussions and consultations.

The nature of the impact evaluation was mostly quantitative, with some qualitative
descriptive data that would be fed into the process evaluation. Appropriate statistical
analyses were performed, as data sets were large enough.

Evaluation of the Universal Integrated Framework

This section demonstrates how the evaluation of the UIF was carried out in one of
the case studies described in Chapter 9. In this case study, the coaching and mentoring programme was introduced in a health and social care setting. The programme
required delegates to commit to mentoring or coaching for up to four days, over a
12-month period. They were introduced to the UIF via a wide range of coaching and
mentoring techniques and practical exercises (see Chapter 8). According to the
guiding principle of coach and coachee fluidity (see Chapter 6), all participants first
became coachees or mentees and were paired with appropriate coaches or mentors
within the organization. They then became coaches or mentors for the others once
they were competent enough to act as such.

As described in Chapter 6, the UIF aims to help participants in the programme to get feedback on their performance from their coachees; an online tool – the cultural and social competence self-assessment questionnaire (CSC SAQ) – was developed, which embedded cross-cultural coaching and mentoring competence. This tool generally provides assessments on the personal effectiveness of coaches and mentors and helps them to generate a personal development plan for use in supervision. In the case study under review, individuals were asked to assess themselves on coaching indicators by using the online tool. The CSC was developed on the basis of the UIF. It aimed to help mentors and coaches especially in their development of emotional intelligence from a cultural perspective. In total, the tool had four dimensions (personal, social, cultural and professional) and 18 elements with 110 questions.

The UIF framework benefit that the case study identified was that it enabled participants to embed the core skills and the process into the organization in a sustainable way; as a result, these core skills significantly impacted upon the way in which the coachees and mentees worked.

To realize this benefit, the team measured how supervision and continuous professional development (CPD) contributed to the success of the leadership programme. The online CSC tool provided information as well as feedback through supervision, which yielded qualitative data. These data allowed the team to gather evidence on best practice and to make recommendations for future practice.

In order to ensure that the CSC tool was amenable to statistical analysis, the key performance indicator (KPI) and the evidence of increase in work performance and progress would need to be decided in terms of:

- quality;
- quantity;
- personal effectiveness;
- the overall effectiveness of the organization.

For the statistical evaluation of the CSC tool with the 18 elements described in Chapter 6, a linear multi-variate regression can be used. The general equation is in the following form:

$$Y = b_0 + b_1 X_i + u_j \qquad (10.1)$$

where

Y represents KPI;
X_i represents the elements of CSC $X_1, X_2, \ldots X_n$;
b_0 is the 'intercept' of the linear regression;
b_1 represents the coefficients of the EI elements; and
u_j represents the random variables.

The demographic element and the ethnicity – as well as the CSC scores (across the three dimensions of the UIF) of the participants in the coaching programme – could also be used as explanatory variables X_i. Thus the CSC tool should have the participant's categories according to the census. One also needs to decide what KPI should be used for the variable Y. This may be coaching competence, salary earned or scores from the 360-degree feedback.

As stated earlier, a full evaluation of the mentoring and coaching strategy and of its implementation as an approach to support leadership development was carried out using questionnaires, focus groups and the coaching competence online CSC tool, the results of which were presented to the Special Group in the Second Coaching Psychology Annual National Conference (Law, Ireland and Hussain, 2005) and subsequently published (Law, Ireland and Hussain, 2006).

Results

The data from the online CSC tool were statistically analysed by using the participant competency scores against overall rating scores. Owing to missing values in some data fields, the initial 49 respondents were reduced to 23 (the complete data set after the

Table 10.1 Correlations between each of the UIF dimension and the coaching competence

		Personal	Social	Cultural	EI	Coaching
Personal	Pearson correlation	1	0.653**	0.415*	0.739**	0.644**
	Sig. (2-tailed)		0.001	0.049	0.000	0.001
	Sum of squares and cross-products	0.602	0.577	0.443	0.543	0.344
	Covariance	0.027	0.026	0.020	0.025	0.016
	N	23	23	23	23	23
Social	Pearson correlation	0.653**	1	0.713**	0.925**	0.538**
	Sig. (2-tailed)	0.001		0.000	0.000	0.008
	Sum of squares and cross-products	0.577	1.298	1.117	0.998	0.422
	Covariance	0.026	0.059	0.051	0.045	0.019
	N	23	23	23	23	23
Cultural	Pearson correlation	0.415*	0.713**	1	0.882**	0.367
	Sig. (2-tailed)	0.049	0.000		0.000	0.085
	Sum of squares and cross-products	0.443	1.117	1.890	1.149	0.347
	Covariance	0.020	0.051	0.086	0.052	0.016
	N	23	23	23	23	23
EI	Pearson correlation	0.739**	0.925**	0.882**	1	0.572**
	Sig. (2-tailed)	0.000	0.000	0.000		0.004
	Sum of squares and cross-products	0.543	0.998	1.149	0.897	0.373
	Covariance	0.025	0.045	0.052	0.041	0.017
	N	23	23	23	23	23
Coaching	Pearson correlation	0.644**	0.538**	0.367	0.572**	1
	Sig. (2-tailed)	0.001	0.008	0.085	0.004	
	Sum of squares and cross-products	0.344	0.422	0.347	0.373	0.474
	Covariance	0.016	0.019	0.016	0.017	0.022
	N	23	23	23	23	23

**Correlation is significant at the 0.01 level (2-tailed).
*Correlation is significant at the 0.05 level (2-tailed).

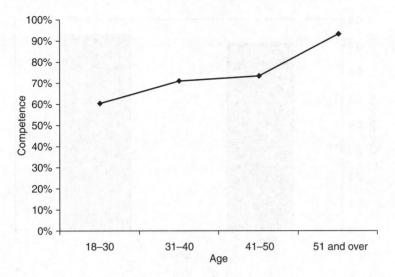

Figure 10.4 Competence increased with age

missing data were excluded in the analyses). The findings supported the survey and the use of the UIF model for coaching and mentoring. The results are summarized as follows:

- *UIF dimensions* There were significant correlations between personal competence, social competence (understanding, empowering, communication, facilitation of conflict, leadership facilitation, team coaching and coaching for change), cultural competence (appreciation of, respect for and championing different ways of being or doing) and coaching competence (measured by the 360-degree feedback questionnaire) (overall $p < 0.05$). See Table 10.1 for the summary of the statistics. Social competence, with its link with authenticity, was the best predictor of all-round competency (overall $p < 0.01$).
- *Age* Competence increased with age/life experience; see Figure 10.4 (ANOVA $F(3, 31) = 9.66$; $p < 0.00015$).
- *Gender* There were no gender differences; see Figure 10.4 ($t(17) = 2.11$; $p = 0.52$).
- *Ethnicity and culture* Like in the survey, the highest rated coaches and mentors were black participants, followed by Asians and then by whites in the analysis of total competency scores; see Figure 10.5 (ANOVA $F(2, 23) = 6.57$; $p = 0.006$). The result implies that people with cross-cultural experience or dual cultural heritage (in this case, indicated by the ethnicity within the UK context) may significantly leverage change by utilizing their cultural competence.

Benefits of Coaching and Mentoring to Organizations

The practical benefits of coaching and mentoring have been widely documented. The literature review undertaken by Garvey and Garrett (2005) for the East Mentoring Forum describes the main benefits as being broadly in the areas of motivational

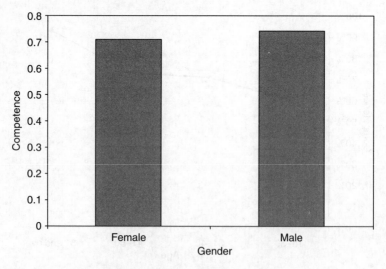

Figure 10.5   Coaching competence: female vs male participants

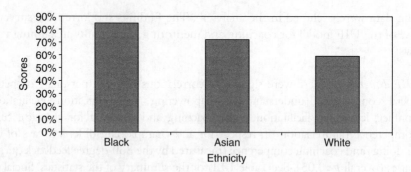

Figure 10.6   Coaching competence: differences between ethnic groups

aptitude, knowledge and skills development, managing change and succession, and business performance benefits; both coaches and coachees were shown to gain from the relationship.

Commonly, motivational benefits for the mentee in the research literature are cited in terms of career advancement, improved commitment to business and organization, improved job satisfaction and increased income. Knowledge and skills development for mentees are cited in terms of improved abilities and skills, faster learning, enhanced decision making, and improved understanding of business and organizational work-ings (e.g. politics, policies, enhanced positive risk-taking and improved support for innovation).

By managing change and succession, mentees gain in confidence and well-being. This is part of the development of their leadership abilities and behaviours, which in turn are supportive of change. For coaches and mentors, research studies cite improved job performance through an enhanced understanding and knowledge of other perspectives, improved communication, increased appreciation of cultures, improved self-awareness, job satisfaction and loyalty, rejuvenation, and opening up to new opportunities. Business benefits identified through the review of the literature include reduction in staff turn-over, improvement in retention, improved flow of communication, opportunity for talent management, improvement in organizational learning, increased knowledge transfer, effective and cost-effective training.

The benefits for the health and social care sector have also been cited in research commissioned in 2004 by the leadership centre of the NHS and the department of health. They include the impact of mentoring on doctors, identified improved reflection skills, support for dealing with specific problems, and findings to the effect that coaching and mentoring promote nurses' growth and development into future leaders (Madison, 1994). Benefits identified by nurses include: enhanced thinking, risk taking, increased self-esteem, greater wisdom, political awareness, job enrichment and performance. Developing strategies to deal with and resolve problems was identified by doctors as an organizational benefit. Coachees and mentees mentioned benefits in the area of support for changing the way things were done and for making significant changes of direction, confidence building in decision making, improved self-worth and job satisfaction. Mentors stated that their motivation and job satisfaction had increased too: they reported, namely, greater satisfaction about developing talents. They also experienced improved relations with colleagues and patients through an enhanced awareness of others' perspectives and enhanced problem-solving skills.

In some approaches coaches and mentors may benefit as much as the coachees and mentees, if not even more (this is often the case when chief executives are involved); but, overall, coachees and mentees benefit more than others. More studies cite motivational benefits, business and organizational performance improvement, and skills and knowledge development as the primary benefits. In short, the main benefits to coachees and mentees are improved performance and productivity, career opportunities and advancement, improved knowledge and skills, and greater confidence and well-being. For coaches and mentors, the primary benefits are improved performance, greater satisfaction, loyalty and self-awareness, and leadership development. Business outcomes are primarily staff retention, improved motivation and relationships and enhanced knowledge and organizational learning.

However, mentoring and coaching have a specific contribution to make to a learning organization dealing with an evolving and complex agenda. The mentor or coach is required to move between the spectrum of coaching or mentoring seamlessly, paying attention to how the individual is responding to change at a personal level and balancing that person's whole life with the requirement to facilitate the meeting of short-term targets at the same time as constantly reworking longer term scenarios and planning for them. Participants gain from having time to think, reflect and review their learning in a safe environment, to the benefit of the organization as well as for their personal development. A regular focus on learning is useful to ensure that their thinking and action are sustainable. A review of any changes in the environment is essential.

In a region-wide NHS survey of the benefits of coaching and mentoring in 2004, 82 per cent of the participants found the experience good or excellent. Benefits to the mentees were grouped into four areas: motivation and positive view of work; learning and skills acquisition; career development; change management and innovation. In the motivation category, coachees and mentees described feeling valued and making a positive contribution. One of them stated: 'Even in these difficult times, I feel I am learning new things and my morale is high when people around me want to give up.' Another co-coachee described the experience as 'life-changing', and another one stated: 'It has enabled me to see where I can go and the route to being the manager that I want to be.' Under learning and skills acquisition, many identified 'increased political awareness and how the wider system works' as a key learning area. Six members of staff identified career development through promotion and attributed it to the mentoring or coaching experience to some degree; but many more in group and individual responses identified increased 'role activity', such as taking on more and diverse roles, working across boundaries, wider networking, joining new groups and project streams, and having a 'fuller participation in the work of the Trust as a whole'. Under change management participants identified that they were 'more likely to take calculated risks to achieve a goal and feel more resilient in this fickle system'.

Benefits to coaches and mentors were cited in similar categories. In the motivation category, chief executives and directors reported motivation through an 'enjoyment of real relationships outside the line, discussions beyond the short term, nurturing talent'. They described learning about 'different perspectives and blocks in the system that I didn't know were there, re-honing my skill base in a way that I can transfer to how I deal with other colleagues and staff and learning from others about implementing best practice on black and minority ethnic issues'. Some mentors and coaches described a 'buzz of supporting others in leading innovation – helping them get over the barriers'. Benefits for coaches and mentors were increased for those who also attended supervision.

Organizational benefits were cited as 'working with new Trustees on the Foundation Trust boards to understand their role and impact more quickly'; 'development of confident creative leaders'; 'new out-the-line communication which brings new life into the system and different perspectives'; and 'value for money because it is working on real issues and a way to spot and harness talent'.

The number of coaches and mentees looking for new ways to access e-mentoring has increased enormously. E-mentoring has been shown to be effective at enabling coaching and mentoring to work beyond boundaries, breaking down cross-cultural barriers, combating isolation and making early links with innovative practice. It has formed part of the organization's fast-track programmes and supported international BME (black, minority and ethnic) programmes. Sheffield Hallam University (Megginson, Stokes and Garrett-Harris, 2003) found that 75 per cent of the mentees using e-mentoring stated that they had gained a lot from the experience.

Chapter Summary and Reflection

This chapter has shown that conducting an evaluation of a coaching and mentoring programme can be labour intensive. Such evaluation should therefore be carried out collaboratively wherever this is possible: among programme managers, coaches and mentors, coachees and mentees, and all other stakeholders. Leading responsibilities need to be defined in the early stages of the programme, so that accountability is understood. Although evaluation may seem technical in terms of methods, coaches and programme managers should not regard it as a specialist activity, otherwise the evaluation runs the risk of being sidelined.

The results of the evaluation of the UIF have shown a positive correlation between personal competence, social competence and cultural competence. The results should come as no surprise, as they are in line with the theoretical perspective of emotional intelligence (EI). When people are more self-aware, they manage social and cultural situations more competently. However, the implication of our study to the current debate in EI research in terms of its concept, measurement and evaluation may be quite profound, as will be discussed in the final chapter.

The findings of the evaluation investigated here may also be attributed to the more comprehensive training of diverse leaders through the coaching and mentoring programme – especially BME leaders compared with white senior managers, who relied on previous training and experience. We thus recommend that more coaching and mentoring programmes be warranted as part of the diversity training for white staff working with BME groups as coaches and mentors. From the feedback of those who participated in the programme, white delegates have much to gain by including BME participants in coaching and mentoring – as well as in organizational change. BME participants seem to show an aptitude for a higher cultural appreciation when they apply their experience to the work context, as well as in their engagement with the players. This may be due to the fact that the majority of them were likely to have had cross-cultural experiences or a dual cultural heritage. This aptitude adds support to the approach of integrated work streams of coaches and mentors to make the most of talent pools; it also backs the UIF approach, which emphasizes the importance of having coaches and mentors who have cultural appreciation as part of any wider coaching and mentoring initiative.

Further research is being carried out to explore the validity of individual elements of the UIF by increasing the size of a sample and by showing how the UIF can be utilized to aid coaches and mentors to develop their competence. Some practical recommendations can be made here. To ensure a coordinated approach to conducting the evaluation of a coaching and mentoring programme, organizations should consider how evaluation is integrated into the decision-making processes and corporate governance structures. Coaches and programme managers should:

- establish a formal evaluation process as part of the coaching and mentoring programme;
- formalize access to internal and external coaches and mentors;
- discuss evaluation methodology with the sponsors;
- provide incentives for conducting thorough and timely evaluations;
- maintain an accessible archive of the lessons learnt.

11
Conclusion, Discussion, Future Research and Development

Introduction

This chapter not only provides a summary of our 'conversation' so far about the psychology of coaching, mentoring and learning; it also discusses the research and development that need to be done from this point on, and it offers recommendations for better learning through coaching and mentoring. In doing so, it draws together the diverse strands of theories and practice in coaching, mentoring and learning processes.

From the evaluation report in Chapter 10 as well as from my continuous coaching practice, it has become clear to me that diversity has been, and will continue to be, high on many organizations' agendas. From this perspective, the discussion focuses on the following areas:

- matching between coaches and coachees;
- emotional intelligence and cross-cultural competence;
- evidence-based research and impact assessment;
- supervision;
- training;
- coaching and mentoring standards;
- ethics and code of conducts;
- the broader legal framework.

Matching between Coaches and Coachees

Viewed through the lens of diversity, matching is an important stage in the coaching process. Getting the right match between coaches and coachees ensures the success of the coaching outcome. It is an effective way of leveraging cultural change and

Table 11.1   Matching matrix on the basis of UIF vs CBT

Matching criteria	Coachee/ Mentee	Coach/ Mentor	Funder/ Owner	Team/Group/ Community	Culture (includes organizational)
Objectives					
Problems/issues					
Strategies					
Options					
Socio-demographics					
X-factor					
Matching decision					

diversity within organizations. Organizations have therefore focused on the development of sound matching systems, including electronic database access, to deliver close matches in a range of organizational, technological and interpersonal contexts.

One approach is systematically working through a matching matrix. A matching matrix can be constructed on the basis of the universal integrated framework (UIF)/ integrative learning system (ILS) and cognitive behavioural therapy (CBT) models described in Chapters 6 and 7 (see Table 11.1).

Translating the matrix into the matching process takes the following steps (working through each row and column):

1   establishing the goal/purpose of each stakeholder (coach, coachee) and establishing the overall objective/priority of the team/group/community, taking the cultural and organizational perspectives into account;

2   identifying possible barriers or problems that all the stakeholders may face during the coaching journey;

3   identifying possible strategies to overcome those barriers or problems;

4   setting out a number of coaching options in terms of styles, techniques and orientation;

5   considering the socio-demographic factors – for example, age, belief systems/ faiths/religions, culture/race, gender and social barrier/disability;

6   considering the X-factor – for example, attributes, creativity, personality, emotional intelligence, cultural and professional competence and so on;

7   drawing a conclusion about how to match the rows and columns in Table 11.1.

Humphrey and Holland (2006) suggest that, by working through the matching matrix, one can 'deselect those coaches whose purpose is not identified'. However, in my view, from a cross-cultural perspective and according to the UIF/ILS, the community/organizational culture takes precedence. In other words decision makers should tolerate some ambiguity in the setting of personal coaching goals, provided that the group's, community's or organization's goals are clear. This allows the goal to develop through the coaching journey. Moreover, one should realize that not all the factors in the matching matrix are of equal weight. For example, shared values and goals are more important than individual styles and approaches in effective collaboration.

Constructing matching criteria is the first and probably the easiest step in the coaching process. There are many ways of designing a matching matrix, depending on individual or organizational requirements (see Humphrey and Holland, 2006). You can construct your own matrix and be your own matchmaker.

Successful matching is as much about the choice and training of the broker as it is about the criteria of selection. Eastern cultures have long recognized the role of brokers in relationship matching. A broker brings together potential partners, often on the basis of background – education, status and qualities that are compatible. Yet the role and impact of the matchmaker as undertaken by the coordinator has rarely been examined in coaching psychology research.

Bearing in mind the lack of research on the role of the coordinator, previously we focused on the criteria for success in matching. One finding was the importance of the matchmaker in helping the client choose someone different from him-or herself. There is a widespread assumption that homogeneous pairings produce better results. Interpersonal attraction research has shown that similarity in attitudes, political beliefs and religiosity predicts attraction (Byrne and Nelson, 1965). Veitch and Griffitt (1976) identified the fact that positive emotional reactions increased liking.

Factors such as geographical proximity and levels of professional and cultural competence also play an important part in successful outcomes (Ireland, Hussain and Law, 2006). These factors have an implication in terms of explaining why it is that the ideal self we portray for matching and our actual self may be different (Buss and Barnes, 1986). Thus the tendency to select coachees with attributes similar to one's own may be mistaken. After all, characteristics that predict initial attraction may not predict long-term satisfaction. The UIF evaluation points in the opposite direction where matching coaches or coachees with mentors or mentees is at stake. It has shown that coaching outcomes are more positive if the coach and the coachee have different temperaments according to the Myers–Briggs Type Indicator.

Matching for success

To summarize the lessons learnt from the evaluation and case studies, the main matching conditions for success include:

- location or geography of both partners;
- appropriate distance in the pairing by level;
- commitment of mentor and mentee to each other;
- early interest and affirmation from the mentor to the mentee;
- choice of diverse ethnic and cultural background of mentor to match the mentees;
- cultural competence of mentors and coaches;
- active involvement in the pairing process;
- option generation of at least two possible matches;
- insight and understanding of each other (coaches and coachees; mentors and mentees) in terms of personality type, strengths and weakness.

All the key points above indicate that the role of the broker/matchmaker was key in less experienced participants. A broker/coordinator was able to move people outside their comfort zone and make them opt for features more dissimilar to their own in order to promote learning. The need for information to fill gaps about potential partners decreased as trust in the broker rose and shared goals or values and mutual commitment became clear. Criterion-based matching using forms alone was rarely sufficient for facilitating a match in mentoring or with inexperienced participants.

The role of electronic mentoring matching

Another implication is about the role of electronic mentoring matching. There are some useful elements in such systems. Advantages include:

- flexibility: coaching and mentoring conversation can take place anywhere, any time, or just in time;
- rich information from the online search: this encourages involvement in the process through self-directed data search;
- time: online research saves time: it alleviates requirements for matchers to offer this initial service and saves the broker intervention for the later, more crucial stages in the process;
- cost: the above advantages also involve a significant cost saving in the matching process.

To ensure cost-effectiveness, electronic database-driven systems should be part of a whole system rather than a standalone, off-the-shelf package (e.g. a web-based programme with mentors and mentees taking responsibility for inputting their own data). This is in effect a self-driven system. As participants mature, matching programmes need to be capable of meeting their changing needs. Coordinators require any system to enable them to keep abreast of matches – types and numbers of registered pairings – so that they can monitor relationship outcomes and engage with participants over supervision and training opportunities.

The roles of the broker in mentoring and coaching matching are:

- negotiation: bringing realism and confirmation of shared values into goal planning and expectation setting;
- mediation and stretch: managing the mismatch of expectations and reality, challenging self-limitations that reduce the learning potential of the pair;
- facilitation: building mutual commitment to working together on shared goals, enabling the sharing of enough information and leveraging the mutual benefits to steer the participants to affirm the match; clarifying confusions and contextualizing information, spotting and diffusing barriers to the match at an individual and pair level;
- synthesis: mirroring back what is agreed between the parties and establishing a framework for moving forward, establishing the psychological contract to work together before the formal introductory letter/email/agreement is sent;
- ongoing support up to session contract/agreement: after this stage, the coach–coachee pair moves on to a collective support system through supervision; the coordinator may then exit at this point.

What to look for in a coordinator

Apart from sharing some of the attributes described in this book for coaches and mentors, a coordinator should have the following attributes:

- emotional intelligence across cultures;
- interpersonal skills evidenced across a range of media (computer literacy);
- networking skills;
- credibility in coaching or mentoring;
- leadership (inspiring people, meeting customer needs, managing change, resources, projects, capability, systems development and planning);
- cultural understanding;
- influencing and negotiation skills (direct and indirect);
- facilitation skills.

As you would notice, many of the above skills are present in effective coaches and mentors; this makes it a natural progression for them to move into a coordinating role. Coaching and mentoring would be more effective if we were to pay more attention to careful matching in terms of the above requirements, as well as respect for diversity and confidentiality as part of the code of ethics.

Emotional Intelligence and Cross-Cultural Competence

This book has been advocating an integrative learning system (ILS) as a coaching and mentoring approach. It has evolved from the initial proposal of the universal integrated framework (UIF), which considers the fluidity of coaches'/mentors' and coachees'/mentees' roles and learning. Evidence from the evaluation of UIF confirms that mentors learn as much, if not more, from mentees as they do from other coaches and mentors. The evaluation also implies that coaching, mentoring and learning are interrelated, as are their measurements (e.g. emotional intelligence (EI) and professional and cultural competence). They should therefore be tackled together in a systemic way, as demonstrated in the case studies. For instance, the debate about whether EI is a cognitive ability or a personality-like trait (Mayer, DiPaolo and Salovey, 1990; Mayer and Salovey, 1993, 1997) has important implications for its measurement, and hence for its evaluation.

In terms of measurement, academic discussion has focused on two key questions:

1 Should EI be measured by self-reporting (as administered in the coaching and mentoring programme reported in our case study)?
2 Should the respondents' performance be measured instead?

Some researchers make a rigid distinction between the EI trait and cognitive EI and propose the following conditional rules (for example, see Petrides, Furnham and Frederickson, 2004; Petrides, Frederickson and Furnham, 2004):

- If one regards EI as a trait like personality, then it should be measured by self-reporting.

- If EI is conceptually treated as a cognitive ability, then the measurement should be performance-based.

It is not helpful to adopt a rigid binary position (either/or) when one is using EI as a learning tool for intervention. Nevertheless, the above distinction may be used to guide us to design and evaluate the research and development of EI and its applications, such as in coaching and mentoring. For example, many current EI measurements in academic research and commercial markets (in the form of tests or inventories) can be evaluated according to the following criteria:

- Do they have a clear theoretical framework?
- Do they have complete coverage of all the relevant dimensions and essential elements?
- Have they addressed measurement issues – defining responses, internal consistency, factor structure and construct validity?
- Have they adequately matched the measurement to the theoretical concept?

The case study has shown that we can use self-reporting complemented by 360-degree feedback to assess EI and infer the correlation between self-perception and performance-based ability in our evaluation. The correlation between personal competence, social competence and cultural competence also supports the view that coaching is never culturally neutral. However, one must be cautious in drawing a conclusion from the results, as a correlation does not mean causation. The results may imply that change is culturally sensitive to context and that the coachees, mentees and the setting need to be fully understood and engaged with to ensure success. Best practice cannot be established and sustained using techniques not tuned to the context for implementation. The players involved need to feel valued and appreciated.

Participants with a cross-cultural background did particularly well in the overall coaching competence ratings. This is consistent with the UIF/ILS, which identifies the importance of cross-cultural working as it applies to individuals and settings. This is a welcome result, since research and the everyday media coverage have tended for too long to focus on the negative representation of other social groups rather than on positive regard for them. For those secure in themselves, comfort lies in the continuity of one's learning and widening friendships. This is called 'allophilia' and may be associated with positive behaviours and/or generalization; but it is always associated with *positive regard* for another social group. It seems that only those who foster allophilia can be positively curious enough to leverage optimum mentoring and coaching opportunities. This attitude is even more important in today's context, not only for living in harmony within our local community, but also globally, for resolving international conflicts, which often involve a complex relationship between cultural and (spiritual) belief dimensions.

Evidence-Based Research: Coaching Assessment and Impact Evaluation

Organizations have an ongoing interest in deriving the benefits they are securing from any change interventions and in establishing benchmarks for performance. As such, the cultural and social competence (CSC) tool has been found to be very effective in helping coaches and mentors to manage their own development and organizational plan to address areas of reduced performance. The CSC tool made the coaching process more transparent but also ensured it was coachee-driven throughout. It takes one more step to help organizations to explore the link between the quality of the coach (or mentor) and the coaching outcomes and to capitalize on it. Impact assessment is an important part of the coaching process, not an add-on. It can be developmental, itself enabling all participants to get involved and increase their knowledge of wider agendas and systems. The impact assessment process can provide new opportunities to re-engage with stakeholders in new ways and establish new approaches forward. Evaluation can be done by consultants, by in-house teams, or through an integrated impact, online management system. The last one is particularly effective when a sponsor wants to establish core baseline assessment and inter-agency comparisons, where there is a cross-cultural and geographical spread of participating agencies in a programme and when the participating entities have access to the Internet.

As coaching is still an emerging industry, demonstrating its benefit through evidence-based research and impact evaluation will be increasingly demanded by sponsors, players and buyers in the field. Coordinators need to make the most of the opportunities they have to influence the strategists and sponsors on the key objectives that have to be assessed and to find new ways of incorporating softer sets of data into a robust mix of evidence. The notion of sustainability needs to be a shared focus for sponsors, stakeholders and coordinators alike. An evidence base is merely the starting point for wider discussions and a lever to do things better. You do not have to wait for the agreement of a strategic plan to get going. In the meantime, it is also useful to compile case studies (see Chapter 9) or simple examples of how coaching or mentoring has helped individuals or organizations improve their performance. Evaluation of coaching programmes is part of the continuous learning cycle designed to help individuals and organizations achieve their aspirations.

Supervision and coaching training

The evaluation of the UIF has confirmed that attention to the personal, the social and the cultural dimensions of settings and players is also required for integrating supervision as part of ILS and of the continuous professional development (CPD) of the coaches and mentors. In the sister study that addressed the benefits of training, these results were also replicated; but they were linked to the importance of training (T) and supervision (S) for the improved quality (Q) of coaches and mentors. The increase in the benefits cited was in direct proportion to the quality of the coach or mentor, thus:

$$B = kQ \qquad\qquad (11.1)$$

where B represents benefits; Q represents the quality of the coach or mentor; and k is a constant.

Constituting the ingredients of the coach's or mentor's quality – that is, T for training and S supervision – we have:

$$B = k(T + S) \qquad\qquad (11.2)$$

The supervision frameworks have focused on the CPD (or D, for short) and on improving the quality of the coach (Q) through reflective practice (R):

$$S = D + Q \tag{11.3}$$

Substituting the components of S in Equation 11.2, we have:

$$B = k(T + D + Q) \tag{11.4}$$

As training in this context is coaching training, we can replace T with C for coaching and formulate the final equation for realizing the coaching benefits:

$$B = k(C + D + Q) \tag{11.5}$$

Representing the above equation in a general form, as described in Chapter 10 – namely:

$$Y = b_0 + b_1 X_i + u_j \tag{10.1}$$

we have:

$$Y = b_0 + b_1(C + D + Q) + u_j \tag{11.6}$$

where Y represents the coaching benefit (B); b_0 means 'intercept'; b_1 stands for the coefficients of the EI elements; and u_j is the random variable.

The CSC tool has been continuously developed in a range of online education programmes, in the UK and internationally. It helps the learners' CPD and development of good practice. Participants in the programmes have been using the CSC elements (X_i) to inform their reflective practice in supervision through peer coaching. Thus we could assess the quality of coaches and their CPD and coaching by using the results of the CSC tool as a proxy measurement. The predicted coaching benefits (Y) can be computed in advance. The effectiveness of the coaching programme, the validity and reliability of the coaching model can be evaluated by comparing the actual outcome with the predicted benefits of any coaching intervention. Future research into the validation of the general coaching equation given above will have an important impact on the evidence-based coaching practice.

The results so far indicate that many coaches feel less confident and less prepared about the personal (EI) and cultural dimensions of their CPD. Future training programmes for mentoring and coaching should therefore:

- include more focus on personal development (especially cross-cultural EI);
- incorporate cultural appreciation as a core element.

These elements are increasingly important in our world of greater complexity and increasing conflicts among beliefs and values, especially for those who work in unfamiliar contexts, with people from a different profession and background.

Coaching and Mentoring Standards

In 2007, at the time of writing the first edition, a lot of work was being done in the development of standards, competencies and kite marks, the requirement for standardization across the coaching and mentoring profession being one of the hottest topics. In 2005, David Lane unveiled the European Mentoring and Coaching Council's (EMCC) kite mark scheme for coaching and mentoring at its annual conference in Zurich. The EMCC aimed to provide a benchmark for others to share these standards. Its kite mark scheme was based on the core competencies. It allows organizations to audit quality in terms of processes, procedures and outputs. The outcomes of coaching and mentoring still needs to be evaluated, though. While EMCC's kite mark scheme has been up and running for more than half of a decade now, during this period of time other professional organizations, such as the Association for Coaching (AC), also followed the trend and developed their own accreditation process. The British Psychological Society's Special Group in Coaching Psychology, after years of negotiation between its consecutive chairs and its various committees and trustees, finally established its first register for coaching psychologists, which was launched at the beginning of 2012. All these new developments signal the maturity of this new profession – coaching. To resonate with my reflection in Chapter 2, coaching (and coaching psychology in particular) is truly coming of age.

While establishing a coaching and mentoring standard may be welcomed by some (especially those involved in the process) as a way to professionalize the industry, many coaches and mentors are still concerned that this may hinder creativity, diversity and the development of coaching and mentoring. A lot is at stake for the coaching and mentoring companies and organizations as commercial enterprises. Many have developed their own standards, competency frameworks and accreditation systems. Moreover, like any industrial standard, benchmarking only works if there are sufficient numbers of organizations signing up for it and individual coaches and mentors going through the assessment process.

Benchmarking itself does not guarantee a standard or an outcome. As different coaching and mentoring bodies have different competing standards, the situation continues to cause confusion among coaches, mentors and clients. However, this is healthy and indicates the developmental process of an evolving discipline. Clients may simply need some information about the diversity of the industry and some guidance as to how to assess and evaluate the coaching supply that will meet their requirements. Just like in the revolution in information technology in the twentieth century, the customers (in this case, the coachees) will be the ones to lead the way in the long run.

While one may celebrate the professionalization of coaching that the move to standardization involves, a word of caution is necessary here. First, coaching has captured the imagination of its participants because it offers flexibility and variety in how it operates. While there are clear features in the process, the latter is looser and less structured than other development methods. That is its niche. The Community Coaching Café described in Chapter 9 is a good example. There is room within the mix to operate across contexts and to meet the needs of different learners at both the micro- and the macro-level. The standardization movement has identified the fact that organizations could be audited on 'quality in terms of processes, procedures and outputs'. This takes scrutiny beyond the level of the coaches' competency, to the shaping of a uniform collective development of an integrative learning system (ILS). This may go counter to the UIF/ILS principles of encouraging creativity and diversity of practice at macro- and micro-levels. The development of the coaching standard is primarily a Western phenomenon that may not be applicable universally across cultures. Quality is rarely linked to one process or to one ideal set of procedures, as shown by the formula described earlier and by the evaluation in Chapter 10. Of course, the use of CSC and of its self-assessment questionnaire (SAQ) in different cultures would need to be adapted and translated into the local context and language (Law and Fitzgerald, 2012).

An inputs-based model of impact assessment, which addresses learning and development (rather than accreditation), involvement and flexibility in CPD (rather than forced compliance) and feedback on universal qualities and competencies – feedback derived from self-assessment, from colleagues and from coachees – embodies a loose but transferable model of practice across different contexts and groups. Further, rigid or specified processes and procedures for development are culturally and contextually bound. Any sustainable standard-setting movement would have to be able to answer the following questions:

- Whose standard and which culture anyway? Bearing in mind that a standardized framework is culturally limited, which culture and individuals would predominate when it comes to identifying good practice and defining aligned processes and procedures?
- Who sets the standard, and what are the selection criteria? How would power and expertise denote who the standard setters were, and how would individuals be selected to be a part of those groups?
- Is the standard universal, or is it culturally mindful? In light of global coaching programmes, would participation in a predominantly European-centred standard be a precursor to involvement?
- Is the standard fit for the purpose of the local community? How much opportunity would there be for distinctive local standard setting? What would be the impact on small organizations and community groups? How does a standardized approach fit with the micro-learning-centred coaching ethos of mutual learning, mutual respect, self-determination and partnership?
- Is the standard practical? How would standards be enforced? What is the cost and who would pay?

Standards and standardization pose challenges at the level of the contextual variation of coaching applications. For example, in some settings the opportunity for coaches to train and receive certification would attract coaches to that programme and would give credibility to a service. In another setting it would act as a barrier to the fluidity of roles in the process and would over-professionalize a service that did not warrant it. Coaching is universal insofar as it crosses contexts; but the levels of coaching intervention and the depth of the practitioners' competence vary according to the specific needs of the coachees and mentees.

The route towards standard setting has been travelled before, in other disciplines, with mixed success in complex settings. As predicted, the current standards set out various requirements for the accredited members' CPD to be audited; this follows from the development of a specialist audit industry designed to fulfil that need. The assessment and audit (and perhaps verification) industry may well be connected to the very agencies that suggested standard setting in the first place! While one recognizes the creativity of a thriving coaching market, there may be real consequences for social enterprises doing very valuable community work, which cannot afford to be accredited. Those same agencies might find that front-line service-funding allocations are reduced to cover the costs of auditing functions. A good example of a similar development is the development of social enterprises. Various agencies were developed and insisted that social enterprises should be registered as community-interest companies (CICs), which requires an additional auditing process. The extra cost and the resources required in the process have distracted many social enterprises' efforts and valuable resources from focusing on their initial social cause.

There is probably a mid-point in this debate, where forces – forces of the market, the requirement to bring greater clarity, uniform status and professionalism to this field, the drive to improve the participants' coaching experiences and opportunities for cross-cultural learning and to create a vigorous, competitive supply sector – come to some new realization of a way forward together. However, a loose input-based structure – a structure capable of being flexible enough to respond to the diverse needs of people and settings and relying on empirical evidence to ascertain the quality of individual coaches – makes a significant contribution to shaping some of this debate and its practice.

Ethics and Code of Conduct

Apart from the business agenda, the drive for standardization in coaching practices underlines an agenda for professionalization in the industries. This raises an important issue, which has often been neglected in the debate on professional competence and standards: the ethics and code of conduct of coaching and mentoring.

Two key questions help us to consider the development of an ethical framework:

1   What forms should ethical thinking take?
2   What is the impact of ethical principles on the practice of coaching and mentoring?

Ethical thinking and its principles are usually embedded in many professional bodies in the form of self-regulation. For example, the members of the BPS are required to commit to ethical standards and to a code of practice. The main aim is to protect clients and the public at large from dangerous practice; and the objectives are to:

- benefit clients;
- ensure safety;
- protect clients;
- manage boundaries;
- manage conflict.

Translating the above objectives into the code of practice requires you as a coach to:

1 do no harm;
2 act in the best interest of your clients and their organization;
3 observe confidentiality;
4 respect differences in culture;
5 apply effectively the best practice in everything you do;
6 help your client to make informed choices and take responsibility to improve his or her performance and well-being;
7 recognize your role as a coaching psychologist.

There are many common aspects between these objectives and codes of practice across a wide range of professions, such as counselling and psychotherapy (for example, see Barnes and Mudin, 2001; Hill and Jones 2003; and the BPS's *Code of Conduct, Ethical Principles and Guidelines*). However, there are also many aspects that are unique to coaching and distinguish coaching psychology from many other disciplines. For example, a coach is asked by a director (the budget holder) to coach a team of senior managers (the job holders) with the objective of improving their performance (see Law, 2003). The term 'client' used within this organizational context is very different from the same term used in the contexts of counselling and psychotherapy. A number of questions would arise from such a coaching process:

• Who are the clients?
• Whose benefit has priority?
• Whose interests is the coaching psychologist serving?
• What is the coach's ethical duty?
• What is the responsibility of the coaching psychologist to manage different values and interests between all the stakeholders?
• How are the differences managed?
• Is there potential for an abuse of power?
• What are the issues of confidentiality?
• What are the implications of vicarious liability?

Managing the multiple boundaries, relationships and conflicts is particularly important in the situation described above – and in coaching psychology in general. Coaching is different from counselling and therapy. It requires us to have different attitudes, knowledge, skills and ethical thinking as part of our professional competence.

Ethical principles have an important impact upon wide areas of practice (Law, 2005a, 2005b, 2006a). These include:

• coaching;
• supervision;
• training;
• teaching.

While many coaches are happy to engage with clients in their inspirational journey of empowerment, they tend to feel uncomfortable when they encounter difficult ethical dilemmas. In order to maximize the clients' benefit and to protect them from dangerous practice, members are required to adhere to ethical standards and to a code of practice in coaching psychology. There are many ethical aspects that are unique to our profession and distinguish it from many other disciplines; for instance, managing multiple boundaries, relationships and conflicts. Handling such aspects requires us to have certain attitudes, knowledge, skills and ethical thinking as part of our professional competence.

As coaches, we are expected to:

- learn as much as we can about ethics;
- see the others' views on ethics;
- look at client management and ethical issues;
- understand the overlap and the differences between coaching and counselling psychology on ethical issues;
- know what to do when things go wrong.

While there are many definitions of ethics and ethical principles, I have found the following definition useful, as it captures many of the essential elements as well as opening up some other avenues for practical exploration:

> Ethical principles are defined as the *rules* which people are *committed* to because they see them as embodying their *values* and *justifying* their *moral judgements*. (Rowson, 2001; emphasis added)

This definition seems quite straightforward in principle. It can be translated into the following cognitive process (see Figure 11.1):

morality → professional judgement → rationale → values → commitment → rules

For example, considering values would require us to question ourselves:

- What are our values?
- What is the relationship between ethics, codes of conduct and practice?

In practice, this often requires the coaches' conscious struggle between conflicting rights and duties (cf. Solomon, 2000, in a counselling context) – while one may argue that the issue of conflict arises in many professions, such as counselling psychology. The typical double triad – the relationship between the client's line-manager, the coach and the coachee – in executive coaching increases the prevalence, complexity and intensity of the conflicts that coaching psychologists may experience (Figure 11.2).

For instance, on the subject of disclosure about our client's performance, the following ethical questions would arise:

- Should I tell the truth even if it might affect the client's well-being?
- Should I respect the client's (or the line manager's, or the subordinate's) autonomy even when this may cause him or her harm?
- Should I tell this to the client's line manager?

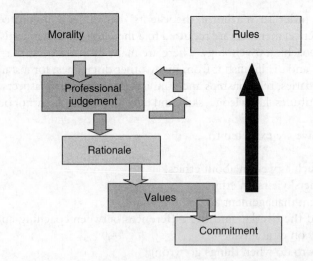

Figure 11.1   Cognitive process in formulation of ethical principles (Law, 2006a)

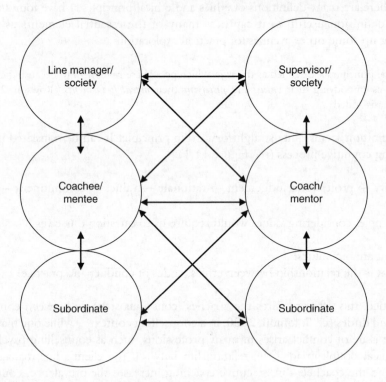

Figure 11.2   A double triad relationship between the client's line-manager, the coach/ mentor and the coachee/mentee (Law, 2006a)

In terms of the three-way information flow, disclosure may come from various stakeholders, which sometimes can have a detrimental effect on the coachee. Coaching psychologists may need to consider the following questions:

- What should I do about this piece of information?
- Why is my coachee's line manager telling me this about him or her?

- Why is the coachee telling me this about his or her line-manager?
- Should I be encouraging the coachee/line manager to report this to the director or higher authorities?

Similar questions might be asked if the coaching psychologist is in the supervisor's position. When making decisions on actions in the area of morality versus opinions, one's professional judgement could be very complex. The conflict resolution depends not only on how we define our meaning in terms of self versus culture, truth versus facts, but also on the ethical principles we adopt.

If one adopts the principle of duty and accords priority to deontological concerns about general and specific duties, one may hold on to the following rules:

- Tell the truth.
- Respect confidentiality.
- Respect autonomy.

If we prefer to apply the teleological principle of utility in our coaching situation, we will formulate rules and apply them so as to achieve the best outcome (rule utilitarianism). This may take the following form:

- Goal: seek the best outcome.
- Action: consider all the options/outcomes before you act (act on the principle of utilitarianism).
- Rule: DO x EXCEPT y

(Note: in the above rule, exceptions are allowed in order to achieve the best outcome. For example, tell the truth unless it would harm the client. Is this ethical? This is an ethical dilemma that calls for one's professional judgement and may require supervision.)

There is not enough space to address all of these issues here (as ethics is not the primary objective of this book). To unpack the complexity of this area would require further research and development; it would call for another book, specifically dedicated to ethical choices in relation to coaching. For the time being, interested readers may request a copy of the *Code of Ethics and Conduct* from the British Psychological Society (BPS, 2009).

Ethics as a Cross-Cultural Phenomenon

Ethics and ethical principles do not translate readily into cross-cultural practice, and this is for a range of reasons. First, our commitment to following rules is leveraged by a belief that the rules are congruent with our values and sense of morality. Our enforcement of rules is also linked to our values. Those beliefs and values are time-bound and subjective, not universally held by people in different cultures, places, spaces and circumstances.

For instance, in the eighteenth and nineteenth centuries the slave trade was seen as an entirely proper way of dealing with the consequences of colonization, in the UK and in Europe. Professions have sometimes indicated that their practice was moral or ethical, only to overturn that practice later. In modern times the appeal to ethical principles among agencies as a reason not to do something has impacted on the effectiveness of collaborations in multi-agency situations.

In China, since Mao's agenda of modernization and in contrast with the country's established culture and tradition, a policy was developed to encourage parents to have only one child, with sanctions in place for those who would not comply. By contrast, in France and other European countries there were incentives to have more children in order to sustain economic growth. In China there were concerns over population growth and its possible dangers for economic growth. Such cultural differences in the employment of a strategy to manage population levels can result in different perceptions of morality, depending on the culture from which you look at it.

There is a view that right and wrong are easily discernible to the moral thinker. However, right and wrong may be less readily discerned in a complex picture, where a whole range of factors are at play and knock-on effects of one action may be damaging or potentially outweigh the benefits. Only a sense of local knowledge, context awareness and experience can help us discern right from wrong in situations where a network of variables interacts with changing local conditions.

This complex picture needs to address the role of history and the experience of all players in a situation. The cross-cultural history of a relationship informs how the presentation of an ethical position is construed. Where one collective culture has been abused or exploited by another and trust is low, ethical principles might be seen as hypocritical. The diminishment of the ethical stance of another culture as a platform for raising one's own standing and for capitalizing on advantage further undermines trust and partnership.

Ethical principles have an uneasy and unclear relationship with actions. If the intention was ethical but the action was wrong and brought much harm, is that moral or immoral? Is there knowledge and are there skills that one can acquire that may support a developing, growing and adaptable morality?

Obviously, the sharing of ethical principles at a broad level is easier than their realization in practice at a local level. The ethical codes of practice, at the level of rules of conduct for micro-practice, may be best limited to the context of their origin, where the point-to-point correspondence on matters of values, systems, equality of access to education and services and work is assured and where hopes and expectations are shared.

Within this context, key questions include:

- Does having codes of conduct and standards make us ethical?
- On whose terms are we ethical?
- And how long will it last?
- Are we flexible and continually changing, to keep up with the requirements of new situations and the moral challenges they pose?

To answer these questions, we need to address the process of formulating ethical principles rather than the output of that process. We need to go back to basics. Our process is driven by our coachees, and as such we need to assess and take stock of their values, their concept of success, their concept of helpfulness and adapt how we work to the local context. We need to consult and be changed rather than assume that we will bring change. We need to be genuine, open and humble. Only then can we build trust. And, if we are lucky, one day someone might describe us as ethical. Perhaps that is the point. The phrase 'ethical practitioner' is a description assigned to us by someone else.

Future Work and Research

From the above discussion, the future work would most likely focus on the following areas:

- refining the universal integrated framework;
- research on the coaching/mentoring-matching attributes of the coach/coachee and mentor/mentee interactions, as well as on the attributes of the matchmaker;
- developing ethical principles in coaching and mentoring;
- identifying the ethical implications for the supervision of coaches and mentors;
- developing quality-control procedures;
- promoting diversity in coaching and mentoring;
- developing training in the psychology of coaching and mentoring;
- embedding ethical principles and the psychology of learning as part of the core competence and continual development in our profession.

Chapter Summary and Reflection

Our ethical discussion shows that resolving an ethical dilemma is a complex decision-making process and that understanding ethical principles could provide us with a decision aid as well as with a rationale for our professional judgement. When making ethical decisions, a coach should not rush to take action but carefully consider the following:

- Aim to serve your coachees well.
- Be informed about legal and employment requirements that override limits on confidentiality for the particular context.
- Make these limits clear to your coachees.
- Consider supplementing your verbal description of limits with a written contract.
- When practising with extended confidentiality, share on a 'need to know' basis.
- Be trustworthy.
- Discuss with your coachees if breaking confidentiality is necessary.
- Understand that helping coachees to act is much better than you (the coach) having to act.
- Accept that life and coaching involve taking risks.
- Discuss the case with a supervisor, a coaching colleague and a manager.
- Where there is a specific duty or legal requirement for disclosure to a third party, warn the coachees during the sessions that, if they tell you more, you will be under an obligation to act.

The UIF/ILS advocated in this book requires you (readers) to have commitment to learn on the basis of your own direct experience. We believe that to work and to live your life this way is both challenging and fulfilling.

I would like to end this book by echoing what is said in the preface. From reading this book, I hope that, at whatever juncture of your coaching or mentoring journey you happen to be (whether you are a coach, a mentor, a coachee, a mentee, or all these), you would by now understand that, although throughout this book we have advocated a scientific approach, we believe that there is a kind of magic to the art of coaching and mentoring. To emphasize the spiritual–magical engagement of coaching and mentoring in action, I recall the exercise that I conducted in one of my coaching sessions for the diverse communities in Peterborough. Inspired by the Oriah Mountain Dreamer's poem 'My Invitation' – adopted from Jean Houston's (1998) *A Passion for the Possible* – I inverted the poem, transforming it into questions. I wrote it on a piece of paper and folded it into a paper-aeroplane. I threw it to the participants as a 'message carried by air'. A participant picked it up, unfolded the message, answered the questions silently and passed it on to the next person in the group, and so on... The questions are listed below. Readers may like to participate in this exercise by answering them – they are not another emotional intelligence test!

1   Do you dare to dream of your heart's belonging?
2   Will you risk looking like a fool for love, for dreams, for the adventure of being alive?
3   Have you touched the centre of your own sorrow?
4   Have you been opened up by life's betrayals?
5   Can you sit with pain, mine or your own, without moving to hide it or make it fade or fix it?
6   Can you be with joy, mine or your own?
7   Can you dance with wildness and let ecstasy fill you to the tips of your fingers and toes without cautioning us to be careful, be realistic, or to remember the limitations of being a human?
8   Can you disappoint another in order to be true to yourself?
9   Can you bear the accusation of betrayal and not betray your own soul?
10   Can you be faithful and therefore trustworthy?
11   Can you see beauty even if it's not pretty everyday?
12   Can you source your life from God's presence?
13   Can you live with failure, yours and mine, and still stand on the edge of a lake and shout to the silver moon, 'Yes!'?
14   Can you get up after a night of grief and despair, weary, bruised to the bone, and do what needs to be done for the children?
15   Will you stand in the centre of the fire with me and not shrink back?
16   Can you sustain yourself from the inside, when all else falls away?
17   Can you be alone with yourself?
18   Do you truly like the company you keep in the empty moments?

If your answers to all of the above questions are 'Yes', congratulations! For all you know, cross-personal/cultural and spiritual intelligence are only a quantum apart.

References

AC (2012). *Coaching definitions*. The Association for Coaching. At http://www.association forcoaching.com/about/about03.htm (accessed 4/8/2012).

Alban-Metcalfe, J. & Mead, G. (2010). Coaching for transactional and transformational leadership. In J. Passmore (ed.), *Leadership in coaching* (pp. 211–28). London: Kogan Page.

Alban-Metcalfe, J. & Alimo-Metcalfe, B. (2007). The development of the private sector version of the (Engaging) Transformational Leadership Questionnaire (ELQ). *Leadership & Organisational Development Journal*, 28(2), 104–21.

Alimo-Metcalfe, B. & Alban Metcalfe, J. (2005). Leadership: Time for a new direction? *Leadership*, 1(1), 51–71.

Alli, A. (1977). *Orientation: Principles, techniques, and philosophy of a ritual technology for self-initiation*. At http://www.paratheatrical.com (accessed 4/8/2012).

Alli, A. (2003). *Towards an archaeology of the soul*. Berkeley, CA: Vertical Pool Publishing.

Allport, G. W. (1954). *The nature of prejudice*. Reading, MA: Addison-Wesley.

Allport, G. W. (1961). *Pattern and growth in personality*. New York: Holt, Rinehart & Winston.

Anderson, A. G., Knowles, Z. & Gilbourne, D. (2004). Reflective practice for sport psychologists: Concepts, models, practical implications on dissemination. *The Sport Psychologist*, 18, 188–203.

Anderson, R. C., Spiro, R. J. & Anderson, M. C. (1978). Schemata as scaffolding for the representation of information in connected discourse. *American Educational Research Journal*, 15, 433–40.

Argyris, C. (1977). Double loop learning in organizations. *Harvard Business Review*, 55(5), 115–25.

Argyris, C. (1999). *On organizational learning* (2nd edn). Oxford: Blackwell.

Argyris, C. & Schön, D. A. (1978). *Organizational learning: A theory of action perspective*. Reading, MA: Addison-Wesley.

Arvedson, L. (1993). Coming to grips with learning organisations. *European Forum for Management*, 1, 5–10.

Ausbel, D. P. (1968). *Educational psychology: A cognitive view*. New York: Holt, Rinehart & Winston.

Austin, E. J. (2008). A reaction time study of responses to trait and ability emotional intelligence test items. *Personality and Individual Differences*, 36, 1855–64.

Bandura, A. (1977). Self-efficacy: Toward a unifying theory of behavioural change. *Psychological Review*, 84, 195–215.

Bandura, A. (1982). Self-efficacy mechanism in human agency. *American Psychologist*, 37, 122–47.

Bandura, A. (1986). *Social foundations of thought and action: A social–cognitive theory.* Englewood Cliffs, NJ: Prentice Hall.

Bandura, A. (1997). *Self-efficacy: The exercise of control.* New York: W. H. Freeman.

Bargh, J. A., McKenna, K. Y. A. & Fitzsimons, G. M. (2002). Can you see the real me? Activation and expressions of the 'true self' on the Internet. *Journal of Social Issues*, 58(1), 33–48.

Barnes, F. P. & Mudin, L. (eds) (2001). *Values and ethics in the practice of psychotherapy and counselling.* Buckingham: Open University Press.

Bartlett, F. C. (1932). *Remembering: A study in experimental and social psychology.* Cambridge: Cambridge University Press.

Bass, B. M. (1998). *Transformational leadership: Industrial, military, and educational impact.* Mahwah, NJ: Lawrence Erlbaum.

Bass, B. M. & Riggio, R. E. (2005). *Transformational leadership.* Mahwah, NJ: Lawrence Erlbaum.

Basseches, M. (1984). *Dialectical thinking and adult development.* Norwood, NJ: Ablex.

Bateson, G. (1972). *Steps to an ecology of mind: Collected essays in anthropology, psychiatry, evolution and epistemology.* Chicago, IL: University of Chicago Press.

Beck, A., Rush, A., Shaw, B. & Emery, G. (1979). *Cognitive therapy of depression.* New York: Guilford Press.

Beisser, A. R. (1970). The paradoxical theory of change. In J. Fagan & I. L. Shepherd (eds), *Gestalt therapy now* (77–80). Palo Alto, CA: Science and Behavior Books. At www.gestalt.org/arnie.htm (accessed 4/8/2012).

Belenky, M. F., Clinchy, B. M., Goldberger, M. R. & Tarule, J. M. (1986). *Woman's ways of knowing: The development of self, voice and mind.* New York: Basic Books.

Bell, J. & Hardiman, R. (1989). The third role: The naturalistic knowledge engineer. In D. Diaper (ed.), *Knowledge elicitation: Principles, techniques and applications* (49–85). Chichester: Ellis Horwood.

Bennet, M. J. (1991). *American cultural patterns: A cross-cultural perspective.* New York: Intercultural Press.

Blackler, F., Crump, N. & McDonald, S. (1999). Organisational learning and organisational forgetting. In M. Easterby-Smith, J. Burgoyne & L. Araujo (eds), *Organisational learning and learning organisation: Development in theory and practice* (194–216). London: Sage.

Bockler, J. (2006). Alchemy: Ritual expeditions into the psyche. Paper presented at the 10th Annual Conference of Transpersonal Psychology, the British Psychological Society.

Bor, R. & Legg, C. (2003). The systems paradigm. In R. Woolfe, W. Dryden & S. Strawbridge (eds), *Handbook of counselling psychology* (2nd edn, 261–76). London: Sage.

Boud, D. (1995). *Enhancing learning through self-assessment.* London: Kogan Page.

Boud, D., Keogh, R. & Walker, D. (1985). *Reflection: Turning experience into learning.* London: Kogan Page.

BPS (2009). *Code of ethics and conduct.* Leicester: The British Psychological Society.

Bresser, F. (2006a). Best implementation of coaching in business: Part 1. *Coach the Coach*, 20 (Fenman Professional Training resources at http://www.fenman.co.uk/; catalogue at http://www.fenman.co.uk/cat/view/Coach-the-Coach-complete.html).

Bresser, F. (2006b). Best implementation of coaching in business: Part 2. *Coach the Coach*, 21 (Fenman Professional Training resources at http://www.fenman.co.uk/; catalogue at http://www.fenman.co.uk/cat/view/Coach-the-Coach-complete.html).

Brookfield, S. D. (1991). *Developing critical thinking: Challenging adults to explore alternative ways of thinking and acting.* San Francisco, CA: Jossey-Bass.

Bruner, J. S. (1964). The course of cognitive growth. *American Psychologist*, 19, 1–15.

Brunner, J. (1986). Actual mind, possible worlds. Cambridge, MA: Harvard University Press.

Burns, J. M. (1978). *Leadership.* New York: Harper & Row.

Buss, D. & Barnes, M. (1986). Preferences in human mate selection. *Journal of Personality and Social Psychology*, 50, 559–70.

Byrne, D. & Nelson, D. (1965). Attraction and linear function of positive reinforcements. *Journal of Personality and Social Psychology*, 1, 659–63.

Campone, F. (2011). The reflective coaching practitioner model. In J. Passmore (ed.), *Supervision in coaching* (11–30). London: Kogan Page.

Cangelosi, V. & Dill, W. R. (1965). Organisational learning: Observations toward a theory. *Administrative Science Quarterly*, 10(2), 175–203.

Cannon-Bowers, J. A. & Salas, E. (1993). Reflections on shared cognition. *Journal of Organizational Behaviour*, 22, 195–202.

Carroll, M. (2006). Key issues in coaching psychology supervision. *Coaching Psychologist*, 2(1), 4–8.

Casida, J. M. (2007). The relationship of nurse managers' leadership styles and nursing unit organizational culture in acute care hospitals in New Jersey. PhD dissertation, Seton Hall University, New Jersey.

Cavanagh, M. & Lane, D. (2012a). Coaching psychology coming of age: The challenges we face in the messy world of complexity. *International Coaching Psychology Review*, 7(1), 75–89.

Cavanagh, M. & Lane, D. (2012b). Coaching psychology coming of age: A response to our discussants. *International Coaching Psychology Review*, 7(1), 127–9.

Chambless, D. L. (1988). Empirically validated treatment. In G. P. Koocher, J. C. Norcross & S. S. Hill (eds), *Psychologists' desk reference* (209–19). New York: Oxford University Press.

Chaplain, R. (2003). *Teaching without disruption.* Vol. 1: *A model for managing pupil behaviour in the secondary school.* Oxford: RoutledgeFalmer.

Chattopadhyay, P., Glick, W. H., Miller, C. C. & Huber, G. P. (1999). Determininants of executive beliefs: Comparing functional conditioning and social influence. *Strategic Management Journal*, 20, 763–89.

Child, R., Woods, M., Willcock, D. & Man, A. (2011). Action learning supervision for coaches. In J. Passmore (ed.), *Supervision in coaching* (31–44). London: Kogan Page.

CIPD (2012). *Coaching and mentoring.* At http://www.cipd.co.uk/hr-topics/coaching-mentoring.aspx#Informationpage (accessed 4/8/2012).

Clore, G. L. & Byrne D. (1974). A reinforcement model of attraction. In T. L. Huston (ed.), *Foundations of interpersonal attraction* (143–70). New York: Academic Press.

Clutterbuck, D. (2004). *Everyone needs a mentor* (4th edn). London: CIPD [Chartered Institute of Personnel and Development].

Clutterbuck, D. & Megginson, D. (2005). *Creating a coaching culture.* London: CIPD.

CMI (2012). Level 3 qualifications in coaching and mentoring (QCF). At http://www.managers.org.uk/training-development-qualifications/personal-development/qualifications/level-3-qualifications-coach (accessed 5/4/2013).

Collins, A. M. & Quillian, M. R. (1969). Retrieval time from semantic memory. *Journal of Verbal Learning and Verbal Behaviour*, 8, 240–7.

Combrink, A., Maree, J. & Mabolo, M. (2006). Breaking the silence: Stories as tool for healing in marginalized communities. Paper presented at the International Narrative Therapy Festive Conference, 1–3 March, Dulwich Centre, Adelaide Australia.

Contino, D. S. (2004). Leadership competencies: Knowledge, skills, and aptitudes: Nurses need to lead organizations effectively. *Critical Care Nurse*, 24(3), 52–64.

Cranton, P. (1996). *Professional development as tranformative learning*. San Francisco, CA: Jossey-Bass.

Csikszentmihalyi, M. (1991). *Flow: The psychology of optimal experience*. New York: Harper Perennial.

Cyert, R. M. & March, J. G. (1963). *A behavioural theory of the firm*. Englewood Cliffs, NJ: Prentice Hall.

Daloz, L. (1999). *Mentor: Guiding the journey of adult learners*. San Francisco, CA: Jossey-Bass.

Downey, M. (1999). *Effective coaching*. London: Orion Business Books.

Drake, D. B. (2006). Narrative coaching: The foundation and framework for a story-based practice. Paper presented at the Narrative Matters International Conference, Wolfville, Nova Scotia.

Drake, D. B. (2007). The art of thinking narratively: Implications for coaching psychology and practice. *Australian Psychologist*, 42(4), 283–94.

Drake, D. B. (2008a). Finding our way home: Coaching's search for identity in a new era. *Coaching: An International Journal of Theory, Research and Practice*, 1(1), 15–26.

Drake, D. B. (2008b). Thrice upon a time: Narrative structure and psychology as a platform for coaching. In D. B. Drake, D. Brennan & K. Gørtz (eds.), *The philosophy and practice of coaching: Issues and insights for a new era* (51–71). San Francisco, CA: Jossey-Bass.

Drake, D. B. (2009). Narrative coaching. In E. Cox, T. Bachkirova & D. Clutterbuck (eds), *The Sage handbook of coaching* (120–31). London: Sage.

Drake, D. B. (2012). Anxiety and complexity in a postprofessional era: The challenge of practising what we preach. *International Coaching Psychology Review*, 7(1), 106–8.

Driscoll, M. P. (2005). *Psychology of learning for instruction*. New York: Pearson Education.

Duncan, R. & Weiss, A. (1979). Organizational learning: Implications for organizational design. In B. Staw (ed.), *Research in organizational behaviour*. Greenwich, CT: JAI Press.

Ebbinghaus, H. (1913). *Memory: A contribution to experimental psychology* [1885]. New York: Columbia University, Teachers College Press.

Ekblom, P., Law, H. C. & Sutton, M. (1996). *Domestic burglary schemes in the Safer Cities Programme* (Home Office RSD Research Findings No. 42). London: Home Office.

Elsbree, L. (1982). *The rituals of life: Pattern in narrative*. New York: Kennikat.

EMCC (2011). *Code of conduct: For coaching and mentoring*. EMCC, June. At http://www.emccouncil.org/src/ultimo/models/Download/102.pdf (accessed 4/8/2012).

Eyerman, R. & Jamison, A. (1991). *Social movements: A cognitive approach*. University Park: Pennsylvania State Press.

Festinger, V., Schachter, S. & Back, K. W. (1950). *Social pressures in informal groups: A study of human factors in housing*. New York: Harper.

Fiol, C. M. & Lyles, M. A. (1985). Organizational learning. *Academy of Management Review*, 10, 803–13.

Fitzsimmons, G. & Guise, S. (2010). Coaching for leadership style. In J. Passmore (ed.), *Leadership coaching* (229–44). London: Kogan Page.

Fowers, B. J. & Richardson, F. C. (1996). Why is multiculturalism good? *American Psychologist*, 51, 609–21.

Freire, P. (1992). *Politics of education*. Greenwich, CT: Brunner/Mazel.

Gale, J. E. (1992). *Conversation analysis of therapeutic discourse: The pursuit of a therapeutic agenda* (Advances in Discourse Processes 41). Norwood, NJ: Ablex.

Gale, J. E. & Newfield, N. (1992). A conversation analysis of a solution-focused marital therapy session. *Journal of Marital and Family Therapy*, 18, 163–5.

Gallwey, T. (2000). *The inner game of work.* New York: Random House.

Gardner, H. (1983). *Frames of mind: The theory of multiple intelligences.* New York: Basic Books.

Garvey, B. (2011). *A very short, fairly interesting and reasonably cheap book about coaching and mentoring.* London: Sage.

Garvey, R. & Garrett, H. R. (2005). The benefits of mentoring: Literature review. Paper presented at the East Mentoring Forum, February, Coaching and Mentoring Research Unit, Sheffield Hallam University, Sheffield.

Garvin, D. A. (1993). Building a learning organisation. *Harvard Business Review,* 71(4), 78–84.

Geertz, C. (1973). *The interpretation of cultures: Selected essays.* New York: Basic Books.

Geertz, C. (1986). Anti-anti-relativism. *American Anthropologist,* 86, 263–78.

Gibb, G. (1988). *Learning by doing: A guide to teaching and learning methods.* Oxford: Oxford Brookes University, Further Education Unit.

Gilbourne, D, (2006). Reflecting on the reflections of others: Support and critique. *Sport and Exercise Psychology Review,* 2(2), 49-54.

Gillie, M. (2009). *I and thou.* New York: Scribner.

Ginsberg, A. (1990). Constructing the business portfolio: A cognitive model of diversification. *Journal of Management Studies,* 26, 417–38.

Goleman, D. (1995). *Emotional intelligence, why it can matter more than IQ.* London: Bloomsbury.

Goleman, D. (1998). *Working with emotional intelligence.* London: Bloomsbury.

Goleman, D., Boyatzis, R. E. & McKee, A. (2003). *The new leaders: Transforming the art of leadership.* London: Sphere.

Grant, A. & Palmer, S. (2002). Coaching psychology. Workshop and meeting held at the Annual Conference of the Division of Counselling Psychology, British Psychological Society, Torquay, 18 May.

Greenberger, D. & Padesky, C. A. (1995). *Mind over mood: Change how you feel by changing the way you think.* New York: Guilford Press.

Grindel, C. G. (2003). Mentoring managers. *Nephrology Nursing Journal,* 30(5), 517–22.

Haberman, J. (1971). *Knowledge and human interest.* London: Heinemann.

Hall, E. T. (1963). *The silent language.* Greenwich, CT: Fawcett Publications.

Hall, E. T. (1976). *Beyond culture.* Garden City, NY: Anchor Press.

Hall, L. (ed.) (2006a). News: Sort it with a story from down under. *Coaching at Work,* 1(2), 8.

Hall, L. (ed.) (2006b). UKAEA turns to coaching to power change. *Coaching at Work,* 1(2), 10.

Hall, L. (ed.) (2006c). The E word. *Coaching at Work,* 1(2), 22–5.

Hamel, G. (1996). Strategy as revolution. *Harvard Business Review,* July–August. At http://89.145.77.23/~crosshea/groupcreative/wp-content/uploads/Strategy-as-revolution-Gary-Hamel.pdf (accessed 27/4/2013).

Handy, C. B. (1989). *The age of unreason.* London: Business Books.

Hanson, P. C. (1973). The Johari Window: A model for soliciting and giving feedback. In J. Jones & J. W. Pfeiffer (eds), *The 1973 Annual Handbook for Group Facilitators* (114–119). LaJolla, CA: University Associates.

Hardingham, A., Brearley, M., Moorhouse, A. & Venter, B. (eds) (2004). *The coach's coach: Personal development for personal developers.* London: CIPD.

Hartley, J., Whomsley, S. & Clarke, I. (2006). Transpersonal encounter: honouring people's stories as a route to recovery. *The Transpersonal Psychology Review,* 10(1), 93–101.

Hartman, S. & Crow, S. (2002). Executive development in healthcare during times of turbulence. *Journal of Management in Medicine,* 16(5), 359–70.

Hawkins, P. & Smith, N. (2006). *Coaching, mentoring and organizational consultancy: Supervision and development.* Maidenhead: McGraw-Hill.

Hefferon, K. & Boniwell, I. (2011). *Positive psychology: Theory, research and applications*. London: McGraw-Hill.

Hergenhan, B. R. H. & Olson, M. H.(1997). *An introduction to theories of learning*. Cambridge: Pearson.

Heron, J. (1981a). Experiential research methodology. In P. Reason & J. Rowan (eds), *Human enquiry: A sourcebook of new paradigm research* (153–66). Chichester: John Wiley.

Heron, J. (1981b). Philosophical basis for a new paradigm. In P. Reason & J. Rowan (eds), *Human enquiry: A sourcebook of new paradigm research* (19–36). Chichester: John Wiley.

Higgins, J. (2005). Oil change. *Director* (December), 46–9.

Hill, D. & Jones, C. (eds) (2003). *Forms of ethical thinking in therapeutic practice*. Buckingham: Open University Press.

Hilpern, K. (2006). Driving force. *Coaching at Work*, 1(2), 30–1.

HMSO (1997). *Green book: Appraisal and evaluation in central government*. London: Stationary Office.

Hodgkinson, G. P. & Sparrow, P. R. (2002). *The competent organisation*. Buckingham: Open University Press.

Hofstede, G. H. (1980). *Culture's consequences: International differences in work-related values*. Beverly Hills, CA: Sage.

Hofstede, G. H. (1991). *Cultures and organizations: Software of the mind*. London: McGraw-Hill. (Republished by McGraw-Hill in New York in 1997 and 2004.)

Hounsell, D. (1984). Understanding teaching and teaching understanding. In F. Marton, D. Hounsell & N. Entwistle (eds), *The experience of learning* (238–57). Edinburgh: Scottish Academic Press.

Houston J. (1998). *A passion for the possible*. London: Thorsons.

Huber, G. P. (1991). Organizational learning: The contributing process and the literatures. *Organization Science*, 2(1), 88–115.

Humphrey, S. & Holland, S. (2006). A chemistry lesson. *Coaching at Work*, 1(2), 22–5.

Hunt, K. (2005) E-mentoring: solving the issue of mentoring across distances. *Development and Learning in Organizations*, 19(5), 7–10.

ICF (2013). At www.coachfederation.org/ (accessed 22/4/2013).

ICF & PricewaterhouseCoopers (2012). *ICF global coaching study: Executive summary*. At http://www.coachfederation.org/coachingstudy2012/ (accessed 10/6/2012).

Ireland, S., Hussain, Z. & Law, H. C. (2006). The perfect matchmaker: CIPD. *Coaching at Work*, 1(2), 26–9.

Jahoda, M. (1958). *Current concepts of positive mental health*. New York: Basic Books.

James, W. (1960). *The variety of religious experience: A study of human nature* [1902]. London: Fontana.

Jarvis, P. (1987). Meaningful and meaningless experience: Towards an analysis of learning from life. *Adult Education Quarterly*, 37(3), 164–72.

Jarvis, P. (1992). *Paradox of learning: On becoming an individual in society*. San Francisco, CA: Jossey-Bass.

Johnson, G. & Scholes, K. (1999). *Exploring corporate strategy: Text and cases* (5th edn). London: Prentice Hall.

Johnson-Laird, P. N. (1983). *Mental models*. Cambridge: Cambridge University Press.

Jørgensen, I. S. & Nafstad, H. E. (2004). Positive psychology: Historical, philosophical and epistemological perspectives. In P. A. Linley & S. Joseph (eds.), *Positive psychology in practice* (15–34). Hoboken, NJ: Wiley.

Jung, C. (1933). *Modern man in search of a soul*. New York: Harcourt, Brace, & World.

Kadushin, A. (1992). What's wrong, what's right with social work supervision. *The Clinical Supervisor*, 10(1), 3–19.

Kauffman, C. & Scouler, A. (2004). Toward a positive psychology of executive coaching. In P. A. Linley & S. Joseph (eds), *Positive psychology in practice* (287–302). Hoboken, NJ: Wiley.

Kegan, R. (1982). *The evolving self: Problem and process in human development*. Cambridge, MA: Harvard University Press.

Kegan, R. (1994). *In over our head: The mental demands of modern life*. Cambridge, MA: Harvard University Press.

Keller, J. M. (1984). The use of the ARCS model of motivation in teacher training. In K. E. Shaw (ed.), *Aspects of educational technology*. Vol. 17: *Staff development and career updating* (140–5). New York: Nichols.

Kessels, J. W. M. (1996). Knowledge productivity and the corporate curriculum. In J. F. Schreinemakers (ed.), *Knowledge management: Organization, competence and methodology. Proceedings of 4th international ISMICK symposium*, 21–2 October (168–73). Rotterdam: Ergon.

Kiesler, S., Siegel, J. & McGuire, T. W. (1984). Social psychological aspects of computer-mediated communication. *American Psychologist*, 39, 1123–34.

Kirkpatrick, D. (1994). *Evaluating training programs: The four levels* [1959]. San Francisco, CA: Berrett-Koehler.

Koffka, K. (1935). *The principles of gestalt psychology*. Princeton, NJ: Brace and World.

Kogan, M. (1998). The politics of making meaning: Discourse analysis of a 'postmodern' interview. *Journal of Marital and Family Therapy*, 20, 229–51.

Kogan, S. M. & Gale, J. E. (1997). Decentering therapy: Textual analysis of a narrative therapy session. *Family Process*, 36, 101–26.

Kohlberg, L. (1981). *The philosophy of modern development. Moral stage and the idea of justice*. New York: Harper & Row.

Kolb, D. A. (1984). *Experiential learning: Experience as the source of learning and development*. Englewood Cliffs, NJ: Prentice Hall.

Kondo, D. (1990). *Crafting selves: Power, gender and discourses of identity in a Japanese workplace* (9, 11–24). Chicago: University of Chicago Press.

Koskela, L. (1992). Application of the new production philosophy in construction (Technical Report No. 72). Stanford, CA: Stanford University, Center for Integrated Facility Engineering (CFIFE).

Kram, K. E. & Hall, D. T. (1996). Mentoring in the context of diversity and turbulence. In E. E. Kossek & S. A. Lobel (eds), *Managing human resource strategies for transforming the workplace* (108–36). Cambridge, MA: Blackwell Business.

Krause, I.-B. (1998). *Therapy across culture*. London: Sage.

Lane, D. (2005). Building a model for coaching psychology practice. Workshop held at the Second National Conference of the Special Group in Coaching Psychology in the UK, British Psychological Society.

Lave, J. & Wenger, E. (1991). *Situated learning: Legitimate peripheral participation*. Cambridge: Cambridge University Press.

Law, H. C. (2002). Coaching psychology interest group: An introduction. *The Occupational Psychologist*, 47, 31–2.

Law, H. C. (2003). Applying psychology in executive coaching programmes for organisations. *The Occupational Psychologist*, 49, 12–19.

Law, H. C. (2004a). Arts of healing across cultures: Dissertation on intercultural therapy. Postgraduate certificate dissertation, Goldsmiths, University of London.

Law, H. C. (2004b). Transcultural aspects of healing. *Transpersonal Psychology Review*, 8(2), 46–54.

Law, H. C. (2005a). The role of ethical principles in coaching psychology. *Coaching Psychologist*, 1(1), 19–20.

Law, H. C. (2005b). The new code of ethics, human rights, and coaching psychology. *Coaching Psychologist*, 1(2), 13–15.

Law, H. C. (2006a). Ethical principles in coaching psychology. *Coaching Psychologist*, 2(1), 13–16.

Law, H. C. (2006b). Can coaches be good in any context? *Coaching at Work*, 1(2), 14.

Law, H. C. (2011). What are the striking parallels between cognitive neuroscience and spiritual traditions? Or why counselling psychologists should embrace transpersonal psychology. Dr Ho Law in conversation with Professor Les Lancaster. *Counselling Psychology Quarterly*, 24(4), 331–9.

Law, H. C. (2012). The application of mindfulness, *Counselling Psychology Quarterly*. DOI: 10.1080/09515070.2012.708476

Law, H. C. (2013). *Coaching psychology: A practitioner's manual.* Chichester: Wiley.

Law, H. C. & Fitzgerald, R. (2012). Coaching psychology in education: Evaluation of coach training in Bahrain. In *SGCP annual conference 2012: Putting coaching psychology into practice: An evidence based approach* (unpublished). Aston University, Birmingham. (Abstract at http://abstracts.bps.org.uk/index.cfm?&ResultsType=Abstracts&Result Set_ID=8977&FormDisplayMode=view&frmShowSelected=true&localAction=details, accessed 27/4/2013.)

Law, H. C., Aga, S. & Hill, J. (2006). Creating a 'camp fire' at home: Narrative coaching: Community coaching and mentoring network conference report and reflection. *The Cutting Edge* (e-journal, ISSN 1366-8005), 7(1), 1–2.

Law, H. C., Ireland, S. & Hussain, Z. (2005). Evaluation of coaching competence self-review on-line tool within an NHS leadership development programme. Paper presented at the SGCP annual conference, December. British Psychological Society/City University, London.

Law, H. C., Ireland, S. & Hussain, Z. (2006). Evaluation of the coaching competence self-review on-line tool within an NHS leadership development programme. *International Coaching Psychology Review*, 1(2), 56–67.

Law, H. C., Ireland, S. & Hussain, Z. (2007). *Psychology of coaching, mentoring and learning.* Chichester: John Wiley & Sons.

Law, H. C., Laulusa, L. & Cheng G. (2009). When Far East meets West: Seeking cultural synthesis through coaching. In Michel Moral & Geoffrey Abbott (eds), *The Routledge companion to international business coaching* (241–55). East Sussex: Routledge.

Lee, H., Spiers, J. A., Yurtseven, O., Cummings, G. G., Showlow, J., Bhatti, A. & Germann, P. (2010). Impact of leadership development on emotional health in healthcare managers. *Journal of Nursing Management*, 18(8), 1027–39.

Lee, S. M. & Roberts, S. (2010). Sequential dynamic classification using latent variable models. *The Computer Journal.* DOI: 10.1093/comjnl/bxp127

Leonard, N. H., Scholl, R. W. & Kowalski, B. (1999). Information processing style and decision making. *Journal of Organizational Behaviour*, 20, 407–20. Chichester: John Wiley & Sons.

Levi-Strauss, C. (1966). *The savage mind.* London: Weidenfeld & Nicolson.

Levinson, D. J. (1997). *The season of a woman's life.* New York: Ballantine Books.

Levinson, D. J., Darrow, D. N., Klein, E. B., Levinson, M. H. & McKee, B. (1978). *The season of a man's life.* New York: Knopf.

Levitt, B. & March, J. G. (1988). Organizational learning. *Annual Review of Sociology*, 14, 319–40.

Lincoln, Y. S. & Guba, E. G. (1984). *Naturalistic enquiry.* Beverly Hills, CA: Sage.

Linley, P. A. (2004). Coaching psychology: The positive psychology foundations. Paper presented at the International Positive Psychology Summit, October. Washington, DC.

Linley, P. A. & Harrington, S. (2005). Positive psychology and coaching psychology: Perspectives on integration. *The Coaching Psychologist*, 1 (July), 13–14.

Linley, P. A. & Harrington, S. (2006). Strengths coaching: A potential-guided approach to coaching psychology. *International Coaching Psychology Review*, 1, 37–46.

Linley, P. A. & Joseph, S. (2004a). Applied positive psychology: A new perspective for professional practice. In P. A. Linley & S. Joseph (eds), *Positive psychology in practice* (3–12). Hoboken, NJ: Wiley.

Linley, P. A. & Joseph, S. (eds) (2004b). *Positive psychology in practice*. Hoboken, NJ: Wiley.

Lioukas, S. & Chambers, D. (1998). Strategic decision-making process: The role of management and context. *Strategic Management Journal*, 19, 39–58.

Lipman-Blumen, J. (1996). *Connective leadership: Managing in a changing world*. New York: Oxford University Press

Locke, E. A., Shaw, K. N., Saari, L. M. & Latham, G. P. (1981). Goal setting and task performance: 1969–1980. *Psychological Bulletin*, 90, 125–52.

Loevinger, J. & Blasi, A. (1976). *Ego development*. San Francisco: Jossey-Bass.

Luft, J. (1970). *Group processes: An introduction to group dynamics* (2nd edn). Palo Alto, CA: National Press Books.

Madison, J. (1994). The value of mentoring in nursing leadership: A descriptive study. *Nursing Forum*, 29(4), 16–23.

Magee, W. (2006). Two heads, one mind. *Director*. At http://www.director.co.uk/ MAGAZINE/2006/11%20Nov/mentoring_60_4.html (accessed 24/4/2013).

Magerman, M. H. & Leahy, M. J. (2009). The lone ranger is dying: Gestalt coaching as support and challenge. *International Gestalt Journal*, 32(1), 173–96.

Marienau, C. (1999). Self-assessment at work: Outcome of adult reflections on practice. *Adult Education Quarterly*, 49(3), 135–46.

Markoczy, L. (1997). Measuring beliefs: Accept no substitutes. *Academy of Management Journal*, 40, 1228–42.

Maslow A. H. (1954). *Motivation and personality*. New York: Harper & Row.

Maslow, A. H. (1968). *Toward a psychology of being* (2nd edn). New York: Van Nostrand Reinhold.

Mathena, K. A. (2002). Nursing manager leadership skills. *Journal of Nursing Administration*, 32, 136–42.

Mayer, J. D. & Salovey, P. (1993). The intelligence of emotional intelligence. *Intelligence*, 22, 89–113.

Mayer, J. D. & Salovey, P. (1997). What is emotional intelligence? In P. Salovey & D. Sluyter (eds), *Emotional development and emotional intelligence* (3–31). New York: Basic Books.

Mayer, J. D., DiPaolo, M. T. & Salovey, P. (1990). Perceiving affective content in ambiguous visual stimuli: A component of emotional intelligence. *Journal of Personality Assessment*, 54, 772–81.

McAlearney, A. S. (2006). Leadership development in healthcare: A qualitative study. *Journal of Organizational Behavior*, 27, 967–82.

McGoven, J., Lindemann, M., Vergara, M., Murphy, S., Barker, L. & Warrenfeltz, R. (2001). Maximising the impact of executive coaching. *Manchester Review*, 6(1), 1–32.

McKenna, D. & Davis, S. (2009). Hidden in plain sight. *Industrial and organizational psychology: An exchange of perspectives on science and practice*, 3(2), 244–60.

Megginson, D. & Clutterbuck, D. (1995). *Techniques for coaching and mentoring*. Oxford: Elsevier Butterworth-Heinemann.

Megginson, D., Stokes, P. & Garrett-Harris, R. (2003). Passport to export mentoring pilot scheme: East Midlands. *An evaluation report on behalf of trade partners UK* (1–3). Sheffield: MRCU Sheffield Hallam University.

Melnick, J. & Nevis, S. (2005). Gestalt methodology. In A. Woldt and S. Toman (eds), *Gestalt therapy: History, theory and practice* (101–14). Thousand Oaks, CA: Sage.

Mentkowski, M. (2000). *Learning that lasts: Integrating learning, development and performance in college and beyond.* San Francisco, CA: Jossey-Bass.

Merriam, S. (1994). Learning and life experience: The connection in adulthood. In J. Sinnott (ed.), *Interdisciplinary handbook of adult learning* (74–89). Westport, CT: Greenwood Press.

Merton, R. K. (1948). The self-fulfilling prophecy. *Antioch Review*, 8, 193–210.

Mezirow, J. (1990). *Fostering critical reflection in adulthood: A guide to transformative and emancipatory learning.* San Francisco, CA: Jossey-Bass.

Mezirow, J. (1991). *Transformative dimensions of adult learning.* San Francisco, CA: Jossey-Bass.

Mezirow, J. (1996). Contemporary paradigms of learning. *Adult Education Quarterly*, 44(3), 158–73.

Mezirow, J. (2000). *Learning as transformation: Critical perspectives on a theory in progress.* San Francisco, CA: Jossey-Bass.

Mikolajczak, M., Luminet, O., Leroy, C. & Roy, E. (2007). Psychometric properties of the Trait Emotional Intelligence Questionnaire. *Journal of Personality Assessment*, 88, 338–53.

Miller, C. C., Burke, L. M. & Glick, W. H. (1998) Cognitive diversity among upper-echelon executives: Implications for strategic decision process. *Strategic Management Journal*, 19, 39–58.

Mintzberg, H. (1994). The fall and rise of strategic planning. *Harvard Business Review* (January). At http://hbr.org/1994/01/the-fall-and-rise-of-strategic-planning/ar/1 (accessed 27/4/2013).

Mohammed, S., Klimoski, R. & Rentsch, J. (2000). The measurement of team mental models: We have no shared schema. *Organisational Research Methods*, 3, 123–65.

Moreland, R. L. (2000). Transactive memory: Learning who knows what in work groups and organisations. In L. Thompson, D. Messick & J. Levine (eds), *Shared cognition in organisations: The management of knowledge* (3–31). Hillsdale, NJ: Lawrence Erlbaum.

Murray, A. (1989). Top management group heterogeneity and firm performance. *Strategic Management Journal*, 10, 125–41.

Myerhoff, B. (1980). *Number our days.* New York: Simon & Schuster.

Myerhoff, B. (1982). Life history among the elderly: Performance, visibility and re-membering. In J. Ruby (ed.), *A crack in the mirror: Reflexive perspectives in anthropology* (99–120). Philadelphia: University of Pennsylvania Press.

Myerhoff, B. (1986). Life not death in Venice: Its second life. In V. Turner & E. Brunner (eds), *The anthology of experience* (261–86). Chicago: University of Illinois Press.

Myers, I. B. (1962). *The Myers Briggs type indicator.* Palo Alto, CA: Consulting Psychologists Press.

Naranjo, C. (1993). *Gestalt therapy: The attitude and practice of an atheoretical experientialism.* Carmarthen, Wales: Crown House Publishing.

Neenan, M. & Palmer, S. (2001). Cognitive behavioural coaching. *Stress News*, 13(3), 15–18.

Nonaka, I. (1991). The knowledge-creating company. *Harvard Business Review*, November–December, 96–104.

Nonaka, I., Takeuchi, H. & Umemoto, K. (1996). A theory of organisational knowledge creation. *International Journal of Technology Management*, 11(7–8): 833–45.

Norman, D. A. (1983). Some observations on mental models. In D. Gentner & A. L. Stevens (eds), *Mental models* (7–14). Hillsdale, NJ: Lawrence Erlbaum.

Palmer, S. & Whybrow, A. (2004). Coaching psychology survey: Taking stock. Paper presented at the BPS SGCP Inaugural Conference, 15 December, City University, London.

Palmer, S. & Whybrow, A. (2006). The coaching psychology movement and its development within the British Psychological Society. *International Coaching Psychology Review*, 1(1), 56–70.

Palmer, S. & Whybrow, A. (2007). *The handbook of coaching psycholohy*. Hove, Sussex: Routledge.

Parks, M. R. & Floyd, K. (1996). Making friends in cyberspace. *Journal of communication*, 46, 80–96.

Parsloe, E. (1995). *Coaching, mentoring and assessing: A practical guide to developing competence* [1992]. New York: Kogan Page.

Pask R. & Joy, B. (2007), *Mentoring–coaching: A handbook for education professionals*. Milton Keynes: Open University Press.

Passmore, J. (ed.) (2011). *Supervision in coaching*. London: Kogan Page.

Patterson, M., Wilcox, S. & Higgs, J. (2006). Exploring dimensions of artistry in reflective practice. *Reflective Practice*, 7(4), 455–68.

Pedlar, M. M., Burgoyne, J. & Boydel, T. (1991). *The learning company: A strategy for sustainable development*. London. McGraw-Hill.

Perls, F. S. (1969). *Gestalt therapy verbatim*. Utah: Real People Press.

Perls, F. S. (1973). *The Gestalt approach and eye witness to therapy*. Palo Alto, CA: Science and Behaviour Book.

Perry, W. G. (1970). Cognitive and ethical growth: The making of meaning. In A. W. Chickering (ed.), *The modern American college* (76–116). San Francisco, CA: Jossey-Bass.

Peterson, D. B. (2009). Book review. *Coaching: An International Journal of Theory, Research and Practice*, 2(1), 89.

Peterson, C. & Seligman, M. E. P. (2004). *Character strengths and virtues: A handbook and classification*. New York: Oxford University Press.

Petrides, K. V. & Furnham, A. (2001). Trait emotional intelligence: Psychometric investigation with reference to established trait taxonomies. *European Journal of Personality*, 15, 425–48.

Petrides, K. V., Frederickson, N. & Furnham, A. (2004). The role of trait emotional intelligence in academic performance and deviant behaviour at school. *Personality and Individual Differences*, 36, 277–93.

Petrides, K. V., Furnham, A. & Frederickson, N. (2004). Emotional intelligence. *The Psychologist*, 17(10), 574–7.

Piaget, J. (1954). *The construction of reality in the child*. New York: Basic Books.

Porter, M. (1996). What is strategy? *Harvard Business Review* (November–December), 61–78. At http://www.ipocongress.ru/download/guide/article/what_is_strategy.pdf (accessed 28/4/2013).

Potter, G. (2012). *Sacred paths entwine*. St Albans: Academy Press.

Reason, P. (ed.) (1988). *Human enquiry in action*. Thousand Oaks, CA: Sage.

Reason, P. & Rowan, J. (eds) (1981). *Human enquiry: A sourcebook of new paradigm research*. Chichester: John Wiley.

Rentsch, J. R. & Hall, R. J. (1994). Members of great teams think alike: A model of team effectiveness and schema similarity among team members. *Advances in Interdisciplinary Studies of Work Teams*, 1, 223–61.

Roberts, J. (1994). *Tales and transformations: Stories in families and family therapy*. New York: Norton.

Rogers, C. R. (1963). Toward a science of the person. *Journal of Humanistic Psychology*, 3, 79–92. (Reprinted in T. W. Wann (ed.), *Behaviorism and phenomenology: Contrasting bases for modern psychology*, Chicago, IL: University of Chicago Press, 1964.)

Rosenbaum, M. E. (1986). The repulsion hypothesis: On the nondevelopment of relationships. *Journal of Personality & Social Psychology*, 50, 729–36.

Rosinski, P. (2003). *Coaching across cultures*, London: Nicholas Brealey.

Rosinski, P. (2006). Cross cultural coaching. In J. Passmore (ed.), *Excellence in coaching* (153–69). London: Kogan Page.

Rothbaum, B. O., Mesdows, E. A., Resick, P. & Foy, D. W. (2000). Cognitive behavioural therapy. *Journal of Traumatic Stress*, 13, 558–63.

Rotter, J. B. (1956). *Social learning and clinical psychology*. Englewood Cliffs, NJ: Prentice Hall.

Rowson, R. (2001). Ethical principles. In F. P. Barnes & L. Mudin (eds), *Values and ethics in the practice of psychotherapy and counselling* (6–22). Buckingham: Open University Press.

Rumelhart, D. E. (1980). Schemata: The building blocks of cognition. In R. J. Spiro, B. C. Bruce & W. F. Brewer (eds), *Theoretical issues in reading comprehension* (33–58). Hillsdale, NJ: Lawrence Erlbaum.

Rumelhart, D. E. & Norman, D. A. (1978). Accretion, tuning, and restructuring: Three modes of learning. In J. W. Cotton & R. L. Klatzky (eds), *Semantic factors in cognition* (37–53). Hillsdale, NJ: Lawrence Erlbaum.

Rumelhart, D. E. & Norman, D. A. (1981). Analogical processes in learning. In J. R. Anderson (ed.), *Cognitive skills and their acquisition* (335–59). Hillsdale, NJ: Lawrence Erlbaum.

Rushall, B. S. (2003). Coaching development and the second law of thermodynamics [or belief-based versus evidence-based coaching development]. At http://coachsci.sdsu.edu/csa/thermo/thermo.htm (accessed 15/5/2013).

Ryde, J. (2000). Supervising across difference. *International Journal of Psychotherapy*, 5(1), 37–48.

Sackmann, S. A. (1991). *Cultural knowledge in organisations: Exploring the collective mind*. Newbury Park, CA: Sage.

Sackmann, S. A. (1992). Culture and sub-cultures: An analysis of organisational knowledge. *Administrative Science Quarterly*, 37, 140–61.

Safran, J. D. (1990). Towards a refinement of cognitive therapy in light of interpersonal theory. *Clinical Psychological Review*, 10, 87–105.

Salovey, P. & Mayer, J. D. (1990). Emotional intelligence. *Imagination, Cognition and Personality*, 9, 185–211.

Schön, D. A. (1983). *The reflective practitioner*. New York: Basic Books.

Schön, D. A. (1991). *The reflective practitioner: How professionals think in action*. London: Ashgate.

Schwartz, S. (1994a). Theory of cultural values and some implications for work. *Applied Psychology*, 48(1), 23–47.

Schwartz, S. H. (1994b). Beyond individualism/collectivism: New dimensions of values. In U. Kim, H. C. Triandis, C. Kagitçiabasi, S. C. Choi & G. Yoon (eds), *Individualism and collectivism: Theory, method and applications* (85–119). Newbury Park, CA: Sage.

Seligman, M. E. P. & Csikszentmihalyi, M. (2000). Positive psychology: An introduction. *American Psychologist*, 55, 5–14.

Senge, P. (1990). *The fifth discipline: The art and practice of learning organisations*. London: Doubleday.

Shams, M. & Law, H. (2012). Peer coaching framework: An exploratory technique. *The Coaching Psychologist*, 8(1), 46–9.

Sheehy, G. (1976). *Passages: Predictable crises of adult life*. New York: Ballantine Books.

Sheehy, G. (1996). *New passages*. New York: Ballantine Books.

Simon, S. N. (2009). Applying gestalt theory to coaching. *Gestalt Review*, 13(3), 230–9.

Smith K. G., Olian, J. D., Smith, K. A. & Flood, P. (1999). Top management team diversity, group process and strategic consensus. *Strategic management Journal*, 20, 445–65. Chichester: John Wiley & Sons.

Smith, L., Ciarrochi, J. & Heaven, P. C. L. (2008). The stability and change of trait emotional intelligence, conflict communication patterns, and relationship satisfaction: A one-year longitudinal study. *Personality and Individual Differences*, 45, 738–43.

Snowden, D. & Boone, M. (2007). A leader's framework for decision making. *Harvard Business Review*, 85(11), 68–76.

Solomon, H. M. (2000). The ethical self. In E. Christopher & H. M. Solomon (eds), *Jungian thought in the modern world* (191–216). London: Free Association.

Spence, G. B., Cavanagh, M. J. & Grant, A. M. (2006). Duty of care in an unregulated industry: Initial findings on the diversity and practices of Australian coaches. *International Coaching Psychology Review*, 1(1), 71–85.

Spinelli, E. (2006). Applying existential psychology in a coaching psychology practice: The question of conflict. Paper presented at the Second National Coaching Psychology Conference, 19–20 December, British Psychological Society.

Spreitzer, G. M. (1995). Psychological empowerment in the workplace: Construct definition, measurement and validation. *Academy of Management Journal*, 38(5), 1442–65.

Stacey, R. D. (1996). *Strategic management and organisational dynamics: The challenge of complexity* (2nd edn). London: Financial Times.

Stacey, R. (2012). Comment on debate article: Coaching psychology coming of age: The challenges we face in the messy world of complexity. *International Coaching Psychology Review*, 7(1), 91–5.

Staples, D. S., Greenaway, K. & McKeen, J. D. (2001). Opportunities for research about managing the knowledge-based enterprise. *International Journal of Management Review*, 3(1), 1–20.

Stelter, R. (2007). Coaching: A process of personal and social meaning making. *International Coaching Psychology Review*, 2(2), 191–201.

Stelter, R. (2009). Coaching as a reflective space in a society of growing diversity: Towards a narrative, postmodern paradigm. *International Coaching Psychology Review*, 4(2), 207–17.

Stelter, R. & Law, H. (2009). Narrative coaching: Towards personal and social meaning-making. Master class at the Second European Conference of Coaching Psychology, December, London.

Stelter, R. & Law, H. (2010). Coaching: Narrative–collaborative practice. *International Coaching Psychology Review*, 5(2), 152–64.

Storey, J. (2010). Signs of change: 'Damned rascals' and beyond. In J. Storey (ed.), *Leadership in organizations: Current issues and key trends* (2nd edn, 3–13). Abingdon: Routledge.

Strata, R. (1989). Organisational learning: The key to management innovation. *Sloan Management Review*, 30, 63–74.

Strawson, M. (1996). In deep sympathy. Toward a natural history of virtue: Review of M. Ridley, *The origin of virtue*. *Times Literary Supplement*, 29 November, 3–4.

Sue, D. W. & Sue, D. (1990). *Counselling the cultural difference*. New York: Wiley.

Sutcliffe, K. M. & Huber, G. P. (1998). Firm and industry as determinants of executive perspective perception. *Strategic Management Journal*, 19, 793–807.

Swann, W. B., Jr. (1990). To be adored or to be known: The interplay of self-enhancement and self-verification. In R. M. Sorrentino & E. T Higgins (eds), *Handbook of motivation and cognition*, vol. 2 (408–48). New York: Guildford Press.

Taylor, K., Marienau, C. & Fiddler, M. (2000). *Developing adult learners: Strategies for teachers and trainers*. San Francisco, CA: Jossey-Bass.

Thorndike, E. L. (1920). Intelligence and its use. *Harper's Magazine*, 140, 227–35.

Tichy, N. & Devanna, M. A. (1986). *Transformational leadership*. New York: John Wiley & Sons.

Tidwell, L. C. & Walther, J. B. (2002). Computer-mediated communication effects on disclosure, impressions, and interpersonal evaluations: Getting to know one another a bit at a time. *Human Communication Research*, 28, 317–48.

Trompenaars, F. & Hampden-Turner, C. (1997). *Riding the waves of culture*, 2nd edn. London: Nicholas Brealey.

Turner, V. (1967). *The forest of symbols: Aspects of Ndembu ritual.* Ithaca, NY: Cornel Paperbacks.

Turner V. & Brunner E. (eds) (1986). *The anthology of experience.* Chicago: University of Illinois Press.

Vaill, P. (1996). *Learning as a way of being: Strategies of how to survive in permanent white water.* San Francisco, CA: Jossey-Bass.

van Nieuwerburgh, C. (2012). *Coaching in education: Getting better results for students, educators and parents.* London: Karnac Books.

Veitch, R. & Griffitt, W. (1976). Good news, bad news: Affective interpersonal effects. *Journal of Applied Social Psychology,* 6, 69–75.

Verity, P. (2006). Planning for growth. In A. Jolly (ed.), *The growing business handbook* (3–7). London: Kogan Page.

Vosniadou, S. & Brewer, W. F. (1987). Theories of knowledge restructuring in development. *Review of Educational Research,* 57, 51–67.

Vroom, V. (1964). *Work and motivation.* New York: Wiley.

Vygotsky, L. S. (1962). *Thought and language* [1926]. Cambridge, MA: MIT Press.

Vygotsky, L. S. (1978). *Mind in society* [1926]. Cambridge, MA: Harvard University Press.

Ward, P. (1997). *360-degree feedback.* London: Institute of Personnel and Development.

Weick, K. E. (1995). *Sensemaking in organizations.* Thousand Oaks, CA: Sage.

Weick, K. E. & Roberts, K. H. (1993). Collective mind in organisation: Heedful interrelating on flight decks. *Administrative Science Quarterly,* 38, 357–81.

Weissman, A. (2008). Lesson learnt from Enron: A lawyer's perspective on business ethics. Keynote address at the 'Real World Real People: Professional Ethics Conference', 1–3 July, Kingston University, Surrey, UK.

Wenger, E. (1998). *Communities of practice: Learning, meaning, and identity.* Cambridge: Cambridge University Press.

Wenger, E. (2009). Social learning capability: Four essays on innovation and learning in social systems. *Social Innovation, Sociedade e Trabalho Booklets,* 12 (supplement, MTSS/GEP & EQUAL Portugal, Lisbon).

Wenger, E. (2011). *What is a community of practice?* Posted by Team BE on 28 December in FAQ. At http://wenger-trayner.com/resources/what-is-a-community-of-practice/ (accessed 4/8/20012).

Wenger, E., McDermott, R. & Snyder, W. (2002). *Cultivating communities of practice: A guide to managing knowledge.* Harvard, MA: Harvard Business School Press.

Wenger, E., White, N. & Smith, J. D. (2009). *Digital habitats: Stewarding technology for communities.* Portland, OR: CPsquare.

White, M. (1995a). *Re-authoring lives: Interviews and essays.* Adelaide, S. Australia: Dulwich Centre Publications.

White, M. (1995b). Reflecting team-work as definitional ceremony. In M. White, *Re-authoring lives: Interviews and essays.* Adelaide, S. Australia: Dulwich Centre Publications.

White, M. (1997). Definitional ceremony. In M. White, *Narratives of therapists' lives.* Adelaide, S. Australia: Dulwich Centre Publications.

White, M. (2000). Reflecting team-work as definitional ceremony revisited. In M. White, *Reflections on narrative practice* (59–85). Adelaide, S. Australia: Dulwich Centre Publications.

White, M. (2006). Narrative Therapy Intensive Workshop, 20–24 February, Adelaide, S. Australia: Dulwich Centre.

White, M. (2007). *Maps of narrative practice.* New York: Norton.

Whiteley, P. (2006). Pioneering medicine. *Coaching at Work,* 1(2), 30–1.

Whitmore, J. (2002). *Coaching for performance.* London: Nicholas Brealey.

Whybrow, A. (2008). Coaching psychology: Coming of age? *International Coaching Psychology Review,* 3(3), 227–40.

Whybrow, A. & Palmer, S. (2006). Shifting perspectives: One year into the development of the British Psychological Society Special Group in Psychology in the UK. *International Coaching Psychology Review*, 1(2), 75–85.

Wiersema, M. F. & Bantel, K. A. (1992). Top management team demography and corporate strategic change. *Academy of Management Journal*, 35, 91–121.

Willis, P. (2005). Standards research. Paper presented at the 12th European Mentoring and Coaching Conference, Zurich.

Wills, T. A. (1991). Social support and interpersonal relationships. In M. S. Clark (ed.), *Review of Personality and Social Psychology*, 2, 26–89.

Winnicott, D. W. (1971). *Playing and reality*. New York: Basic Books.

Witkin, H. A. (1962). *Psychological differentiation: Studies of development*. New York: John Wiley & Sons.

Zack, M. (1999). Managing codified knowledge. *Sloan Management Review*, 40(4), 37–56.

Index

Note: page numbers in *italics* refer to figures; those in **bold** to tables.

abstract conception, *33*, 34
AC *see* Association for Coaching
ACT *see* adaptive control of thought model
acting/identification Gestalt techniques, 127–8
acting out, 170, 172–3
action/action plans, *204*
    case studies, 177–8, 181–2, 187–8, 190–5,
        197–8
    CBT, 133, 158
    CPD, *94*
    GROW model, 143, 144, 145, 149
    narrative coaching, 28, 135–6, 137,
        139, 194
    reflective practice, *33*, 34, 36, *93*,
        155–6, 157
    Vygotsky's distancing tasks, 41, 134
adaptive control of thought (ACT) model, 43
Aga, S., 191
age, 39, 213
agreement/certainty matrix, 17–18
Alli, A., 169, 170, 171
Anderson, R.C., 43
appraisal/implementation
    business case for coaching/mentoring
        programme, 77–8
    ROAMEF evaluation framework, 204,
        206–7

appreciation, 109–10
ARCS model of motivational design, 31
articulation, 71, 72
association, principle of, 29
Association for Coaching (AC), 57,
        186–9, 227
Athena, 53, *54*
Ausbel, D., 43
automatic thought, 130
axiomatic knowledge, 69, *70*, 87

barriers to learning/change
    adapting to the future, 47, 49, 51
    CBT, 132–3
    in coachee–coach matching, 220
    corporate coaching/mentoring
        programmes, 79–80
    identifying/overcoming exercise,
        156, 157
    input analysis, 58
    Kodak, 65
    negative experiences, 27–8
    self-fulfilling prophecy, 31
Bartlett, F.C., 43
befriending behaviour, 83
belief-based practice, ix
Bell, J., 72, 73

BME (black and ethnic minority) leadership
    project (case study), 176–81, 208–13,
    214, 215–16, 217
BPS *see* British Psychological Society
Bresser, F., 187, 188
British eclectic model, 149
British Psychological Society (BPS), Special
    Group in Coaching Psychology (SGCP),
    2, 11–12, 58, 60, 92, 212, 227, 229
Bruner, J.S., 40
Buddhism, 100, 122
business consultancies, 13–14

campfire (Peterborough case study), 191
case studies
    Community Coaching Café, 196–200
    Maltese Healthcare leadership coaching
        programme, 181–6
    Peterborough, narrative coaching in
        communities, 190–6
    transatlantic e-coaching, 186–9
    UK healthcare system, 176–81, 208–13,
        214, 215–16
Cavanagh, M., 17, 18, 19
CBA *see* cost–benefit analysis
CBT *see* cognitive behavioural techniques
CEA *see* cost-effectiveness analysis
certainty/agreement matrix, 17–18
chains of association, 41, 134
change, paradoxical theory of, 124–6
Chartered Institute of Personnel and
    Development (CIPD), 11, 55
Chartered Management Institute (CMI), 11,
    13, 75
child development, 37–8, 40, 83
CIPD *see* Chartered Institute of Personnel
    and Development
classic conditioning, 29
clients, ethics/codes of conduct, 229–30,
    231, *232*
Clutterbuck, D., 20, 149
CMI *see* Chartered Management Institute
CMSI *see* cross-cultural coaching/mentoring
    and social intelligence model
coaching/mentoring
    industry/market *see* industry
    skills/competence, 21, 88–9, 156, 201,
        212, 214
    terminology, 3, 4–5, 7, 53–8, 101

coaching psychology
    coming of age, 16–19
    defined, 59–60
    see also learning theories
codes of conduct/practice, 229–33, 234
cognitive behavioural techniques (CBT), x,
    130–4, 143, 144, 150, 157–8, 220
collaborative learning
    bridging collective/individual
        purpose, 147
    coach–coachee relationship, 15, 40,
        130–1
    community of practice, 42, 44, 45, 46,
        86–7, 154
    group learning defined, 57
    narrative coaching, 42, 140–1, 167–9,
        189–96
    organizational learning, 64, 66, 82, 84–6
    reinforcement affect model, 29–30
    social support, 83–4
communication
    cultural environment, 95, 97–8, 99
    feedback mechanism, 92, 113–14
    Internet technology, 19, 20–1, 69
    in organizations, 19, 66, 69, 70–1, 75, 82,
        183, 216
    social competence, 61, 108, **111**,
        185, 213
Community Coaching Café (case study),
    196–200
community learning
    Community Coaching Café (case study),
        196–200
    goals in matching matrix, 220
    impact of registration requirements, 229
    narrative coaching, 140–1, 189–96
    of practice, 42, 44, 45, 46, 86–7, 154
    social support, 83–4
complaints, 64, 82, 187–8
conclusion and recommendation, 36, 41, *93*,
    134, *138*, 139, 157
    see also action/action plans
conditioned stimulus/response, 29
confidence/self-esteem, 83, 105, 133–4,
    155, 200, 214, 215
conflict resolution, 69, 108, 128–9, 224,
    231–3
Confucius, 53, *54*
conscientiousness, 106, **111**, 184

consciousness, landscape mapping (narrative coaching), 28, 136–9, 164, 194
see also externalizing conversations
constructive-developmental theories
  individual meaning making, 42–4
  Levinson's life structure theory, 38–40
  Piaget's theory of child development, 37–8
  Vygotsky's zone of proximal development, 40–1, 42, 61, 134, 135
consultancies, 13–14
continuous professional development (CPD) cycle, 13, 92–5, **111**, 153–5, 178, 228, 229
control model of learning, 32–3
coordinators
  attributes, 223
  in case studies, 176, 177, 178, 187, 188, 196, 199, 200
  as matchmakers, 177, 178, 221–2
  to promote evidence-based practice, 225
cost–benefit analysis (CBA), 206
cost-effectiveness analysis (CEA), 206
counselling, *12*, 16, 88, 130, 230, 231
CPD *see* continuous professional development cycle
creativity
  management ILA/learning, 184, 185
  personal competence, 107, 111, 145, 149, 171
  positive psychology, 23, 25
  and standardization, 227, 228
cross-cultural coaching/mentoring and social intelligence model (CMSI), 104 *see also* cultural and social competence self-assessment questionnaire
cross-cultural practice
  applicability of Western cultural values, 30, 33, 39–40, 100, 102
  ethics, 233–4
  experience–competence link, 213
  framework for, 22, 91 *see also* universal integrated framework (UIF)/integrative learning system (ILS)
  spirituality, 149
  terminology/definitions, 3, 60
  see also case studies; diversity
CSC SAQ *see* cultural and social competence self-assessment questionnaire

Csikszentmihalyi, M., 23, 170, 193
cultural competence
  adapting to, 49
  allophilia, 224
  case studies, 178–80, 186, **212**, 213, 217
  CPD, 226
  cultural-agility development, 145–7, 149, 150
  cultural environments, 92, 95–101
  intercultural coaching psychology, 60
  Levinson's life structure theory, 39–40
  organizational, 15, 77, 81–2, 88, 89, 109, 110, **111**
  pragmatic model, *103*, **111**
  self-assessment questions, 109–12
  sensitivity, 5 *see also* narrative coaching
  spirituality, 149
  structuring reflective logs, 156
  UIF/development intention model, **113**
  Western cultural values, 30, 33, 39–40, 100, 102
  see also cross-cultural practice
cultural and social competence self-assessment questionnaire (CSC SAQ), xv, 104–13, 155, 211–13, 224–5, 226

Daloz, L., 54
Davis, S., 16–17
de-centred coaching posture, 142
decision-making, appraising coaching proposals, 18, 76, 206
definitional ceremonies, 140–1, 164, 168–9, 189
description
  narrative coaching, 136–7, *138*, 139
  organizational directory knowledge, 69
  reflection, 36, 93, 155, 157
  Vygotsky's distancing tasks, 41, 134
development *see* constructive-developmental theories
development intention model, 112, **113**
dictionary knowledge, 69, *70*, 87
directory knowledge, 69, *70*, 87
disillusionment story (Peterborough case study), 193
distance learning *see* e-coaching/mentoring

diversity
  champions/social artists, 51, 77, 109,
    110, 180
  coach–coachee matching, 219–20,
    221, 223
  future focus, 235
  skills/competence, 5, 78, 88, 89, 109,
    110, **111**
  threat by standardization, 227, 228
  top team, 73, *74*
  see also cross-cultural practice
double triad, 231–2
Drake, D., 18, 19, 41
Driscoll, M., 58, 59
dynamic learning model, 46–50, 92, *93*, 113

Ebbinghaus, H., 29, 42
e-coaching/mentoring, 14, 19–21, 154,
  186–9, 216
economic benefits/costs, 13, 15, 78
effect, law of, 29
EI *see* emotional intelligence
electronic mentoring matching, 222
Embedded Figure Test, 76
EMCC *see* European Mentoring and
  Coaching Council
emotional intelligence (EI), 92, 102–3,
  104–10, **212**, 217, 223–4, 226
empathy, 47, 50, 88, 107, **111**, 154
employers *see* organizations/employers
empowerment
  community, 82, 141, 164, 190, 192
  management skill, 89, 107–8, **111**, 183, *184*
empty chair technique, 163–4
enactive representation, 40
Enron, 64, 65
epistemological approach to learning, 28
esteem/confidence, 83, 105, 133–4, 155,
  200, 214, 215
ethics, 13, 229–35
ethnicity, 99–100, 110, 114, 211, 213, *214*
European Mentoring and Coaching Council
  (EMCC), definitions of coaching/
  mentoring, 54, 55, 56–7, 227
evaluation
  case studies, 179–81, 185–6, 188–9,
    195–6, 198–9, 208–16
  CBT, 131
  generic methodology, 203–10

goal-based/appreciative, 30
re-authoring (narrative coaching), 134,
  138–9
ROAMEF framework, 207–10
UIF/ILS, 93–4, 199, 209, 210–13, 217,
  223, 225–6
evidence-based practice, ix–x, xi, xiii, 19, 67
  see also evaluation
executive coaching/leadership training, 10,
  15, 57, 89, 131, 132, 150, 154
  Malta leadership coaching programme
    (case study), 181–6
  transatlantic e-coaching project (case
    study), 186–9
  UK coaching and mentoring programme
    (case study), 176–81, 208–16
expectancy valence theory, 32
experimental approach to learning, 28, 29
explication/translation and Gestalt
  techniques, 127
explicit knowledge, 68, 71, 73, 87, 88
expressive Gestalt techniques, 126–7, 150
externalizing conversations, 136–7, 140,
  142, 144, 150
  see also re-authoring

face-to-face with computer-mediated
  coaching/mentoring, 20–1
family influence, 96–7, 100, 147
feedback mechanism (UIF), 93, 113–14,
  136, 185, 211
field dependence, 76
flexibility, 105, 106–7, **111**
fluidity of coach/coachee roles, 101, 210
friendship, 83
Furnham, A., 102, 110, **111**, 112
future work, 235

Gallwey, T., 16, 56
gender, 213, *214*
Gestalt therapy/coaching
  approach to change, 124–6
  background, 121–2
  dos and don'ts, 129–30
  focus on being/present, 123–4, 150
  integration with GROW, 143, 144
  practical exercises, 158–64, 173
  techniques/exercises, 126–30, 150,
    158–64

theory of learning, 29
transpersonal aspect, 122–3
Gibb, G., 36
global coaching survey (ICF), xi, 10
goal setting
as constraint, 30, 148
GROW model revisited, 143–4
organizational, 69, 77, 84, 85
self-efficacy, 35
see also objectives
Goleman, D., 102, 103
Greenberger, D., 130
group coaching, 57, 82, 109, 161–2, 167–9,
170, 171, 172
see also community learning
GROW model, 99, 115, 117, 143–5, 153,
182, 183

Haberman, J., 37
Hall, E.T., 97
Hampden-Turner, C., 98
Handbook of Coaching Psychology, The
(Palmer and Whybrow), 16
happiness, 24, 25, 59, 96, **111**
Hardiman, R., 72, 73
healthcare systems
Malta leadership coaching programme
(case study), 181–6
management challenges, 175–6
National Health Service (NHS), 83, 131,
176–81, 208–16
Hofstede, G.H., 97, 98
Holland, S., 15, 220
human strengths, 25–7
Humphrey, S., 220

ice-skating and ice-hockey story
(Peterborough case study), 193
ICF *see* International Coaching Federation
iconic representation, 40
idealized leadership attributes (ILAs), 181,
183–4
identification/acting Gestalt techniques,
127–8
ILA *see* idealized leadership attributes
ILS *see* universal integrated framework
(UIF)/integrative learning system (ILS)
impact evaluation, 85, 208, 209–10,
225–6

industry
codes and ethics, 229–35
overview, 9–14
standards, 227–9
insightful learning, 29
inspirational distortions, 79
integration
Gestalt techniques, 128, 150
knowledge transfer matrix, 71
intercultural coaching, 60
see also cross-cultural practice
interdisciplinary overlap, 3, *4*, 16–19, 22, 59
International Coaching Federation (ICF),
xiv, 10, 56
International Society for Coaching
Psychology (ISCP), 12–13
Internet
communities of practice, 86, 87
e-coaching/mentoring, 14, 19–21, 154,
186–9, 216
electronic mentoring matching, 222
self-review online tools, 104, 209
UIF, 91, 118 *see also* cultural and social
competence self-assessment
questionnaire
interpretivism, 28
'Invitation, The' (Oriah Mountain Dreamer)
(poem), 236
Ireland, S., 145
ISCP *see* International Society for Coaching
Psychology
I/you exercises (Gestalt-based coaching),
159–60

Johari window, 113, *113*, 136
Johnson, G., 67
journey metaphor, xiv, 15, 21, 33, 55
Jung, C., 201
justification, 134, *138*, 139

Kai Sin, xiv
Kandola, P., 24
Kirkpatrick, D., 207
kite mark scheme, 227
knowledge transfer, 67, 69–74, 87–8, 214
see also learning theories
Kodak, 64–5
Kolb, D.A., 33, 34, 35, 73
Kowalski, B., 76

landscape mapping, 28, 135–9, 164, 194
Lane, D., 17, 18, 19, 92, 227
Lave, J., 44, 86
law of effect, 29
leadership
    in changing business environment, 64–5,
        66, 175–6
    in a coaching culture/learning
        organization, 77, 81, 88–9, *184*
    competence/performance, 74–6, 89, 180,
        181, 183–4
    executive coaching, 10, 15, 57, 89, 131,
        132, 150, 154
    Malta leadership coaching programme
        (case study), 181–6
    as mentors/coaches, 14, 132
    top team diversity, 73, *74*
    transatlantic e-coaching project (case
        study), 186–9
    UIF/ILS framework, 102, 108, 111, *114*
    UK coaching and mentoring programme
        (case study), 176–81, 208–16
learning organizations
    benefits of coaching/mentoring, 6, 13,
        15, 68, 75–6, 213–16
    changing business environment, 6, 64–6,
        85, 91
    coaching programmes, 75–82, 88–9,
        101–2, 133 *see also* case studies
    communities of practice, 86–7
    equation with competence/performance,
        66–9, 101–2
    knowledge types, 69–70, 87
    leadership styles/competencies, 74–6, 88
    psychology of learning/knowledge flow,
        70–4
    social/community application, 82–7
learning theories
    coaching/mentoring frameworks, 14, 15,
        21 *see also* universal integrated
        framework (UIF)/integrative learning
        system (ILS)
    constructive-developmental theories,
        37–44
    learning context, 27–8
    learning process, 3, 33–7, 51, 58–9, 70–4
    literature review, 28–33
    positive psychology, 9, 16, 21, 22, 23–7,
        50, 59

social learning, 44–6
    Vygotsky's zone of proximal development,
        40–1, 42, 61, 134, 135
Leonard, N.H., 76
Levinson, D.J., 38, 39
life coaches/coaching, 13, 14, 57, 132
life stages, 38–40, 145, 149
life structure theory, 38–40
line-dancing story (Peterborough case
    study), 192
living in the moment practice, 124, 159, 161
locus of control model of learning, 32–3, 35

Maltese leadership coaching programme
    (case study), 181–6
market overview, 9–14
marriage brokering, 221
matching coaches/coachees, 79, 80, 177,
    178, 198, 219–23, 235
Mayer, J.D., 102
MBTI *see* Myers-Briggs Types Indicators
McKenna, D., 16–17
meaning
    dynamic learning model, 49, *50*
    Ebbinghaus' principle of association, 29
    individual meaning making, 42–4
    positive psychology, 23, 24, 25, 26
    social interaction, 42, 44–6
    through narrative, 44, 135
    through reflective practice, 34, 36, 37
    using metaphors, 148
meaningful reception learning theory, 43
meditation, 100, 122
men's life structure, 38–9
mentoring/coaching
    industry/market *see* industry
    skills/competence, 21, 88–9, 156, 201,
        212, 214
    terminology, 3, 4–5, 7, 53–8, 101
meta-models, 92, 112, 119
    see also universal integrated Framework
        (UIF)/integrative learning system (ILS)
mindfulness, 100, 123, 134, 159
minority group success, 31–2
monitoring (ROAMEF evaluation
    framework), 207
motivation, 30–1, 105, 105–6, 214, 215–16
    see also self-efficacy
multiculturalism, 22

Myerhoff, B., 45, 134, 139, 189
Myers-Briggs Types Indicators (MBTI),
　　76, 221

narrative coaching
　coaching attitude/posture, 141–2
　complexity debate, 18
　group situations, 140–1
　landscape mapping, 28, 135–9, 164, 194
　narrative psychodrama, 169–73
　Peterborough case study, 189–96
　remembering conversations, 139–40
　storytelling exercises, 164–9
　theoretical foundation, 41–2
　Vygotsky's levels of learning, 134–5
narrative psychodrama, physical exercises,
　　169–73
National Health Service (NHS), 83, 131,
　　176–81, 208–16
naturalistic knowledge engineering (NKE), 72
nature–nurture debate, 32
negative learning experiences (exercise), 156
niche/speciality coaching, 57
NKE *see* naturalistic knowledge engineering
nurture–nature debate, 32

objectives
　case studies, 177, 181, 186–7, 190,
　　197, 208
　coach–coachee matching, **220**
　codes of practice, 229–30
　CPD cycle, *94*
　evaluation, 203, 204, 205–6, 207, 208,
　　209–10
　learning organizations, 66, 67, 77, 78, 79,
　　80, 105
　motivational, 31, 105
　SMARTER, 78, 79, 131, 132, **133**, 144
　UIF competencies, 105, 108
objectivism, 28
'off-piste coaching', 145–9
options (GROW model revisited), 144
organizations/employers
　360-degree feedback, *114*
　analysis tools, 66
　coaching benefits, 6, 13, 15, 68, 75–6,
　　213–16
　coaching/mentoring market, 9–10, 13–14
　communications technology, 19–21

corporate coaching defined, 57
　goals in matching matrix, 220
　importance of leadership, 65–6
　internal coaching/mentoring, 14
　see also learning organizations
outsider witness retelling, 140, 141, 164,
　　167–8

Padesky, C.A., 130
Palmer, S., 12, 16, 59, 130
paradoxical theory of change, 124–6
paratheatre, 169
parenting, 16, 37
peer review, 113–14
people knowledge, 69, *70*, 87
Perls, F., 122, 128
personal competence
　case studies, 179, 185, 186, **212**, 213,
　　214, 215, 217
　CPD, 226
　creativity, 107, 111, 145, 149, 171
　definition of personal strength, 59
　pragmatic model, *103*, **111**
　self-assessment questions, 104–7, **111**
　self-efficacy, 30–1, 35, 41, 102–3
　self-esteem/confidence, 31, 83, 105,
　　133–4, 155, 200, 214, 215
　structuring reflective logs, 155–6
　techniques/tools, 120–1, 147, 150 *see also*
　　cognitive behavioural techniques;
　　Gestalt therapy/coaching
　UIF/development intention model, **113**
Peterborough, narrative coaching in
　communities (case study), 190–6
Peterson, C., 24, 25, 27
Peterson, D., 16
Petrides, K.V., 102, 110, **111**, 112
Piaget, J., 37–8
positive psychology, 9, 16, 21, 22, 23–7,
　　50, 59
practical exercises
　CBT, 157–8
　Gestalt coaching, 158–64
　narrative psychodrama, 169–73
　storytelling exercises, 164–9
pragmatism, 28
prejudice, 47–8
principle of association, 29
prisons, 83

procedural knowledge (recipe/directory
    knowledge), 69, *70*
process evaluation, 208, 209
professional competence
    case studies, 180, 186, 214–15
    leaders, 74–6, 89, 180, 181, 183–4
    learning organizations, 66–9, 101–2
    narrative coaching, notes for coaches,
        164–5, 166–7
    pragmatic model, *103*, **111**
    self-assessment questions, 112–13
    structuring reflective logs, 156
professional cultures, 100
professionalism (coaching/mentoring)
    coaching psychology debates, 19
    ethics, 13, 229–35
    standards, 227–9
professional organizations, xiii, 10–13
    Association for Coaching (AC), 57,
        186–9, 227
    British Psychological Society (BPS),
        Special Group in Coaching Psychology
        (SGCP), 2, 11–12, 58, 60, 92, 212,
        227, 229
    Chartered Institute of Personnel and
        Development (CIPD), 11, 55
    Chartered Management Institute (CMI),
        11, 13, 75
    European Mentoring and Coaching
        Council (EMCC), definitions of
        coaching/mentoring, 54, 55, 56–7, 227
    International Coaching Federation (ICF),
        10, 56
prophecy, 145, 149
proximal development, Vygotsky's zones of,
    40–1, 42, 61, 134, 135
psychology
    coming of age, 16–19
    definitions, 59–60
    transpersonal, 16, 122, 169
    see also learning theories
psychometric tests, 76
psychotherapy, 2, 16–17, 24, 51, 122, 134, 230
public-sector coaching programmes, 15 *see*
    also National Health Service

quality
    ethics, 229–35
    standardization, 13, 227–9

rationale, objectives, appraisal, monitoring,
    evaluation and feedback framework
    (ROAMEF), 204–10
rationale (ROAMEF evaluation framework),
    204–5
Ratner, G., 84
realism, 105
realistic goals, 78, 132, 143, 144
reality, 5, 28, 143, 144
    see also meaning
re-authoring (narrative coaching), 136,
    137–9, 164–5
receptiveness to coaching, 153, 156–7
recipe knowledge, 69, *70*
reflective practice
    case studies, 178, 183, 199–200
    coaching/mentoring framework, 46–7,
        48, *49*, *50*, **111**
    CPD cycle, 92, 93, 94
    decision-making behaviour, 76
    diaries/logs, 36, 130, 155, 157–8
    learning theories, *33*, *34*, 35–7, 42–4, 47, 48
    logs/accounts, 36, 130, 155, 157–8
    organizational learning, 71, *72*, 73
    role of coaching, 18
    Vygotsky's levels of learning, 41, 134
remembering conversations, 139–40, 164,
    165–7
reputation, 84, 87
resilience, 75, 105, 126, 185, 193
resistance to change, 125–6
respect, 110
Rice University e-coaching (case study), 186–9
ROAMEF *see* rationale, objectives, appraisal,
    monitoring, evaluation and feedback
    framework
Rosinski, P., 60, 98, 99, 146

Salovey, P., 102
schema theory, 43–4
Scholes, K., 67
Scholl, R.W., 76
schools, 83–4
self-confidence, 31, 83, 105, 133–4, 155,
    200, 214, 215
self-development
    defining coaching/mentoring, 53–4,
        55–7, 59–60
    see also personal competence

self-efficacy, 30–1, 35, 41, 102–3
self-fulfilling prophecy, 31
Seligman, M., 23, 24, 25, 27
skills/competence in coaching/mentoring, 21, 88–9, 156, 201, **212**, 214
SMARTER objectives, 78, 79, 131, 132, **133**, 144
social artists/diversity champions, 51, 77, 109, 110, **111**, 180
social competence
    case studies, 179, 185, **212**, 213, 217
    mentoring link, 54
    pragmatic model, *103*, **111**
    self-assessment questions, 107–9, **111**
    structuring reflective logs, 156
    tools/techniques, 145, 147, 148, 149, 150
    UIF/development intention model, **113**
social learning
    communities of practice, 42, 44, 45, 46, 86–7, 154
    Community Coaching Café (case study), 196–200
    families, 96–7, 100, 147
    knowledge transfer, 71
    locus of control model of learning, 32–3, 35
    narrative-based, 42, 140–1, 167–9, 189–96
    in organizations, 64–6, 82, 84–6
    reinforcement affect model, 29–30
    support, 83–4
speciality/niche coaching, 57
Spinelli, E., 69
spirituality, 25, 26, 122, 149, 169, 224
sports coaching, 16, 34, 55
Stacey, R.D., 17–18, 84
standardization, 13, 227–9
storytelling approach *see* narrative coaching
strategic management, 66–7, 77–8
styles of coaching, 14, 57–8, 97, 98, 130
supervision, 92–5, 153, 154, 162, 197, 225–6
suppressive Gestalt techniques, 126, 150
symbolic representation, 40
systems thinking, 17–18

tacit knowledge, 68, 71, 72, 87, 88
targets *see* goal setting; objectives
techniques/tools, 17
    adapting the GROW model, 143–5
    'coaching off-piste', 145–9

reflective logs, 36, 130, 155, 157–8
    see also cognitive behavioural techniques; Gestalt therapy/coaching; narrative coaching
technology *see* Internet
temporary states, 145, 147–8
terminology, 3, 4–5, 7, 53–60, 101
three-chair exercise, 163–4
tools *see* techniques/tools
top dog–underdog dichotomy, 128–9, 163–4
transatlantic e-coaching project (case study), 186–9
translation/explication Gestalt techniques, 127
transpersonal psychology, 16, 122, 169
Trompenaars, F., 98
trust
    ethical coaching, 235
    online relationships, 20
    self-assessment questions, 105, 106, 107, **111**

UIF *see* universal integrated framework (UIF)/integrative learning system (ILS)
universal integrated framework (UIF)/ integrative learning system (ILS), 91
    basis for matching matrix, 220, 221
    CPD/supervision, 92–5, 154–5, 225–6, 228, 235
    cultural/cross-cultural appreciation, 95–103, 224
    dimensions/development areas, 60–1, 104–13
    encouraging creativity, 145, 228
    evaluation, 93–4, 155, 199, 209, 210–13, 217, 223, 225–6
    feedback mechanism, 93, 113–14
    integrative continuum, 101–2
    in practice *see* case studies
    role flexibility, 101, 210
    standardization/creativity, 228
    structuring a reflective log, 155–6
    tools/techniques, 119, 145–51
    to structure training, 153–4, 155, 173, 185
    UIF revisited, 115–17
    UIF updated, 5, 17, 118
    see also dynamic learning model

van Nieuwerburgh, C., 56
Vroom, V., 32
Vygotsky, L.S. *see* zone of proximal
    development

web meetings, 19, 21
Wenger, E., 44–6, 77, 86
Western cultural values, 33, 39–40, 100,
    102, 115
White, M., 42, 134, 135, 137, 140, 142
Whitmore, J., 16, 143
Whybrow, A., 16, 17, 130

will (GROW model revisited), 144–5
women's life structure, 39

Yorkshire-pudding story (Peterborough case
    study), 192–3
you/I exercises (Gestalt-based coaching),
    159–60
you-ness (Gestalt exercise), 160
young people, 83–4, 196

zone of proximal development (Vygotsky),
    40–1, 42, 61, 134, 135